Circumnavigating the Globe:

Amazing Race 10 to 14 and Amazing Race Asia 1 to 3

Arthur E. Perkins, Jr.

authorHOUSE®

AuthorHouse™
1663 Liberty Drive
Bloomington, IN 47403
www.authorhouse.com
Phone: 1-800-839-8640

First published by AuthorHouse 11/17/2009

ISBN: 978-1-4490-1119-2 (sc)
ISBN: 978-1-4490-1120-8 (e)

Printed in the United States of America
Bloomington, Indiana

This book is printed on acid-free paper.

ACKNOWLEDGEMENTS

The person who got me started writing for a publication was Susan Wallingford. She noticed my writing skills in various reality show forums and introduced me to the owner of www.realitywanted.com, Mark Yawitz. Mark assigned me initially to Hell's Kitchen 4. Later he requested Hell's Kitchen 5, Top Chef 4 and 5 and Amazing Race 13 and 14. Writing recaps for www.realitywanted.com was good practice for writing this book. Thank you, Mark for giving me the column space for my assignments and for encouraging my writing.

I owe a debt of gratitude to the creators of the Amazing Race concept, Elise Doganieri and Bertram van Munster. They have developed an amazing reality show that is my favorite television show of all time. The competition implied in that statement that is a tall order, but the Amazing Race leaves its pit stop and consistently finishes first. Mark McKay of Active TV in Australia adapted the U.S. Amazing Race format to Asia and has produced seasons that are comparable to the U.S. Amazing Race in viewing enjoyment.

When I think writing skills, there is one person far back who encouraged me to develop these. Miss Esther Urie was my eleventh grade English teacher and she always insisted on good and lucid writing. I improved my writing under her tutelage.

I want to thank my family and friends. My brother-in-law Ray Hughes was especially helpful in providing information on AR13 in the Auckland area. My friend Gary Geoghegan helped me with technical assistance on PC issues and verb tense conflicts and with extensive feedback related to this book. My friend Tony Vandermude has written two books and he assured me that it could be done. My aunt, Ruth Bergman, has been a major inspiration to me throughout my life. My children Arthur III and Gerri have not had an easy time in life, but they persevere. I thank them for providing me reasons to write well. Finally, my biggest source of support is my wife Terry. She has been through a lot of challenges with me but has also persevered. Her work has provided me with the resources I need on a daily basis. I asked multiple people whose writing skills I admire to help me; Terry came through with help on critiquing several drafts of this book and she turned my cover ideas into something I think is special. Terry, I want to thank you for your support. This book is dedicated to you.

TABLE OF CONTENTS

INTRODUCTION

This book could have been titled "the greatest show on earth" because I think the Amazing Race is that. However, anticipation of feedback from Ringling Brothers, Barnum and Bailey Circus caused me to go in a slightly different direction. This book is titled "Circumnavigating the Globe: The Amazing Race 10 to 14 and Amazing Race Asia 1 to 3". I know one person who has circumnavigated by both air and sea travel. There are airline passengers who have circled the globe, but it is so grueling that most never attempt it. I have been all over the globe, but never even considered circumnavigation in one continuous trip. Yet my favorite television show routinely does that each season. I use this name convention: for all Amazing Races - AR1 to AR14 and for all Amazing Race Asias - ARA1 to ARA3. This book contains my take on the action in AR10 to AR14 and ARA1 to ARA3. The reason for not covering (except to a limited extent in the analysis chapters) AR1 to AR9 is they plus additional information can be found in Adam-Troy Castro's fine book "My Ox is Broken" (BenBella Books, Inc.). In addition to the 8 Amazing Races I cover, I will be exploring a variety of other topics covering all Amazing Races.

I and all Amazing Race fans owe a huge debt of gratitude to Elise Doganieri and Bertram van Munster. She invented the concept of the Amazing Race and he determined how good it was, formed World Race Productions (frequently referred to in this book by initials WRP), and convinced CBS to telecast the first season of the Amazing Race. They both participate in the scouting of locations for each Amazing Race and he is active in the supervision of all filming (she may or may not be; that is unclear) and they are Co-Executive Producers. The Amazing Race owes much of its vigor to the host of every Amazing Race to date, Phil Keoghan. His adventure credentials, genial nature and wit make him a fan favorite host. Amazing Race Asia was spun off from the U.S. Amazing Race production machine, with Van Munster and Doganieri having invested as part-owners, and Michael McKay of Active TV (Australia) being the major owner in charge of ARA productions. The also genial and witty Allan Wu is the host of ARA's first three seasons.

Since some readers of this book will not be fans of The Amazing Race, I will summarize how these races occur. Teams of 2 with a pre-existing relationship apply for, audition for and are selected for the cast of a specific Amazing Race. WRP develops a route and the details of all tasks and production aspects in advance. This includes hiring locals in every country visited and having them manage or facilitate tasks. There are rotating cameraman/soundman teams who travel with each still-active Amazing Race team and handle direct production. When a team asks for two airplane tickets on camera in reality they have to get 4. The distances between the 11 to 13 legs (that is the historical range) average about 2000 miles in Amazing Races, so air transportation is involved for most legs. Some prior coordination with appropriate airlines may occur.

Other forms of transportation include trains, ship/boat, buses, taxis and self-driving. There is a separate chapter for each mode of transportation because transportation is frequently more important than task performance in the outcomes of Amazing Races and Amazing Race Asias. Transportation and Hours of Operation create Bunching opportunities (which I acknowledge with capital "B" to highlight them) to keep most teams together. Teams earn or find clues throughout each leg. Once teams "arrive" they have to do tasks, which will almost always include ROADBLOCKs and DETOURs and general tasks that are neither. For definitions of ROADBLOCK and DETOUR, see the Vocabulary Chapter. On some selected legs a FAST FORWARD may give one team the opportunity to move ahead (and usually that means further ahead since these are usually desirable and the leading teams want to win them) or INTERSECTION (temporary joining of two teams into one) applies. There can be a U-Turn (also do the other DETOUR) or YIELD (stop for about 30 minutes). Teams completing the last task of a leg are directed to a pit stop where host Phil Keoghan checks them into a specific placing. The first place teams typically win a prize. The last place team is eliminated each leg unless it is a predetermined non-elimination leg (NEL). In that case there is a penalty, varied over the course of the seasons covered in this book. It currently necessitates the team receiving it to do a SPEEDBUMP, which is typically a 30 minute total task including transportation. Other penalties apply when rules are violated. When at the pit stop, the CBS mantra is "Eat, Relax and Mingle". However, that does not appear fully consistent with reality. Teams undergo lengthy questioning particularly designed to bring out conflict between teams. Pit stops vary in length but with the common 12 hour version there is barely time for racers to get a good rest. Amazing Races and Amazing Race Asias are as much as anything else a contest of stamina and endurance, as long transportation segments and other race elements drain vitality. When an Amazing Race filming is done, then the editors take over for post-production.

The extent of circumnavigation in Amazing Races can be analyzed. Not all Amazing Race seasons completed a 360 degree trip. There can be minor differentials from 360 degrees. Let's take a look at the start and stop points for every race to date and see what we learn:
AR1 start New York City, finish New York City, 360 degrees
AR2 start Las Vegas, finish San Francisco, 353 degrees
AR3 start Florida Everglades near Miami, finish Seattle, 318 degree
AR4 start Los Angeles, finish Phoenix, 366 degrees
AR5 start Santa Monica, finish Dallas, 381 degrees
AR6 start Chicago, finish Chicago, 360 degrees
AR7 start Long Beach, finish Ft. Lauderdale; only did half the globe
AR8 - never leaves North America, so this calculation not relevant
AR9 start Denver, finish Denver, 360 degrees
AR10 start Seattle, finish San Francisco, 360 degrees west-to-east
AR11 start Miami, finish suburbs north of New York City, 397 deg.
AR12 start Los Angeles, finish Anchorage, 299 degrees
AR13 start Los Angeles, finish Portland OR, 360 degrees
AR14 start Los Angeles, finish Maui Hawaiian islands, 325 degrees

The first thing you learn from this analysis is that many major places on the West Coast are at 122 West Longitude. That includes Seattle, Portland, San Francisco, Santa Monica, Los Angeles and Long Beach. Also, Oakland and San Jose CA are at 122 degrees. When you look at the specifics, you can see that 2 Amazing Races never attempted circumnavigation. AR7 went as far east as 81 degrees east Longitude at Lucknow India and then looped back to Istanbul Turkey and London England before reaching North America at Jamaica. The total of 203 degrees was more than half the globe going eastward and 161 degrees back to the west, for a total longitude traverse of 364 degrees even though not unidirect- ional. In AR8 WRP decided to limit where the teams would go to North America. They went down the East Coast, through multiple southern states, flew to Panama City and worked their way up Central America. They reentered the U.S. in Arizona and drove through many Mountain states. They did the most driving of any

Amazing Race, but limited flying. Of the other races, five of them went a full 360 degrees, three of those by finishing in the same metropolitan area as their starting point. Three races went more than 360 degrees overlapping starting point and continuing east. One race was only slightly short of circumnavigation at 353 degrees. Three were short at 325, 318, and 299 degrees.

Amazing Race Asias to date have not circumnavigated, but that could happen in the future and I expect it to. The farthest east and west points and longitudinal difference for each one has been:
ARA1– Queenstown New Zealand to Dubai, 114 degrees
ARA2– Rotorua New Zealand to Frankfurt, 172 degrees
ARA3– Taipei to Muscat Oman, 63 degrees

I want to pay homage to the individual who first demonstrated the earth could be circumnavigated, Ferdinand Magellan. He went west on his around-the-world trip in 1519 and his expedition did not return to Spain until 1522. 3 years to complete the voyage proved how difficult it was back then. More evidence of that is provided by Magellan's being killed at the battle of Mactan on Cebu in the Philippines April 27, 1521, so he did not live to finish the voyage. In fact, 5 ships and 237 men started the voyage but only 18 of them returned to Spain to complete the circumnavigation mission. The Amazing Race has paid a tribute to Magellan when Amazing Race All-Stars (also known as AR11) visited Punta Arenas, Chile next to the Straits of Magellan on their way to Ushuaia, Argentina. The first major task was the DETOUR Sign It involving a publicly displayed Magellan's Map.

I want to review the organization of this book. After this Introduction, there is an Appendix for the visits of Amazing Races and Amazing Race Asias to each country and an Amazing Race Vocabulary. The major chapters are for Amazing Races 10, 11, 12, 13 and 14, then Amazing Race Asias 1, 2 and 3. Each one has its own chapter and each chapter is organized by episode. Then there is a section of analyses of several different types. Finally, I review Amazing Race Transportation in several chapters. This book finishes with an Index of Amazing Racers and Races and an Index of Places in this book.

AMAZING RACE VOCABULARY

A number of terms have special meanings in Amazing Races, so let's look at those for any Amazing Race or Amazing Race Asia:

AIRLINE FLIGHTS--the heart and soul of international travel; teams must take airline flights in most legs to get from country A to country B. Teams that know airline codes, airport codes, and how to read a listing of flights from A to B have an advantage. So do teams that make judicious use of travel agents. Problems with international flights often occur and provide the most interesting and exciting parts of many Amazing Races. An example was Uchenna and Joyce in AR11, Ep.9. Their decision to fly Krakow to Frankfurt to Kuala Lumpur combined with unfortunate problems by Lufthansa Airlines caused last place on arrival and elimination. They had the opposite luck in the AR7 finale in the San Juan pullback decision. See the chapter on Air Travel for more.

BEGGING– teams have motivations for raising funds by begging: the need to have cash after stripped of their funds or somehow lost them (such as Dallas in AR13 Ep.10) or to enable buying treats when traveling or to create a strategic reserve for situations like paying taxi drivers extra to obtain maximum performance. WRP permits use of begging under specified conditions but not at U.S. airports or when illegal. When "take all your money" non-eliminations were used I can't remember a non-eliminated team not finding the funds to keep going. How did they do it? You know this one. I find begging most Amazing Race teams do demeaning to WRP and to the Race. I think a rule ought to prohibit all begging.

BUNCHING—teams are forced together by any of several different factors. Bunching is a method for getting multiple teams to the pit stop in the same time frame so there is some excitement to the finish of many Amazing Race episodes. Most common is waiting for airline flights at airports. Second is waiting for hours of operation to commence. Waiting for other transportation modes like train, bus or boat is the third most common in my AR viewing experience. Bunching, referred to with a capital B for the remainder of this book, prevents the leading teams from getting far ahead of the weaker teams, making the coordination of the production easier as a result. Bunching started in AR2 in response to the AR1 leap ahead by Rob

/Brennan and Frank/Margarita without the means to retard them.

CLUE—Amazing Race clues detail instructions for next task or what not to do (like take a taxi when the clue directs to walk). When a team completes the task, it's eligible for another clue. Clues are usually found in a marked cluebox but sometimes are photos or objects (a replica of a boat, for example)or newspapers that arrive from which the requisite action must be deduced.

DETOUR—these are done by the team. As with the ROADBLOCK, only sketchy information on the nature of the real tasks is available before a selection is required. You have to choose option A or Option B. Successful task completion makes you eligible for the next clue. The decision on which task to attempt is solely made by the team. A team may choose to switch tasks as many times as they wish with no penalty other than time lost in attempting the tasks and traveling between task locations. If U-Turned, they must also do the other option.

ELIMINATION "In the Field" – applies to Marshall/Lance Season 5 Ep.6, Lena/Kristy Season 6 Ep.3 and Toni/Dallas Season 13 Ep.10.

ELIMINATION LEG—finishing regular legs automatically results in elimination of last team to check in. About 75% to 80% of AR legs are elimination, but it's risky to assume a leg will be non-elimination.

FAST FORWARD—in early Amazing Races, there was a FAST FORWARD opportunity most legs of the race. That has changed dramatically and now there are typically only 2 or 3 the entire race and sometimes they are unattractive and unused. Once a team uses the FAST FORWARD, usually when they are leading the race they cannot use another one in the race, so selection of when to go for it can be a difficult decision. FAST FORWARD information is placed into a selected clue packet. The first team that gets to the FAST FORWARD must complete a task of varying difficulty (some have included head shaving and others tattoos). If successful that team goes straight to the pit stop and almost always (only 4 exceptions in 14 seasons) finishes first that leg. Recent trends have made FAST FORWARDs harder, with small time savings versus the normal tasks. See the FAST FORWARD chapter.

FERN—a local in a place visited by an Amazing Race helps a team by leading it directly to the next place. Often the transportation is by car. Sometimes it is by the "follow that car" method. There has been too much eagerness by Amazing Race and Amazing Race Asia competitors to solve their navigation problems through hijacking locals to help them. The name "Fern" became attached to these practices as the first fern person helping in an Amazing Race was actually named Fern.

GUIDOED - when a team does not finish the final leg of their Amazing Race. Examples are Joe/Bill stuck in Alaska in AR1, who gave their team name to this happening, and David/Jeff stuck in Hawaii in AR4 due to their making a bad choice of flights. Only these 2 times in Amazing Race history have Final 3 teams been thousands of miles away from the FINISH LINE as the race ended. Team Guido (Joe and Bill) was unable to finish AR1 as they had been running a day behind and were in Alaska 24 hours behind the other 2 teams. In Cairns Australia in AR4, David/Jeff made the fateful and incorrect decision to fly to Sydney when they should have gone to Tokyo to get to Hawaii. They were in Hawaii when the race finished in Phoenix. In both cases WRP staffers placed messages for those teams telling them the race was over and please stop racing. The name some have assigned to this practice is "Guidoed" in honor of Joe/Bill's team name.

INTERSECTION—introduced in AR10, it has only been used to pair up two teams or maybe to slow one down. The first team to reach an INTERSECTION will have to wait until another team arrives that is willing to pair up with them and so on. The motivation to get the pairings established is excellent because teams must wait until they do get a pairing before they can leave the Intersection point. Those 2 teams then work together on tasks until an instruction is received in a clue or otherwise that the Intersection is over. It may also include a FAST FORWARD, which is allowed to be claimed by one full group of two teams working together, regardless of whether either team has already claimed their FAST FORWARD; teams that claim a FAST FORWARD during an Intersection are free to claim a non-Intersected Fast Forward if one is available after that point. A prerequisite for Intersections is an even number of teams left.

MARKED CAR or TAXI—directions in most Amazing Race seasons

for finding a car like in an arrival airport parking lot or taxi clearly identified by logo as being associated with the Amazing Race.

MARKED FOR ELIMINATION—starting with AR10, the penalty for non-elimination changed to Marked for Elimination. That team must finish first on the next leg or receive a 30 minute penalty. The last team may stay last, but frequently last place teams come in not more than 30 minutes ahead of the last team, in which case this penalty eliminates them. An example is David/Mary in AR10 Marked for Elimination in Mauritius for placing last, which caused them to get a 30 minute penalty for the Antananarivo, Madagascar leg which eliminated them.

MONEY—at the beginning of each leg of the race, each team receives an allowance of cash with their first clue and subsequently at most pit stops. During the race, all expenses (food, transportation, lodging, attraction admission, supplies) must be purchased from this allowance. The exception to this is the purchase of airline tickets, which the teams pay for using a credit card supplied by WRP. Any money left over after a leg of the race can be used on subsequent legs. Previous seasons have allowed teams to use the credit card for phone and online reservations, but teams in Season 12 could only use the credit card to pay for tickets in person. A predetermined (by recent exchange rates and estimates of local costs) amount of money is given to each team in cash U.S. Dollars; sometimes that amount is zero. Some teams supplement their cash receipts by begging for more money.

NON-ELIMINATION LEG—when a leg ends, the last team to be checked in at the pit stop finds out if it is eliminated or must face a significant penalty. The penalties were initially to have all money confiscated but then concerns about whether teams were actually giving all of it up led to the confiscation of all clothing (except what was on their bodies and medications and passport) and of all other possessions. From AR1 to AR4 there was no penalty for finishing a non-elimination leg last. From AR5 to AR9, teams were penalized for finishing last on a non-elimination leg. Teams were forced to surrender all money and would not be given any to start the subsequent leg. From Season 7 to Season 9, the penalty for arriving last during a non-elimination leg became more severe. In addition to being stripped of all their money and starting the next leg without an allowance, teams were forced to surrender all their possessions, except for their passports and the clothes they were wearing, for the remainder of the Race. Then in AR10 the Marked for Elimination penalty of 30 minutes if you failed to place first in the following leg (note - to the best of my knowledge no team has ever won that first place except for David and Mary in AR10) was introduced. More recently the trend is a SpeedBump to penalize teams for the non-elimination last-place finishers, which is roughly equivalent to a 30 minute penalty the typical YIELD incurs.

PENALTIES—a summary of some well-known Amazing Race penalties:
24 hours will be assessed for not flying economy class or for not completing a DETOUR (or both DETOURs when a U-TURN is involved); Nancy/Emily incurred this is Thailand in AR1.
4 hours is assessed for failure to complete a ROADBLOCK (4 racers accepted this penalty to avoid eating gigantic portions of meat in Mendoza, Argentina)
2 hours will be assessed for each instance of bartering personal property for services unless purchased during the race (Mark/Michael incurred this twice for their actions during Bangkok leg)
The general-purpose penalty is 30 minutes plus possibly time gained as a result of the action causing the penalty (Heather/Eve in AR3 Lisbon got an additional 7 minutes, eliminating them from the race).
There used to be negative penalties, "production credits", awarded to make up losses from unusual events. These have seldom been seen in recent seasons. When a vehicle breaks down, it may be replaced without time credits. Production credits may be invisible to viewers.

PHILIMINATION—one camp says this is for last place finishes on any leg, the other only for non-elimination legs. So pick one of these camps in your usage of this term, Phil Keoghan involved either way.

PIT STOP—the end of each leg of the race has a pit stop unless it is a To Be Continued (TBC) leg. Teams have their check-in time recorded on arrival at and release from the pit stop. The last team to check in is either ELIMINATED or NON-ELIMINATED. There are times where teams arriving at the pit stop have been sent back to complete tasks; an example is Andrew/Dan in Almaty returning to walk to the pit stop). Each Pit Stop is a mandatory rest period which allows teams to "eat, sleep, and mingle"; earlier seasons showed some of these periods of rest for racers, but not much in recent seasons probably due to higher priorities for screen time. The production staff provides highly variable lodging and food for the teams at the Pit Stops. During the Pit Stop, teams are interviewed to provide commentary and voice-overs.

PIT STOP DURATION—the interval of a pit stop can be important as it influences actual departure from the area based on which transportation schedules apply. Timings used in past Amazing Races are:
Less than 12 hours—rare, but it is used occasionally; in AR13 Finale, the pit stop from end leg 10 to beginning leg 11 was 7 hours
12 hours—the most general-purpose standard pit stop timing
18 hours—a rarely used timing
24 hours—can occur, usually based on transportation constraints
36 hours—an extended pit stop, 12 hour pit stop plus 1 full day
60 hours—only example is AR1, Ep.5 in Tunisia delay due to sandstorms

PRODUCTION— U.S. ARs are produced by Jerry Bruckheimer with Bertram van Munster an Executive Producer and in charge. The camera/sound 2 person units rotate among the teams. Prior arrangements are made in each country visited for local production support. There are WRP staff traveling either ahead of or with the entourage who expedite, coordinate and assist. Route selection and task design and sequencing decisions are critical and made months in advance of the beginning of each race. Amazing Race Asias use the same basic methods, with Active TV of Australia and Michael McKay in charge.

ROADBLOCK—a team reaching this gets a general (and frequently misleading) description of the task. Based only on this vague clue and any observations of their surroundings and/or other teams, they must decide which team member is best suited to complete it before being allowed to read the rest of the task description. Once a choice has been made, the teammates cannot switch roles and must stay on the sidelines unless directed by the clue to participate, which occasionally happens. Once the task is completed, the team will receive a new clue.

11

ROADBLOCK BALANCE RULE—Through AR5, there was only a minimal requirement on splitting the ROADBLOCKs between the 2 members of each team. Starting AR6 and continuing, there has been a rule that the final ROADBLOCK count show each member of a team within a specific differential of each other. In an 11 leg race like AR13, which had no ROADBLOCKS in the first or last leg, that split was 6/3. Variance of more than one from equal is allowed.

ROUTE INFORMATION—Route Information clues instruct teams where to go next. The clue usually only provides the name of the team's next destination and it's up to the teams to figure out how to get there. The clue may direct how the teams have to travel. For example, the very first clue of the race traditionally specifies which flights teams may take. Teams may be required to walk, take public transportation, or drive a marked car or other vehicle, according to the clue's instructions. The Route Information clues may specify a specific location in another city or country, another location within the team's present city, the Pit Stop of the leg, or the Finish Line of the race.

ROUTE MARKERS—are flags that mark the places where teams must go. Most Route Markers are attached to boxes that contain clue envelopes, but some mark places where the teams go to complete tasks. Route Markers are usually colored yellow and red. The original Route Markers used in Season 1 were colored yellow and white. The current colors (with red added) were adopted so that teams could more easily spot them. AR3 visited Vietnam with solid yellow-colored flag and Season 10's were yellow and white when the show visited Vietnam again, both for specific reasons. Route Markers in Season 8, the Family Edition, were colored yellow, white, and black.

RULES—here is a summary of well-known condensed rules:
1. Teams must be within 20 feet of each other and near camera/sound.
2. Off-camera, teams must purchase 4 tickets for themselves and camera/sound team. Tickets are economy class only and paid for with a credit card supplied by World Race Productions.
3. Teams are prohibited from contacting any family, friends or acquaintances for the duration of the race. Under direction from

production, they may at designated times communicate briefly once.

4. Excluding use of the U-TURN or YIELD, teams are prohibited from hindering the performance of other teams.

5. Teams may not start the race with any cell phones, personal computer equipment, maps or travel books but they may purchase maps or travel books. Bags of teams may be inspected any time.

7. Teams are expected to keep their Amazing Race-supplied pouch for passports, travel documents and money with them at all times.

8. Teams are prohibited from begging in U.S. Airports or whenever otherwise specified or in any countries where begging is illegal.

9. Teams must abide by the local laws of each country.

10. Cell phones may be borrowed, at least to call airlines/travel agents.

11. Teams may use only public transportation, not get rides in personal vehicles. If they violate this, penalties apply.

SELF-DRIVING—occasionally clues provide cars and some sort of map to get from point A to Point B. I consider a very few racers to be good navigators. Most have very limited navigational skills (with the trend to GPS this will get worse in the future). When in a non-English speaking country you can count on this experience to be nerve-wracking for the racers and a delight for the viewers. One of the few exceptions I can think of was AR6 Ep.1 in Iceland where there was only one road to take and many miles before reaching the next crossing road. A classic example of what I am talking about was ARA2, Ep.7 through South Korea. See the SELF-DRIVING chapter.

SPEEDBUMP– introduced in AR12, on the leg after you finish last in a non-elimination leg an extra task is added only for the team incurring it. This task plus transportation has typically been taking 30 minutes.

To Be CONTINUED (TBC) -- a leg which is too long to fit into the full hour showing of a regular episode. On rare occasions there have been 90 minute legs or back-to-back one hour episodes. However, TBC is neither one. It lasts for 2 hours and is typically telecast over 2 weeks. In the first episode teams racing to a mat find no greeter and Phil Keoghan or Allan Wu hand them a clue "We are still racing" and start the next episode with their next task.

This style has fallen out of favor and has not been used in many seasons until AR14 in Beijing. Prior ones I remember were in Hungary for AR6, Lucknow India for AR7, Yellowstone National Park/Wyoming for AR8 or Finland/Ukraine for AR10.

U-TURN– introduced in AR12, this applies to DETOURS. A team may U-Turn a team behind them by forcing the DETOUR task they originally didn't choose. The team suffering the U-Turn when they finish the usual part of the DETOUR sees that U-Turn has been activated on them and will then have to go back and do the other DETOUR. This typically takes around 30 minutes. Similar to the YIELD, teams that lose their "Courtesy Of" picture during the Race lose their right to use the U-Turn. In AR14 the BLIND U-TURN eliminated the need for a team to identify itself when triggering the U-Turn as Margie/Luke BLIND U-Turned Amanda/Kris, who were eliminated that leg as a direct result. The underlying logic is to encourage use of the U-Turn earlier by allowing teams to remain anonymous in exercising the BLIND U-Turn and by allowing teams both one U-Turn and one Blind U-Turn.

YIELD– introduced in AR5, this is an order to stop immediately, turn the hourglass and not proceed until the hourglass runs out maybe 30 minutes later. Only then can you proceed to the next cluebox or task. The YIELD is implemented by teams deciding Yes or No to use the YIELD (most vote No), then if Yes placing the picture of the team you are yielding on the board and your team's much smaller picture below it. There have been at least 2 instances in AR and ARA where a team did not have their own picture and could not YIELD any team. Only a team behind you can be yielded and each team can only use the YIELD once during a race. There have been multiple wasted attempts to YIELD a team that is ahead, which nullifies the YIELD attempt.

COUNTRIES VISITED BY AMAZING RACE SEASON

6X
India 1-Delhi, Agra, Jaipur, 4-Cochin, Mumbai, Alleppey, 5-Kolkata, 7-Lucknow, Jodhpur, 10-Chennai, 12-Mumbai, 13-Delhi, 14-Jaipur
China (including Hong Kong and Macau) 1-Beijing, 2-Hong Kong, 6-Shanghai, Xian, 10-Beijing, 11-Hong Kong, Macau, 14-Guilin, Beijing

4X
France 1-Paris, Marseille, 4-Paris, Marseille, 6-Ajaccio(Corsica), Nice, 10-Paris
Germany 3-Munich, Fussen, 6-Berlin, 9-Frankfurt, Stuttgart, 14-Bavaria
Italy 1-Rome, Modena, 4-Venice, Cortina D'Ampezzo, Milan, 9-Palermo, Segesta, Catania, Syracuse (all in Sicily), 12-Ancona, Empoli, Florence
Russia 5-St. Petersburg, Pushkin, 9-Moscow, 13-Moscow, 14-Krasnoyarsk, Novosibirsk
Thailand 1-Bangkok, Phuket, 2-Bangkok, Chiang Mai, 9-Bangkok, 14-Phuket, Bangkok

3X
Argentina 5-Buenos Aires, Bariloche, 7-Buenos Aires, Mendoza, 11-Ushuaia
Australia 2-Sydney, Adelaide, 4-Brisbane, Mooloolaba, Cairns, 9-Perth, Freemantle, Darwin
Austria 3-Innsbruck, 4-Vienna, 14-Salzburg
Brazil 2-Rio de Janeiro, Iguassu Falls, 9-Sao Paulo, 13-Salvador, Fortaleza
Malaysia 3-Kuala Lumpur, 4-Kota Kinabalu-Sandakan, 11-Kuala Lumpur
New Zealand 2-Auckland, Queenstown, 5-Auckland, Rotorua, 13-Auckland, Tauranga

2X
Chile 7-Santiago, 11-Santiago, San Pedro de Atacama, Puerto Montt, Punta Arenas
Japan 9-Tokyo, 12-Osaka
Morocco 3-Tangier, Fez, Marrakesh, Casablanca, 10-Casablanca, Ouarzazate

Netherlands 4-Amsterdam, 12-Amsterdam
South Africa 2-Capetown, 7-Capetown, Soweto
Spain 3-Algeciras 10-Barcelona
Switzerland 3-Geneva, Grindelwald, Kanderstag, Montreux, Zurich
14-Locarno, Interlaken
Tanzania 5-Arusha, 11-Dar Es Salaam, Zanzibar
United Kingdom 3-Cambridge, 7-London
Vietnam 3-Ho Chi Minh City, Hoi An, Hanoi, Danang, 10-Hanoi,
HaLong Bay

<u>1X</u>
Bolivia 13-LaPaz, El Alto
Botswana 7-Gaborone, Francisville
Burkina Faso 12-Ouagadougou
Cambodia 13-Siem Reap
Costa Rica 8–San Jose
Croatia 12-Dubrovnik, Split
Ecuador 11-Quito
Egypt 5-Cairo, Giza, Luxor
Ethiopia 6-Addis Ababa, Laibela
Finland 10-Helsinki
Greece 9-Athens, Corinth
Guam 11-western coast
Hungary 6-Budapest
Iceland 6-Keflavik
Ireland 12-Shannon, Cleggan, Clifden
Jamaica 7-Kingston, Port Antonio, Montego Bay
Kazakhstan 13-Almaty
Kuwait 10-Kuwait City
Lithuania 12-Vilnius
Madagascar 10-Antananarivo
Mauritius 10-Plaisance
Mongolia 10-Ulaanbaatar
Mozambique 11-Maputo
Namibia 2-Walvis Bay, Swakopmund
Norway 6-Oslo, Voss
Oman 9-Muscat
Panama 8-Panama City
Peru 7– Lima, Cuzco, Arequipa
Philippines 5-Manila, El Nido Island
Poland 11-Warsaw, Krakow

Portugal 3-Porto, Lisbon
Puerto Rico 7-San Juan
Romania 14-Bucharest, Brasov, Bran
Scotland 3-Aberdeen
Senegal 6-Dakar
Singapore 3-Singapore
South Korea 4-Incheon, Seoul
Sri Lanka 6-Colombo, Kandy
Sweden 6-Stockholm
Taiwan 12-Taipei
Tanzania 5-Arusha, Lake Manyara
Tunisia 1-Tunis
Turkey 7-Istanbul
Ukraine 10-Kiev
United Arab Emirates 5-Dubai
Uruguay 5-Montevideo, Punta del Este
Zambia 1-Livingstone

U.S. Locations
Anchorage 1, 2, 9, 12
Chicago 6 (start and finish)
Dallas 5
Denver 9 (start and finish)
Ft. Lauderdale 11
Ft. Worth 5
Golden 9
Hilo 4
Honolulu 3, 6, 11
Lanai 11
Las Vegas 2
Los Angeles 4, 5, 7, 12, 13, 14
Maui 2, 14
Miami 3, 7, 11
New York 1 (start and finish), 10
Oakland 11
Phoenix 4
Portland 13
Seattle 3, 10
San Francisco 2, 11

MEXICO Locations
Cancun 3
Mexico City 3
Tulum 3

CANADA Locations
Banff 5
Calgary 5
Montreal 8
Toronto 8

Notes: Guam is a territory controlled by the U.S. as is Puerto Rico.

The same information for AMAZING RACE ASIA 1 through 3 is:

<u>2X</u>
China A1, A2
India A1, A3
New Zealand A1, A2
Singapore A1, A2
Thailand A1, A3

<u>1X</u>
Australia A1
Czech Republic A2
Germany A2
Hungary A2
Indonesia A2
Japan A2
Malaysia A1
Oman A3
Malaysia A1
Oman A3
Philippines A2
South Africa A2
South Korea A2
Taiwan A3
United Arab Emirates A1
Vietnam A3

AMAZING RACE 10

There were a lot of innovations in AR10, the use of a double elimination in one leg, the introduction of the Intersection (see AR Vocabulary) and the substitution of Marked for Elimination (see AR vocabulary) for the "take all your possessions" penalty. This means that a team Marked for Elimination must place first in the following leg or incur a 30 minute penalty in addition to the handicap of starting last. There is also a leg with 2 DETOURS and 2 ROADBLOCKS that is, not surprisingly, twice as long. One final innovation is that AR10 is the first Amazing Race circumnavigation from east to west. Phil Keoghan tells teams what they might have learned from studying past Amazing Races may not apply as there will be surprises in AR10. Teams for AR10:

Dustin and Kandice, Beauty Queens (recent Miss California and Miss New York), marketing director and Radio City Rockette, age 24 and 24
Mary and David, husband and wife, a coal miner and housewife from Kentucky, age 32 and 31
Tom and Terry, gay dating couple from New York City, admissions director and special events director, age 39 and 45
Lyn and Karlyn, Team Alabama, best friends and single Mothers, teacher and program analyst, age 32 and 32
Tyler/James, the Alpha Male team from Los Angeles, models, age 29 and 27
Rob and Kimberly, a dating couple from Los Angeles, bartender/student and public relations, age 31 and 28
Erwin/Godwin, the Cho brothers from San Francisco, insurance manager and financial analyst, age 32 and 29
Billel/Saeed, the Islamic team, best friends from Cleveland, medical technician and power lineman, age 37 and 39
Vipul/Arti, the Indian-American team, husband and wife, salesman and educator, age 29 and 26
Kellie/Jamie, best friends, student and recent college graduates from South Carolina, age 22 and 22
Duke/Lauren, father and daughter from Rhode Island, tour company operator and speech/language pathologist, age 52 and 26
Peter /Sarah, recently dating from California, clinical prosthetist and motivational speaker, age 35 and 31
Ep.1 "Real Fast. Quack! Quack!"

World Race Productions wanted to showcase continuity with a past race. AR3 ended in Seattle's Gas Works Park, so AR10 begins in Seattle Gas Works Park. Teams found that their first destination is Beijing, China and raced to the Seattle-Tacoma airport for one of the two flights permitted (United Airlines and Korean Airlines). Erwin/Godwin briefly used their squirt guns on each other, bringing the attention of airport security. Sarah has an artificial leg, as disabled qualifying her for early boarding and probably preferential seating on flights. Teams on the first flight were Dustin/Kandice, David/Mary, Duke/Lauren, Peter/Sarah, Tyler/James and Lyn/Karlyn. The second flight had Tom/Terry, Rob/Kimberly, Erwin/Godwin, Kellie/Jamie, Vipul/Arti and Billel/Saeed. The scheduled arrival gap between the 2 flights was expected to be 60 minutes, but it ended up being only 38 minutes.

The first clue in Beijing took them to the Gold House restaurant for a ROADBLOCK "Who's hungry to stay in this race?" This is to consume the fish eyes in a bowl of fish head soup, which didn't seem to change team positions much. Dustin/Kandice were delayed by a bad taxi driver and arrived about the same time as the earliest from the second flight. The next clue led to the Forbidden City and its Meridian Gate, where teams had to find the kiosk with tags for the next morning departure times 700am, 715am and 730am plus "Last Team". The last two teams to leave the restaurant were Billal/Saeed and Erwin/Godwin (who had been delayed by an inept taxi driver going to Gold House). Now it is Billel/Saeed who had problems and Erwin/Godwin got the final 730am tag, leaving Billel/Saeed with the Last Team tag. They are directed to a finish line mat and to Phil, who miraculously appeared to state "you are the last team to arrive at this point in the race. I told you there would be surprises—even though this is not a Pit Stop I am sorry to tell you that you've both been eliminated from the Race."

The next morning teams set out in motorcycle sidecars to the intersection of 14 HouHai Road and Northbank Road to meet a pedicab manager. Any guesses as to what is ahead? How about a pedicab ride? I was only partly right and so might you be as next is a DETOUR Labor or Leisure. Labor is a 1 mile pedicab trip followed by a pattern match to fill in a 45 square foot square area using traditional methods with bricks of different sizes so that there it matches the model. This is a challenge best handled by the mathematically inclined. James/Tyler did particularly well by studying the pattern before laying bricks. Leisure is 2 miles in a pedicab followed by learning and performing a Chinese relaxation ritual, Taiji Bailong Qui balancing a White Dragon Ball on a paddle. Kellie/Jamie and Tom/Terry were the only Leisure teams.

The next clue takes teams by taxi to Juyongguan, one of the closest gateways to the Great Wall of China. Once teams arrived there expecting a pit stop, they got another surprise, having to climb the Great Wall first before they could check in at the finish mat. World Race Productions was kind to them by providing foot loops that surely weren't part of the original Great Wall, to help racers climb it. Tyler/James had an easy time and got first place. Sarah was at a distinct disadvantage in doing this. Kellie/Jamie used athleticism to improve 4 places from their position on arrival. Mary had difficulty with the rock climb but did not appreciate the advice and encouragement she received from David. At its conclusion she hugged everyone but David; Phil asked her to also hug her husband. Vipul/Arti had been trailing most of the race and they finished last and were eliminated. Sarah's artificial leg was leaking hydraulic fluid throughout the day.

Finish order was:
Tyler/James
Duke/Lauren
Peter/Sarah
Dustin/Kandice
Rob/Kimberly
Kellie/Jamie
Erwin/Godwin
Tom/Terry
Lyn/Karlyn
David/Mary
Vipul/Arti, eliminated

AR10, Ep.2 "Can Horses Smell Fear?"

The pit stop release times are:
Tyler/James   904am

Duke/Lauren   907am
Peter/Sarah   922am
Dustin/Kandice 936am
Rob/Kimberly   951am
Kellie/Jamie   956am
Erwin/Godwin   Unknown, likely between 956am and 1002am;
screen showed 702pm which isn't right
Tom/Terry   1002am
Lyn/Karlyn   1019am
David/Mary   1029am

Tyler/James reached the local bus terminal and booked a midnight bus. They are joined by the next 4 teams. The other 5 teams will leave at 2am. Both buses arrive at the Erenhot train station on the Chinese side of the China/Mongolia border on the Beijing to Ulaanbaatar rail line. The train is at 4am, so all teams make it in ample time. It is the second complete Bunching of AR10 (the first being at Sea-Tac Airport).

The train arrived in Ulaanbaatar and taxis took teams to the Choijin Lama Monastery. Kellie/Jamie, Tom/Terry and Rob/Kimberly arrived first for the every 10 minutes performance starting at 900am. It was a native dance performed by people in costumes and masks representing ancient spirits, followed by the host presenting the next clue.

That clue led to hand-cranked Russian military jeeps. Teams self-drive the jeeps to the nearby Gorkhi-Terelj National Park 43 miles away where they mounted 2 horses. Team members had to don a Russian army hat. Once on horseback teams had a guide to get them to a meadow 2.5 miles away. The cluebox is plainly visible in that meadow. One team Kellie/Jamie headed off clueless about where they are going. Sarah/Peter and Erwin/Godwin got a map. Dustin/Kandice got directions from a local. However, the prize for the transportation here went to David/Mary who got a local to take them to the horses (see FERN in AR Vocabulary). Lyn/Karlyn also found a man to go with them. Leaving the temple in last place was Erwin/Godwin with a map.

Tyler/James got a flat tire and their jack is out of commission; some teams passing them attempted to help and some don't, but nobody succeeded. This allowed the crew for Tyler/James to call for a replacement vehicle, but before it can arrive, a local driving a similar vehicle and having a jack helped them and got them on their way. While changing contact lenses, Kellie/Jamie stalled their vehicle and can't restart it. Eventually they succeeded in restarting it. As you can tell while viewing this, self-driving in a country with a different language has resulted in complete chaos and excellent reality TV.

Peter/Sarah were first to have its members on horses. Dustin/ Kandice arrived second. In an effort to save time, David took their vehicle off-road and gets stuck. He failed to listen to any helpful advice from Mary. Next at the horses were Erwin/Godwin, Duke/ Lauren, Tom/Terry, Rob/Kimberly and Lyn/Karlyn. Kimberly had a close encounter with a large tree branch and the branch won. She was swept off the seat of her horse and her handler had to go bring the horse back. Sarah took a tumble after losing her balance.

The next clue led to a DETOUR Take It Down or Fill It Up. Take It Down teams take down a yurt, roll it up and pack it tightly, then attach it to a camel. Fill It Up requires leading a hynik (like an ox) and cart back and forth 500 meters to a river to fill up 4 water containers, which are transferred into a barrel with a line indicating how much is needed.

The success of Fill It up is dependent on the cooperation of the ox to direction. The success of Take It Down is dependent on ability to tie tight knots. Peter/Sarah started first and chose Take It Down. After a lack of success, they switched to Fill It Up but their hynik ran away, causing them to reevaluate Take It Down and return to it. Dustin/ Kandice did Fill It Up and were the first to receive the next clue. But the army hat for both came off in their wild ride to the site and it is required for them to ride back to their vehicle. Erwin/ Godwin had the same problem, losing one hat. The guide for Dustin/Kandice found their missing hats on foot. By this time Duke/ Lauren, Peter/Sarah and Rob/Kimberly passed Dustin/ Kandice.

The next clue had teams drive their vehicles 47 miles to Hotel Mongolia. Lyn/Karlyn and Kellie/Jamie seem to be battling to avoid last place. The vehicle for each team was not running and they have to get it operational or they will be eliminated. Kellie/Jamie

23

watched as a local comes by and used the hand crank to start their vehicle. Lyn/Karlyn saw and copied that technique. That low-tech method is perfectly suited to these vehicles and worked instantly for Kellie/Jamie and, after help from that local, for Lyn/Karlyn. Kellie/Jamie made a navigational mistake and were on the road to nowhere. Lyn/Karlyn got to Hotel Mongolia in next to last place.

At Hotel Mongolia the first requirement was to find the clue box, which revealed a ROADBLOCK "Who's ready to aim high?" That meant to use a bow to shoot a real flaming arrow 160 feet into a 6 foot diameter pan of oil at the target area. Peter was battling James for first place; Peter won first place by landing his arrow in the target area. Phil asks if they thought that "two legs into the race, they'd be in first place?" What a great pun! I hope Phil made it up himself and did not use a scriptwriter for it. Tyler/James finished second. Lauren got third for her team. Tom got 4th for his. Dustin got 5th. Kimberly was 6th, David 7th and Erwin 8th. Lyn set her target ablaze for 9th place before Kellie/Jamie arrived as the result of Kellie/Jamie getting bad directions from a local and heading back in the wrong direction as Lyn/Karlyn were heading correctly for the hotel. It's over before they got to Hotel Mongolia but Kellie tried 117 arrows over hours before they decided to take the 4 hour penalty. They are eliminated before that penalty can be applied. Actual time for teams to complete their tasks in Mongolia was a range of 10 to 12 hours. It was on this leg that Lyn/Karlyn coined the word Backpack for the teams who are finishing far out of the lead. It also applied to David/Mary and Erwin/Godwin.

There are some relationship adjustments this episode. Sarah now knows the real Peter and she doesn't much like what she sees of his qualifications for her life partner. Similarly, Kimberly got exposed to some of the more outrageous aspects of Rob's personality. Even David, married to Mary for over 10 years, got in serious trouble.

The other thing to note is the screen-filling role that animals demand when involved in any Amazing Race. The hynik in this episode stole the show, with the horses ridden by unskilled riders and reacting to their mistakes a close second. Teams doing Take It Down should feel very fortunate their camels were well-behaved. AR10, Ep.3 "Oh, Wow! It's Like One of Those Things You See on TV!"

Here are the pit stop release times:
Peter/Sarah   654am
Tyler/James   707am
Duke/Lauren   745am
Tom/Terry   752am
Dustin/Kandice   811am
Rob/Kimberly   813am
David/Mary   816am
Erwin/Godwin   818am
Lyn/Karlyn   902am

The first clue was travel to Hanoi, Vietnam, 2300 miles away. Teams jockeyed for position at the travel agency to book and ticket. While next in line, Dustin/Kandice noted that Tom/Terry left a travel agent open, so they took it themselves. This caused a good deal of ill will toward them from the other teams. But that's all useless as they Bunched once more waiting for the flight to Beijing, connecting to a flight Beijing to Hanoi.

On arrival teams took taxis to Hoa Lo Prison, the infamous "Hanoi Hilton" where John McCain and other American servicemen were prisoners for multiple years. Duke/Lauren had a bad experience; after meeting a local woman on the plane who volunteers to guide them she sent the taxi 30 minutes away to let her off first. So much for helpful locals! Also Duke/Lauren had $11 carryover funds to start this leg with since they got no additional money. They should have to spend $10 of that, but they managed to stiff the cabdriver. Other teams paid $10. On arrival teams found no hours of operation until 8am the next morning and camped out around it. Once open, teams were given the task of finding the exhibit for the flight suit of John McCain. Erwin/Godwin took a moment to honor servicemen all over the globe, a classy move. The next clue directed them 1.5 miles to a Hanoi Old Quarter District flower shop. Duke and Lauren had to walk with minimal funds left. The differential in travel time of at least 20 minutes could haunt them.

There they found a ROADBLOCK "Who's ready to pedal some dough?" to take flower bicycles out on the streets and sell the fresh cut flowers for 80000 dung, equivalent to about $5 US and keep the proceeds. Duke/Lauren now had $16 for the remainder of this leg.

The next clue sent teams to Vac 30 miles away to find the Dinh Vac Buddhist Temple. 4 public buses take teams to Vac, with Peter/Sarah getting the wrong bus initially and returning to take the correct one, putting them in last place. On the portion of the trip after leaving the bus, Tom and Terry accepted a ride on a motorbike. I don't think they understood at the time, but this is a rules violation causing a penalty. At the temple teams first encounter a dragon puppet show and then DETOUR Fuel or Fowl. Fuel is to make 30 round coal bricks placing wet coal in traditional presses. Those bricks are a main source of fuel for cooking and heating in Vietnam. Erwin/Godwin make the first ones too small. There is a local Vietnamese audience enjoying the problems teams encounter in Fuel. Fowl is to make a specific type of birdcage from a pattern with traditional materials and local methods as instructed. All teams initially headed for Fuel (it looks much more predictable to me and I'm sure to them), but Duke/Lauren couldn't find it and stumbled onto the site for Fowl. After completing this DETOUR teams went a short distance to the Ca Dong Dia rice paddy to the pit stop.

Erwin/Godwin finished first. Tom/Terry were shocked to discover from Phil Keoghan they were assessed a 30 minute penalty for the rules violation and had to step off the mat for that period. All of the other Fuel teams finished and reached the pit stop before Tom/Terry were allowed to check in. The penalty clock finally ran out and they had 8th place at check-in. Duke/Lauren were last and were eliminated. You might think they were out as a result of both having minimal funds and having to walk to the flower shop. As they made the 3rd bus with several other teams, that can't be the reason. Their main reason for elimination appears to be time wasted attempting to find the Fuel option in Vac. They did a reasonable job assembling the birdcage.

AR10, Ep.4 "I Know Phil, Little Ol' Gorgeous Thing"

Teams are released from the pit stop as follows:
Erwin/Godwin   1055pm
Tyler/James   1122pm
Rob/Kimberly   1126pm
Dustin/Kandice   1127pm

Peter/Sarah	1129pm
Lyn/Karlyn	1131pm
David/Mary	1132pm
Tom/Terry	1146pm

Teams took a taxi back to Hanoi and find the Ly Thai To Gardens.
This was strange and befuddled several teams. They were looking
for a type of cricket, but the real purpose was to position them
where they could hear the loudspeaker repeatedly blare the next
clue in Vietnamese, to get to Ben Xi Gia Lam bus station, where
they would take a bus 103 miles to Ben Xe Bai Chai, where they
would find Hydrofoil Harbor. Tyler/James and Peter/Sarah showed
their smarts by bringing their taxi driver into the park to hear the
message. Rob/Kimberly and Tom/Terry copied this approach.
David/Mary showed smarts getting a local to write down the clue in
Vietnamese so it could provide specific guidance to their taxi driver.
There was confusion among drivers understanding the destination.
Some teams had to return and hear the message a second time
after their first try did not reach the intended destination.

Guess what they discovered when all teams were at the bus
station? The answer Bunching shows you are becoming a student
of the Amazing Race. The bus station didn't even open until 5am.
All teams bought tickets for and got on the same bus. Ben Xe Bai
Chai is on famous Ha Long Bay; after 103 miles teams got off and
located Hydrofoil Harbor and the next clue. There was a YIELD
opportunity, but no team wanted to pass up a future YIELD (see AR
Vocabulary) so early in AR10.

Teams took a motorboat to a 90 foot cliff on Hon Yen Ngua rock
island across the harbor. One team member used a mechanical
ascender to reach the top of that cliff in ROADBLOCK "Who's got
strong arms and legs?" Dustin/Kandice raced to the dock for a
specific motorboat and succeeded but Kandice got a cut on her leg
adding to Dustin/Kandice's reputation as cutthroat competitors.
Sarah took this ROADBLOCK but struggled to complete it. Peter
takes none of the heavy physical tasks. There are only 3 ascender
stations; teams must wait their turn.

After getting the clue at the top, the selected individual rappels
down. Lyn encourages Karlyn with this classic line "If you can have

a baby without anesthesia, you can go up this rock." Next was a trip to cluebox at Sung Sot Cave, a DETOUR Over or Under. Over starts with a junk trip to a floating marker to get rowboats, then row to a supply ship to load a specific amount of provisions, then row downstream to a floating village and locate and deliver to 2 addresses and obtain signatures on the invoices. In Under teams take a junk to a marked buoy, then a rowboat to an oyster farm, choose a line of buoys, harvest 30 sunken oyster baskets and deliver them to a pearl farmer. The rowing involved was difficult and time-consuming for most teams due to the strong current, particularly for Tom/Terry. Peter is doing his first heavy physical task by rowing and whining about the difficulty. David/Mary and Dustin/Kandice both switched from Over to Under.

Teams finishing their DETOUR returned to their junk, which took them 9 miles to Soi Sim Island. Tyler/James were delayed and lost one place as their junk crew failed to take up the anchor. Dustin/Kandice lost 1 position misreading the clue trying to row all the way to Soi Sim Island. The finish order was:
Rob/Kimberly
Peter/Sarah
Tyler/James
Erwin/Godwin
David/Mary
Lyn/Karlyn
Dustin/Kandice
Tom/Terry, who were eliminated

AR10, Ep.5 "I Covered His Mouth, Oh My Gosh"

Teams are released from the pit stop on Soi Sim Island as follows:
Rob/Kimberly   147am
Peter/Sarah   217am
James/Tyler   221am
Erwin/Godwin   228am
David/Mary   249am
Lyn/Karlyn   253am
Dustin/Kandice   346am

Teams are instructed to take a train to Hanoi, then a plane from there to Chennai (formerly Madras) India. Teams must visit a travel agent before getting to the Hanoi airport to obtain reservations and tickets. All teams were on the same 5am train. On the train Erwin/Godwin tried to fake out Peter by claiming that they had booked tickets already (using a fake phone), which made Peter work hard to find a cell phone and call for himself and Sarah plus Dustin/Kandice, who had agreed to be allies for flight bookings this leg, to a Hanoi travel agency.

Now it's time for flight booking bingo. Which team got lucky in their selection of route to Chennai? David/Mary and Lyn/Karlyn booked through Bangkok arriving at noon the next day, but they decided to take a risk on the route of Erwin/Godwin (who publicly blab it and diminish the value of their find) through Hong Kong and Delhi, arriving in Chennai at 9am, the final leg standby. The same opportunity was offered to Dustin/Kandice and Peter/Sarah but neither team wanted to take the risk vs their guaranteed seats on the combination arriving at noon. Rob/Kimberly and Tyler/James booked a route through Singapore and Delhi, unclear if they have a guaranteed last leg. The flight combination for Dustin/Kandice and Peter/Sarah was enhanced as arrival in Bangkok revealed a modified route through Kolkata to arrive Chennai at 750am. Standby status got seats for all teams arriving Delhi except David/Mary on a flight one hour later, arriving Chennai at 10am.

Once teams arrived in Chennai they had to get to the bus station and find bus 119 for Mamallapuram 40 miles away. Once off that bus, they looked for their clue at Vallavar Arts and Crafts. The Hours of Operation delayed them briefly at the crafts store because it is unexpectedly closed until 1130am. Then they were off to do the DETOUR Wild Rice or Wild Things. Wild Rice is walk 200 yards to a temple, select a chalk outline on the temple floor of a design and match its pattern by filling it in with colored rice grains. Wild Things requires a taxi 9 miles to a crocodile bank, finding pit 16 and helping 2 wranglers move a crocodile to another pit. Lyn/Karlyn and Erwin/Godwin initially chose Wild Rice but after they found out how hard it was they switched to Wild Things. The only teams that actually finished Wild Rice were Tyler/James, who elected the nearer DETOUR, and David/Mary because Mary wanted to avoid crocodiles. Dustin/Kandice's taxi ride had a flat tire, so Peter/Sarah took the lead from them. Lyn had major difficulty getting over a 3.5

foot wall designed to keep the crocodiles in.

The next clue led back to Chennai returning by bus leaving every 30 minutes. This ROADBLOCK was "Who's the driving force behind this team?" One member of each team had to enroll in the Karthik Driving School and actually learn enough to pass the test for an India Driver's License and a road test. Those drivers were instructed to take their driving school car and instructor and navigate through Chennai, a city of 4 million population, traffic 10 miles to the pit stop Chettinad House.

The finish order of the teams was:
Peter/Sarah
Dustin/Kandice
Rob/Kimberly
Erwin/Godwin
Lyn/Karlyn
Tyler/James, who are threatened by their own poor performance and near elimination
David/Mary - are non-eliminated, first team ever to face the Marked for Elimination penalty (see AR Vocabulary) of 30 minutes if they fail to finish first the next leg.

AR10, Ep.6 "Maybe Steven Segal Will See me and Want Me to Be in One of His Movies"

There was a wide range of release times from the 24 hour pit stop:
Peter/Sarah   1254pm
Dustin/Kandice 106pm
Rob/Kimberly   142pm
Erwin/Godwin   153pm
Lyn/Karlyn   202pm
Tyler/James   337pm
David/Mary   604pm

Peter/Sarah started 3 hours ahead of 6th place Tyler/James, who are another 2.5 hours ahead of David/Mary. The start of this episode was a clue similar to those in the TV show "Treasure Hunters". It is a mobile phone video message with Phil Keoghan saying fly to Kuwait City 2400 miles away and locate a pair of unnamed spherical towers identified by a picture. Teams departed Chennai on multiple flights to Mumbai, but then were Bunched onto one flight from Mumbai to Kuwait City.

Teams got from the airport to Kuwait Towers, the referenced building. What do you do at a tall building in an Amazing Race? It might be bungee jumping; it might be climbing; it might be just finding a clue. In this case it was climbing. Teams selected one individual for ROADBLOCK "Who's strong in both mind and body?" which really means climb up the outside of Kuwait Towers to retrieve puzzle pieces. Safety is obviously an important considera-tion for all Amazing Race tasks. World Race Productions does not want teams incurring a serious injury or droppign out. Teams arri-ving at the Towers pulled sequential numbers for the order of the climb. The tower is 610 feet high and above that is the cone structure the selected individual must climb up ladders on the outside of. At the top, the puzzle pieces were in a satchel to be taken to the ground and the puzzle assembled to reveal the market-place street where at a small shop the next clue can be found.

There was also a FAST FORWARD opportunity, 1 of only 2 in the entire race. Teams drive 18 miles to an oil field, don protective clothing and then use a fire retardant shield to retrieve a clue near the simulated oil well fire. This one looks pretty easy depending on how hot the blaze is. If more than one team goes for the FAST FORWARD, which sometimes happens, then the first team to finish it wins the directions to the pit stop while any losing teams are in deep trouble, well behind the other teams who did not go for the FAST FORWARD. David/Mary correctly deduced they had to try for the FAST FORWARD as it represented their best chance to finish this leg in first place and avoid the 30 minute penalty. Dustin/Kandice were talking about it, so Erwin/Godwin faked that they would also go for it to potentially scare Dustin/Kandice off, which was successful. This was a totally selfless act to aid another member of the Sixpack Alliance (formerly the Backpack) by the other team jeopardized with a later start in the task specified in the regular clue. Erwin/Godwin were willing to aid David/Mary by sacri-ficing one position and were last in the queue for the climb if they faked leaving and returned, costing them critical time. This dis-suaded Dustin/Kandice (who strongly considered it) from going for the FAST FORWARD. David/Mary were uncontested at the oil field.

The next clue was to find the Bead shop on Souk Al-Gharabally St., where they assemble a puzzle. The solution to the puzzle (in Arabic which has to be translated) gave the next clue. Erwin/Godwin were last in assembling the puzzle, but payback for their good deed is immediate. They asked a policeman for directions; he instead gave them a police escort to the designated street. They passed Lyn/Karlyn and Dustin/Kandice for 5th getting the DETOUR clue for Manual/Automatic.

Manual requires self-driving to a Sulaibiyah feed lot and filling ten 110 pound camel feed bags up to the line, then carrying those bags 100 yards to stack on a pallet. Automatic requires teams to self-drive to the Kuwait Camel Racing Club. Then they would strap a voice-activated robotic jockey whip on the back of a camel and use a walkie-talkie that activates it to motivate that camel down the entirety of the 140 yard track. 3 teams went for Manual and 3 for Automatic initially. Dustin/Kandice had to redo filling all 10 bags. However, on the way to the Camel Racing Club while following Lyn/Karlyn there, Erwin/Godwin decided to change to Manual. Tyler/James had planned Manual, but they changed their minds and decided to find Automatic instead.

Peter/Sarah spent many hours finding the Camel Racing Club without success, finally driving by the place the FAST FORWARD had taken place. After sundown they found the feed lot but this is too late to save them; they are directed to the pit stop without doing Manual. It is evident that poor navigational skills are exceptionally dangerous on self-driving tasks. They finish last and are eliminated at the pit stop, the Al Sadiq Water Tower 11 miles from the DETOUR options. In first place, David/Mary were off the hook.

AR10, Ep.7 "I Wonder If This is Going to Make My Fingers Pickle"

The release times are:
David/Mary   1237am
Dustin/Kandice 340am
Rob/Kimberly   353am
Lyn/Karlyn   410am
Erwin/Godwin 418am

Tyler/James   455am

This leg started with flights to Mauritius 560 miles east of Madagascar off the southeast coast of Africa. It is rather hard to believe since the distance to Mauritius from Kuwait is only 3500 miles as crows fly, but the flight bookings are through London, which makes the trip 9400 miles and 19.5 hours flying time plus 3.5 hours connection time in Heathrow plus a one hour time zone differential. The answer to why flights through Dubai were not preferred is that they are limited so that each day of the week they do not operate to all destinations.

On the seat of their marked cars at Mauritius airport was a model of a schooner/yacht. This is an example of excellent clue construction, as the teams have to work with locals to figure out what it is and more importantly where it is. Far too many Amazing Race clues are now of the "Go to" variety. The ship is the Isla Mauritia and it is moored off Grand Baie. Most teams used locals to help them but Tyler/James went from first place out of the airport to last by trying to get information from a hotel (normally a good strategy but not a good one near the Mauritius airport since it is a long way from towns and the one real city on the island). After driving to Grand Baie and parking near it, team members had to change to bathing suits, goggles and protective foot-gear, don life vests and swim to the Isla Mauritia to get the water-proofed clue and swim back to shore. This is where the phantom ROADBLOCK happened, a task (possibly right in Grand Baie) like kayaking somewhere on the coast, but editors removed it from what got on TV. The normal reason for that is it's uninteresting and/or resulted in no change of position, but who knows? Teams drove 49 miles to Casa Noyale and looked for the post office there. 2 automotive mishaps along the way were Dustin driving into the tail of a local bus and Rob/Kimberly's transmission dead and requiring a replacement vehicle.

Next teams drove south for the DETOUR Sea or Salt. Sea was to take a sailboat piloted by a captain with small outboard engine to a close-by island and use a treasure map to search the island for a mast and sail from the boat, then attach them for the trip back. In Salt teams had to drive 2 miles to a salt pen and search 3 giant piles of sand for a small salt shaker with a clue inside. This was the luck-based option. Initially Dustin/Kandice were the only team to do

33

Sea, but after frustrating results at the salt piles (shakers filled with pepper) all but David/Mary switched to Sea. David is afraid of the water. However, continued futility in finding a correct salt shaker motivated him to switch to Sea.

Dustin/Kandice's decision paid off handsomely; they stayed ahead and found the pit stop at Chateau Bel Ombre 12 miles away in first place. Rob/Kimberly lost second place to Tyler/James. The Sixpack alliance worked together up until arrival at the pit stop. There Erwin/Godwin took 4th, Lyn/Karlyn took 5th and David/Mary finished last. They are the luckiest team in this race, as again it was a non-elimination leg but they were Marked for Elimination once again.

AR10, Ep.8 "He Can't Swim but He Can Eat Cow Lips"

Teams are released as follows:
Dustin/Kandice 300am
Tyler/James   305am
Rob/Kimberly   309am
Erwin/Godwin   404am
Lyn/Karlyn   405am
David/Mary   409am

Teams self-drive to the airport and Dustin/Kandice decided to pull a "prank" by taking another team's good condition car and leaving their damaged vehicle for another team, probably the last one. Needless to say, the other teams are outraged by this. Teams flew to Antananarivo Madagascar 700 miles away and that flight did not depart until 11am, leaving teams plenty of time to enjoy being Bunched once again. Tyler said "We're going to try to reach Antanana…Antanana...hey, hey, hey, say goodbye to one of the 6-Pack. We'll make it into a 4-Pack." The first destination in Antanan-anarivo was the Black Angel in Lac Anosy. Lyn commented "Why should we be looking for the Black Angel? I'm the Black angel and I'm right here." Teams find the only statue in the designated place was a white angel. In an anti-apartheid period the citizens of Antan-anarivo repainted the Black Angel white without changing the name.

On arrival teams found an Intersection, its premiere in an Amazing Race. Pairs of teams work together until they are notified the Intersection is over. Tyler/James and Rob/Kimberly arrived first and logically want to team up. Dustin/Kandice arrived seconds behind, but they are not selected by the initial SixPack teams. David/Mary arrived but waited for another SixPack team to arrive instead of pairing with Dustin/Kandice, the smart move. Lyn/Karlyn arrived next and paired with David/Mary. Erwin/Godwin arrived last and had no option but to pair with Dustin/Kandice. If they thought hard about it they should realize how fortunate they were.

Team Tyler/James/Rob/Kimberly elected the FAST FORWARD "Eat Cow Lips." They all had trouble eating this local delicacy at stand #11 in Anakely Market, so time elapsed finishing that task. Then released from Intersection, they compete to the pit stop.

Dustin/Kandice/Erwin/Godwin and David/Mary/Lyn/Karlyn got a DETOUR Long Sleep or Short Letter. Long Sleep requires putting mattress covers on 8 mattresses, carrying them for 2.2 miles and delivering them to a hard-to-find address. Short Letter is make and decorate 28 sheets of paper to the satisfaction of the papermaker. Both chose Long Sleep. Maneuvering their mattresses through busy streets to find the destinations, Dustin/Kandice/Erwin/Godwin were released from the Intersection with the next clue.

Next was the ROADBLOCK "Who can cut through red tape?", take a taxi 4 miles to Tohotohobato Ambondrona Analakely to obtain 4 matching rubber transportation stamps (airplane, boat, train, car) from stamp vendors and walk up the rest of the wide set of steps. Dustin blew through this one and reunited with Kandice (sent ahead by taxi) at the plaza in front of Cathedral Andohalo, the pit stop; they finished first. They even got there in front of the FAST FORWARD teams, who finished Tyler/James #2 and Rob/Kimberly #3. Erwin/Godwin were 4th.

The last 2 teams battled for fifth place. David/Mary had to arrive 30 minutes ahead or the 30 minute penalty would eliminate them. What does Mary do? She helped Karlyn with directions to rubber stamp vendor #1. Mary still finished ahead of Karlyn and arrived at the pit stop to reunite with David and start the penalty clock. Only 10 minutes elapse before Karlyn arrived to reunite with Lyn. They took 5th place and David/Mary were last and eliminated. The old adage from Leo Durocher "nice guys finish last." fits. David/Mary are delightful people (why Rosie O'Donnell gave them valuable gifts after their elimination episode), but they are mediocre racers. I assumed this was the first time in Amazing Race history a FAST FORWARD team didn't place first, but it's the fourth (after Joe/Bill in AR1, Steve/Josh in AR3 and Monica/Sheree in AR4).

AR10 Ep.9 "Being Polite Sucks Sometimes"

Teams are released from the pit stop as follows:
Dustin/Kandice 256am
Tyler/James   308am
Rob/Kimberly   314am
Erwin/Godwin   324am
Lyn/Karlyn   355am

The clue required flying 6000 miles to Helsinki Finland and finding the Kappeli Café coffeehouse to get to access an AOL (product placement) message with the next clue. Teams were given pre-booked flight reservations they could use if they wished. That approach is expected to not give the best flights. Teams were determined to beat the pre-booked reservations to arrive 1130am. The first 4 teams discovered they could go at 5am to Johannesburg, then to Addis Ababa, from there to Frankfurt and then finally to Helsinki arriving at 1020am the next day. Lyn/Karlyn would have been left behind if not for the generosity of the Cho brothers and a helpful Air Madagascar agent, so Bunching continued until arrival in Helsinki. The Email message at Kappeli Cafe was by loved ones and/or relatives of the members of each team. The next clue took them 125 miles to Tampere and the Soppeenharjun Koulu School. Dustin/Kandice and Tyler/James were both lucky to get a taxi at the airport. The other 3 teams have to wait in the queue there. Rob/Kimberly pleaded with locals ahead of them to let them cut the line. Lyn/Karlyn elected to just cut the line, reinforcing their stereotype as Ugly Americans in foreign countries. Erwin/Godwin chose to wait for their turn, which put them a bit behind. Once at the school teams found a DETOUR Swamp This or Swamp That. Swamp This is to put on cross-country skis (in the summer) and finish a 1 mile long course full of mud. Swamp That required being on foot for a 1 mile obstacle course that is even muddier and requires one team member to carry the other through selected parts of the course. Dustin/Kandice chose cross-country. Tyler/James chose obstacle. Lyn/Karlyn chose cross-country and Rob/Kimberly and Erwin/Godwin chose obstacle course.

Completion of the DETOUR earned teams the next clue, train 104 miles to Turku, then self-drive 78 miles to Lohja. There they had to find the Tytyrin Limestone Mine and find the clue in the mine. The irony of the coal miner David eliminated one leg before a mining challenge should be clear to all. Dustin/Kandice and Tyler/James get the 311pm train, which Rob/Kimberly just miss. Rob/Kimberly, Erwin/Godwin and Lyn/Karlyn all have to take the 411pm train, putting them one hour behind. After finding the clue quite deep in the mine, ROADBLOCK "Who's ready for a miner inconvenience?" was ride a bicycle one mile through tunnels and find a pile of marked limestone blocks then select any one and strap it to the bicycle, ride it back through the tunnels, crack it open with tools, and get the clue inside. That directed teams to drive 39 miles back to Helsinki and find Olympic Stadium. Dustin/Kandice and Tyler/James do not appear to lose time navigating any of it. The other 3 teams compete vigorously against each other but to get out of the mine they all took the same tram ride out.

At Olympic Stadium first Tyler/James then Dustin/Kandice after diffi-culties located the correct door, with a new clue sending them up the 236 foot tower so both team members can rappel face-forward down the side of that tower. James is afraid of heights but has to overcome that to do this. Tyler said it's like being Spiderman. At the bottom they found no finish mat. Instead they received a message KEEP RACING. Is this a To Be Continued (TBC) leg? Opinions vary but mine is that it is.

AR10, Ep.10 "Lookin' Like a Blue-Haired Lady on a Sunday Drive"

This is the continuation with the second part of the TBC, starting at the Olympic Tower in Helsinki with the arrival of the lagging 3 teams and their completion of the Face-Down rappel. Some people refer to this as a superleg since two hours TV time are involved, but I think viewing it as the "leg after a TBC leg" is maybe more revealing. The next clue (indirect ones like this are best) is to the capital of the country where Chernobyl, site of the world's largest nuclear disaster, is located and finding the marked cars. I consulted my world atlas. It is Ukraine, whose capital city is Kiev, but teams don't know the Chernobyl part and have to ask around. Since Finland was downwind of the radioactive plume when the wind was blowing north, it caught some of the fallout from the 1986 Chernobyl disaster. Finns were quick to tell teams where to go (no, not the figurative version, just the literal version).

Total mileage to Kiev was 1,900 miles. Tyler/James and Dustin/Kandice were first to Helsinki airport and they got a 825am flight to Vienna, landing in Kiev at 125pm. The other 3 teams booked a 925am flight to Warsaw supposed to arrive at 125pm but was 30 minutes late. Dustin/Kandice sang the Ukrainian bell carol for amusement; it represents most of what they knew about the Ukraine when they received the clue. Most Americans know less.

The first task in the Kiev area was Oster Tank School, which was developed when the Soviet Union existed and Ukraine was part of it. Oster Tank School is 58 miles from the airport; the local language is Cyrillic, not English. Tyler/James, Dustin/Kandice and Rob/Kimberly acted like money is no object and hire taxis to follow (maybe they had done some begging on the side in any of the prior legs and were well-placed financially). As I have said elsewhere in this book, this practice of following taxis ought to be banned by World Race Productions. Erwin/Godwin elected to self-navigate and Lyn/Karlyn elected to play "Follow the Chos". Next was a ROADBLOCK "Who's ready to take command?" requiring one member of each team to take charge of a T-64 tank through a 1.2 mile obstacle course. This had to be the most fun of any ROADBLOCK in AR10! The nascent tank commanders loved this. Rob wants Kimberly to "be able to get some aggression out; she's finding that she's super robo tank girl."

Next teams had to drive 43 miles back to Kiev and find Apt. 33 in building #3 on a specific street. Dustin/Kandice and Tyler/James did without problems. Rob/Kimberly followed a taxi but their ancient car breaks down. Erwin/Godwin elected to wait for their 6-Pack partners Lyn/Karlyn to finish the ROADBLOCK. This made no sense, particularly when later after following the Chos Lyn/Karlyn tired of the Chos' frequent stops for directions and slow driving, deciding to abandon them in Kiev, knowing a 6-Pack team was likely to be eliminated and not wanting it to be themselves. So this strategy of elaborate courtesy by Erwin/Godwin was neither expected nor appreciated by Lyn/Karlyn, ready to jettison them on a moment's notice. Godwin declares "our alliance with Team Alabama is over" and then attempted to follow them.

At that apartment 33, the DETOUR Make the Music or Find the Music is the choice. Make the Music required teams to drive 3 miles to a hip-hop club, write a rap song containing a reference to each country visited previously on AR10, perform the song, and get approval from the emcee who is introduced as Kiev's top rap music artist (he may be, but not-really "All-Star teams" in prior Amazing Races AR have exposed viewers to grandiose claims). The comedy potential for this Make the Music is mind-boggling. Find the Music sent teams 2.5 miles to the National Music Academy of Ukraine where they don formal attire, locate the sheet music for Tchaikovsky's "Concert Fantasy for Piano and Orchestra", search the 120 practice rooms for one of 6 pianists on call, then have it played and receive the clue. Commercial recordings of that piece last about 30 minutes, so I am guessing that World Race Productions' version took about 15% of that. Tyler/James chose Find the Music, did it quickly and were in first place. Dustin/Kandice chose Make the Music for second place. Should they have been required to redo their composition? I was not the judge. Rob/Kimberly did Make the Music and take third. Chos and Team Alabama battled for 4th place. Lyn/Karlyn found the way to the hip-hop club. The Chos attempted to follow but lost them and decided to go for Find the Music. I was rooting for Erwin/Godwin to finish ahead, but Lyn/Karlyn got a rap song of questionable quality past the judge and didn't have to do it twice.

Teams drove 2 miles to the Great Patriotic War Museum for the pit stop. Lyn/Karlyn hired a taxi to lead them, a smart move despite my usual objections, to help stay in this race. Erwin/Godwin, navigating on their own (the way it always should be), drove onto a plaza with a closed-off section and were detained by local police. It didn't matter as they were already too late to stay in the race. They finished 5th and were eliminated. The Good Guys lacked good navigational skills while Lyn/Karlyn remain due to better skills.

AR10, Ep.11 "We Just Won't Die, Like Roaches"

After a 36 hour extended pit stop, teams left Great Patriotic War
Museum at:
Tyler/James   733am
Dustin/Kandice 741am
Rob/Kimberly   819am
Lyn/Karlyn   908am

This could be a pivotal leg since one of the 4 teams will be
eliminated before the final leg. Will it be today? Teams flew 3,000
miles to Ouerzazate, Morocco and found antique store Antiquittes
de Sud to select one of four good-luck medallions to receive the
clue and deliver it to the pit stop. Dustin/Kandice booked through
Milan and Casablanca while the other teams catch up in
Casablanca (via Paris) but Dustin/Kandice arrived (delayed by
having insufficient time by 5 minutes for a 50 minute connection in
Milan) just before the 1055pm Ouerzazate flight.

Teams arrived in the middle of the night, so all searching for the
store was in the dark and quite difficult. Lyn/Karlyn had used their
connect time in Paris to buy and study a map of Ouerzazate, using
it to find the store first and without the "taxi to follow" approach.
They receivevd a medallion plus he clue directed them 6 miles to
Atlas Studios, a famous movie studio back lot where a YIELD
awaited. The studio did not open until 8am (did I hear Bunch?) and
then the burst of energy from 3 teams was extraordinary. Lyn/
Karlyn were not able to keep up and were last to the YIELD. By that
time Dustin/Kandice have YIELDed Lyn/Karlyn. Dustin/Kandice
state "They are going to hate us, but that isn't anything new."

Next was a ROADBLOCK "Who wants to be a gladiator?" which
had the selected individual join a professional charioteer to pilot a
chariot in a race around the course until they had 2 colored
pennants from above the start line. Of course there were cheering
fans (no doubt studio extras). Lyn/Karlyn had about a 30 minute
wait, did the ROADBLOCK quickly, then starting catching up,
getting on the road to Idelssan 22 miles away and passing
Rob/Kimberly with one more flat tire breakdown. Lyn/Karlyn had
their best performance so far on this leg.

At Idelssan teams must find Café Pirgola to get the clue, which has a DETOUR of Throw It or Grind It. Throw It is to go to a pottery 4 miles away, use the local pottery wheel and make two pots acceptable to the proprietor. Grind It requires teams to travel 4 miles to the North Africa Horse Ranch and Olive Farm where they must use an olive mill to pulverize 77 pounds of olives and pack the crushed olives into pressing sleeves. There are 3 workstations so a fourth team will have to wait. Dustin/Kandice shared some of their knowledge about pottery with Tyler/James, which caused Tyler/James to change their choice to Grind It. This should have been easy, but Dustin/Kandice missed the sign and went miles past the farm. By the time they returned to the right place, Rob/Kimberly had fixed the flat and taken the 3rd workstation at the farm. Dustin/Kandice had to wait until Tyler/James were finished to start their work. Remember that if Tyler/James had gone to their original choice Throw It there would have been a workstation for Dustin/Kandice, who arrive a half-hour behind Rob/Kimberly at the pit stop.

The order leaving Grind It was Tyler/James, Lyn/Karlyn, Rob/Kimberly and Dustin/Kandice. The pit stop was a Berber camp off the road about 25 miles away, so there were no position changes. Teams finished in that order. Tyler/James arrived first but then one had to go back to bring the medallion, outracing Lyn/Karlyn who had arrived in the meantime. Rob/Kimberly arrived 3rd and stated "The Blondes better hope it's a non-elimination round." Dustin/Kandice were non-eliminated, a stroke of luck, and get the 30 minute Marked for Elimination penalty. Their future depends on the design of the next leg. A nice Bunch gets them "even" but really 30 minutes behind unless finishing first.

AR10, Ep.12 "Dude, I'm Such a Hot Giant Chick Right Now"

The teams are released from the Berber camp as follows:
Tyler/James   530am
Lyn/Karlyn   531am
Rob/Kimberly   547am
Dustin/Kandice 616am

Teams receive the first clue to drive 275 miles to Casablanca. Once there all teams had to find a Quartier Habous, an international marketplace in a difficult to find location (at least for those not able to read Arabic) and then find the cluebox. It's time for a ROADBLOCK, "Who's got a taste for the unusual?" as the selected individual eats a traditional Moroccan meal of barbecued ground camel meat. Well, it's really a bit more than that. He/she must find the cluebox (a non-trivial task), purchase 1.1 pounds of camel meal, grind it, prepare it on skewers with a traditional Moroccan recipe and then take it to the chef who grills it. Tyler/James and Dustin/Kandice complete it before the other two teams even arrive. However, that lead over the two lagging teams was closed when all teams had to fly 800 miles to Barcelona. One more Bunch! This has the impact of putting Dustin/Kandice in jeopardy because they now will have only a DETOUR and minor tasks in Barcelona to make up at least 30 minutes.

In Barcelona, teams had to take taxis to Parc del Labyrinth d'Horta and search a large hedge maze for their next clue. The park was closed when they arrived and opened at 10am the next morning. Dustin/Kandice requested taxis to be ready for a 1010am departure. Rob/Kimberly and James/Tyler observed and coped that. One of the Beauty Queens finally acknowledged Lyn and Karlyn's brains-over-brawn strategy as having actual merit: "They're calmer - it's pretty smart, actually."

The next task was a DETOUR Lug It or Lob It. Lug It required taking a taxi 4 miles to an area near the Ramblas, main street of downtown Barcelona, then to the Maremagnum Bridge, changing to the 9.5 foot tall costume of a giant and then walking more than a mile to Placa San Felipe Neri to receive their clue. Lob It starts with a 9 mile taxi ride, then is more interesting as a luck-based needle-in-a-haystack tomato experience. In Bunol Spain every year there is in August a La Tomatina Festival where many tons of tomatoes are tossed at anyone and everyone. It is essentially a giant food fight with tomatoes. Lob It reenacts that festival in the Barcelona area.

Dustin/Kandice and Tyler/James elect to Lug It while Rob/Kimberly and Lyn/Karlyn elect to Lob It. I think this was a huge mistake for Dustin/Kandice. They have to make up 30 minutes or be eliminated, so only a luck-based DETOUR had that potential for them. Rob/Kimberly arrived at the Lob It site and they went to the tomato pile while tomatoes rain down. Some of them hit Kimberly in the face, so she wanted to change DETOURs. She retreated to a taxi. Rob was forced to follow her, but learns that switching requires a 20km taxi ride to reach the other DETOUR. He convinced her to finish Lob It. Returning to the tomato pile, he immediately found a clue.

They leave for the pit stop at Montjuic as Lyn/Karlyn arrived. They quickly find a clue too. The 9.5 foot giant costumes proved difficult for the other teams to handle. They have to ask directions a few times before arriving at Placa San Felipe Neri. When they finish they are very close and leave for Montjuic. At Montjuic, Rob/Kimberly discovered that they have to ascend a long set of stairs to get to the National Museum. They finished 1st. Lyn/Karlyn arrived at the bottom about the same time as Tyler/James and Dustin/Kandice. All 3 teams are confused about where the pit stop exact location is. Lyn/Karlyn figured it out first and finished in 2nd place. Tyler/James finished 3rd and Dustin/Kandice 4th. It is not necessary to apply the 30 minute penalty to Dustin/Kandice. They are eliminated and will not be in the Final 3 with the other teams. Tyler/James stuck with Dustin/Kandice throughout the DETOUR and let the 30 minute penalty be their safety factor.

I think Dustin/Kandice in AR10 were exemplary. They made a navigation mistake at a critical time, which prevented them from getting to the final leg. However, they were delightful to watch in action, with some sneakiness from Dustin balancing their brains, beauty, fitness, charm and ability to attract help. Their smiles won them a lot of assistance along the route of AR10. It is wonderful to later discover that Dustin/Kandice will compete in AR11 All-Stars.

The Final 3 are an alpha male team, a good male/female couple and a female/female team that has done unexpectedly well. Who will win $1,000,000 and what will the final leg, with many tasks and airplane flights with all teams expected, require of the Final 3?

The final finish order was:
Rob/Kimberly
Lyn/Karlyn
Tyler/James
Dustin/Kandice

AR10, Ep.13, Finale "Say Your Deepest Prayers Ever"

It is down to the Final 3 teams. They released from the pit stop at:
Rob/Kimberly 1109pm
Lyn/Karlyn   1144pm
Tyler/James   1153pm

The first clue sends teams to "the church which been under construction for 124 years." I have been to Barcelona and know that is the Sagrada Familia, started by Gaudi and still unfinished. They received a clue to fly to Paris France to visit the Eiffel Tower. When they arrive at Barcelona Airport, it is closed until 4am. Rob/Kimberly used their lead to book a 6am flight to Paris-Charles de Gaulle. Tyler/James got one at 7am and Lyn/Karlyn went against the grain and took a 720am flight to Paris-Orly airport. Now many who have been to Paris know that Orly airport is only 6 miles south of the center of Paris while Charles de Gaulle is 16 miles northeast. I would expect that Lyn/Karlyn will be slightly ahead of James/Tyler at the Eiffel Tower and slightly behind Rob/Kimberly. They did even better than that, also getting ahead of Rob/Kimberly. Will we see the first female/female team race victory?

The next clue sent teams to one of Paris' train stations for a 145 mile train trip to Caen, then find Caen airport. Teams are Bunched once again on the 1225pm train. We can expect that for a final leg World Race Productions will design a lot of Bunching points. Teams find ROADBLOCK "Who's ready to storm the beach?" to relive the experience of World War 2 D-Day when paratroopers were dropped onto Omaha Beach. The selected individual is attached in tandem to an experienced skydiver and they jump. Kimberly had prior skydiving experience; Rob did not. He wanted to do this ROADBLOCK, but they had nominated Kimberly so that couldn't be changed. Darn those ROADBLOCK nomination rules!

The next clue took teams from Bayeux (why didn't teams have time to see the world-famous tapestries?) 163 miles back to Paris. From the Caen station all teams Bunched. In Paris the next clue was to Place de la Concorde to search for the cluebox which offered a DETOUR Art or Fashion. Art required a team to pick up a large painting at a gallery and deliver it to an artist waiting at a specific spot near the Seine River. Fashion was go to Academy Fashion Studio, create a woman's jacket to fit a mannequin from the tools and pattern provided by its designer. All three teams chose Fashion (I guess they are tired and want to save their energy for later) and they finished Tyler/James, Lyn/Karlyn and Rob/ Kimberly.

Teams are instructed to fly to New York City and find the News Building. Lyn/Karlyn made what could prove to be a crucial mistake going back to Orly airport, not knowing that there were no flights from there to NYC. They tried to charm their way into two confirmed seats on the sold-out flight Charles de Gaulle airport to JFK. Tyler/James got on the flight at the last minute. By motivating the gate manager, Rob/Kimberly obtained guaranteed seats. Lyn/Karlyn, who believed what they were told that they wouldn't get on that flight (direction that was probably correct), took an alternate flight from Charles de Gaulle to Newark Airport, closer to downtown Manhattan than JFK Airport is. Are they going to pull off another coup? No; they land about 1 hour after the other 2 did at JFK. It was now a 2 team race.

The taxi that Tyler/James got at JFK had a functional EZPass that allowed them to go through with only a minor pause at a Queens toll plaza. The taxi Rob/Kimberly were in didn't have one and had to use the Cash lane, losing precious minutes. Tyler/James' taxi driver knew where the News Building is and Rob/Kimberly's driver did not. James/Tyler reached the News Building first. At this point the race was effectively over even though both teams played it out. Tyler/James received the clue to travel on foot for 2 miles to the outdoor sculpture shown in a picture (which has the name The Alamo). A person in a yellow cap near that cube handed them the next clue, to the pit stop in the NYC exurb of Garrison about 60 miles north of NYC. They had to go get a taxi to St. Basil's Academy, the pit stop.

Tyler/James never relinquished their lead and finished first for the $1 million prize. Phil Keoghan offered a Sprint phone (product placement) for them to call home. Rob/Kimberly finished about 10 minutes behind for second place. Lyn/Karlyn were directed from first arriving in Manhattan to come straight to the Finish Line and they became the first Female/Female team to finish in the Top 3.

Amazing Race All-Stars, AR11

Amazing Race fans, this should be the most interesting race ever. Contesting the $1 million prize and bragging rights are these teams:
Season 1 Joe and Bill (Life Partners), Kevin and Drew (Friends)
Season 2 Oswald and Danny (Best Friends)
Season 3 Ian and Teri (Married), John Vito and Jill (formerly Dating)
Season 4 nobody (Jon and Kelly were invited but declined)
Season 5 Charla and Mirna (Cousins); Colin and Christie declined
Season 6 nobody
Season 7 Rob and Amber(Married), Uchenna and Joyce (Married)
Season 8 nobody
Season 9 Eric and Danielle, forced by producers out of 2 half-teams
Season 10 David and Mary (Coalminer and Wife), Dustin and Kandice (Beauty Queens)

The selection of the cast for AR11 must have been difficult. Once the All-Stars designation for the race was revealed, Amazing Race fans from around the world bombarded the selectors with guidance. It is not All-Stars based on performance, as winners and #2 teams were avoided except for the rematch between Rob/Amber and Uchenna/Joyce and for Ian/Teri and for Eric. Phil introduced them as "most memorable." It is essentially a collection of fan favorites. There was an effort to balance seasons. A favorite with mediocre performance in AR10 was David/Mary. Rob/Amber, newly married in the year before AR11, expect to earn another huge present.

Ep.1 "I Told You Less Martinis and More Cardio"

Teams get the usual briefing from Phil at the start line, Charles Deering Historic Estate on the south side of Miami. They are off to Ecuador on either American Airlines, leaving later and nonstop, or Copa Airlines with a connection in Panama City. In airport parking, Rob held the van door for Oswald and Danny, who had provided a direct route to the airport for Rob/Amber to follow, later stating "It was the first kind gesture I have made, so I wanted it noted. It killed me to do it." David/Mary, discovering they booked the later-landing flight by mistake, attempted to hoodwink Dustin/Kandice onto it misrepresenting their flight as the fastest flight. Dustin/Kandice checked it out and found they had been lied to, but by that time there were no seats left on the American flight, as David/Mary had told Ian/Teri to go for the American flight, filling up the Amazing Race quota on that flight. So endeth the scheming career of David/Mary. The most memorable shot was of tiny Charla running past Drew to the clues and cars. This showed Kevin and Drew are no longer a force to be reckoned with. Their stay in AR11 won't be long. Rob stated that "Amber and I did not drag our asses back for the Amazing Race All-Stars to finish in second place." Rob is prescient; Amber/Rob will not finish second in this race. David and Mary are awed by meeting their heroes, Rob and Amber.

The planes landed and teams located Plaza San Francisco, then went 3 miles to Pim's Restaurant on a mountain overlooking Quito. Teams drew for 700am, 715am, and 730am departure slots for the next morning, ate a fine Ecuadorian meal and slept there on cots during a pseudo-pit stop. Next morning teams searched for a parking garage in downtown Quito for a marked 4 wheel drive SUV.

The clue directed them to drive up and around the slopes of Cotopaxi, a 19,347 foot active volcano south (down the Pan American Highway) and east of Quito over a dicey country road with lots of ruts and problems. The key was to make the turnoff in the right place. Back-tracking costs time. If a team overshot that turnoff, there was a second one down the Highway for a road that turns back to intersect with the first. The country road took teams to Hacienda Yanahurco in Cotopaxi National Park. Team performance self-driving varied. Rob/Amber had no trouble with it, playing "follow the hired cab" part way (so do Oswald/Danny) and arrived first. John Vito/Jill followed a cab for the first part but later overshot and took the less desirable southern entrance road, as did Charla/Mirna. Drew said to Kevin "Peru is nice. It's beautiful out." Kevin told him "I'm sure it's nice in Peru. We're in Ecuador." For another great quip, Joe on Ian: "Everybody always underestimates them (Ian/Teri) because he is crotchety and old-looking." This is ironic because Joe and Ian are and look like about the same age. Charla/Mirna kidnapped a local FERN to assist them navigating.

Teams arriving at Hacienda Yanahurco found a working ranch with horses as well as their accommodations, all at approximately 13,000 feet. The clue offers teams a DETOUR, Wrangle It or Recover It. In Wrangle It a wild horse needing some maintenance is lassoed, any excess of hoof material is cut away and the mane and tail are trimmed. Recover It is a luck-based Treasure hunt. One team member must dress in the uniform of a historical military figure and then both members attempted to find in a large field the epaulette, button and sword that are needed to complete the uniform. Teams then took a challenging path up to a high point where Phil and a greeter waited at a small overlook. This is Mirador Cotopaxi, the pit stop. Rob/Amber attempted Recover It but had serious problems so they switched to Wrangle It and finished first. Kevin/Drew had vehicle problems (a tire blowout that given the tight race motivated them to drive the small remaining distance on the rim) on the drive on the country road and finished 10th. John Vito/Jill can't make up for the time lost after missing the first turn. They finished in 11th and last place after Kevin/Drew.

AR11, Ep.2 "Beauty is Sometimes Skin Deep"

After an 18 hour extended pit stop, teams are released at:

Rob/Amber	742am
Oswald/Danny	753am
Teri/Ian	817am
Eric/Danielle	824am
Joe/Bill	825am
Dustin/Kandice	834am
Uchenna/Joyce	835am
Charla/Mirna	850am
David/Mary	851am
Kevin/Drew	854am

Teams drove out the same road they came in on to return to Quito International Airport. The highlight of this trip was Kevin/Drew's SUV stuck in mud. Kevin pulled a rope to supplement the traction of the SUV. He attached a rope from the SUV to his body and pulled the car out as Drew was spinning the wheels. Unfortunately, it went further as Drew's lack of control of the vehicle nearly sent the still-attached Kevin under the wheels. David/Mary pulled Charla/Mirna out of the mud. Some teams arrived with airplane reservations and tickets and others elected to do that at the airport. Rob/Amber got a 1245pm flight to Guayaguil (and Oswald/ Danny one at 230pm), booking a 6pm flight from Lima arriving Santiago 130am. The other teams had a direct routing to Lima at 6pm and a flight from there at

9pm arriving Santiago 230am. All teams arrived together at the Santiago airport due to the flights delayed from Guayaquil, wiping out the advantage that Rob/Amber and Oswald/Danny had earned. Eric/Danielle used the Internet in Lima airport to look up Codelco, the company whose headquarters was the focus of the next task. It was very intelligent of Eric/Danielle to think ahead while other teams were in a haze, very possibly from the lateness and the Quito and Yanahurco altitude. Teams arrived by car at different times to Codelco, a very large copper mining company 12 miles from Santiago airport.

There teams found a ROADBLOCK "Who has an eye for detail?" 'Executives' were wheeling and dealing at the table and there were letters on lighters, pens, notepads and ties and sleeves. On 10 pictures on the walls were the names of mines. A team member had to deduce that one of the mines is the correct answer, Chuquicamata. Teams ready for it submitted nominations to the security guard, who either gave them their clue or responded "no". It was difficult for most of the teams to figure it out, but Dustin finished in about 2 minutes. Mary deduced the correct picture was Chuquicamata based on the letters she had. She offered to share her method with Charla. Kevin, hanging around near the guard, overheard Mary giving the right answer, then copied it. At the bottom of the pack was Joyce sharing information with Ian/Teri, a questionable act since they were competing for last place.

All teams were now directed to go to Chuquicamata, near Calama in the Atacama Desert in north central Chile. Teams flew 600 miles into the Calama airport and drove to the mine. The timing caused all teams to Bunch at Santiago airport. After landing David/Mary hired a taxi to follow. Dustin/Kandice had a loosely defined agreement to share a taxi with Charla/Mirna. Charla/Mirna hired a taxi to follow for $200. When Dustin/Kandice tried to follow them they rightfully ask for cost sharing. Charla stated that "you can make yourself beautiful with plastic surgery (I think this is a criticism of the Beauty Queens who are beautiful but I doubt having met them ever had plastic surgery) but to have a pure heart and have morals is not easy to make up." Mirna told that driver during an attempted extortion "Muchas gracias amigo. God help you." On arrival at the mine, teams donned mine safety equipment. Next was DETOUR By Hand or By Machine. By Hand Teams had to select a 2 ton tire and fasten it to the wheel by tightening hard all fasteners. By Machine meant members of a team take turns loading up gravel in a massive front loader, moving the vehicle under its power to a spot and dumping the loads there to reach a yellow mark on a stick. Only Rob/Amber and Joe/Bill chose By Machine. Both completed it together.

Teams selected a marked vehicle and drove 71 miles to the Valley of the Moon entrance. Teams are reminded of 40 km/hr speed limit due to the hazard of the road. Once exiting they resume driving at 50 km/hr until they reached the Valley of the Dead, the pit stop. A "T" in the road is just before Valley of the Dead. To the right is San Pedro de Atacama, to the left Valley of the Dead, but signs did not tell you this. Uchenna/Joyce, Dustin/Kandice, Charla/Mirna, David/Mary and Kevin/Drew all made that error. Mary chose "I would think right because it has the most words."

Before that point Kevin/Drew were at 40 km/hr due to a misinterpretation of instructions for the task and passed by all behind them. When they got to the T they would have been OK if they guessed correctly and turned left, but they didn't and lost out to David/Mary. Kevin/Drew were eliminated. It was probably for the best as their physical conditioning had deteriorated from AR1. Finishing first for the second leg in a row was Rob/Amber. Drew did get attention moving bags that David had put into first class above-seat bins so that they would not get an unfair advantage. Charla/Mirna earned David/Mary's wrath after they passed them on the way to the T.

There were a few gems that occured during this leg illustrating the relationship between Rob and Amber. You might expect that he would just run roughshod over her with impunity, but it doesn't appear to happen that way. In Santiago airport she told him they were going on the same plane with all other teams when he wanted to take a flight 20 minutes later to avoid congestion. It would have been a mistake to take the later flight in my opinion; there was a lot to lose if it was delayed. At Quito airport, a new line opened up and Eric grabbed it. Rob complained but Amber told him that he would have done the same thing if he could have. She has his number.

AR11, Ep.3 "I'm Sorry I'm Wearing a Bathing Suit; It is Very Weird I Know"

Teams were released from the pit stop at:
Rob/Amber   1139pm
Danny/Oswald 1218am
Joe/Bill   1232am
Eric/Danielle   1233am
Uchenna/Joyce 1234am
Dustin/Kandice 1248am
Ian/Teri   1250am
David/Mary   1254am
Charla/Mirna   1255am

First task was finding the clue at San Pedro de Atacama church to Puerto Montt (1000 miles south), finding a marked car on arrival. Teams went to Calama airport, not open in the middle of the night, except Rob/Amber found a small travel agency and got it to open up. 4 teams camped at an airline ticket counter. Uchenna/Joyce offered to find a travel agency and book all 4 teams, who gave credit card numbers but only Joe/Bill gave their authorization code. They and Uchenna/Joyce got tickets; Eric/Danielle and Oswald/ Danny didn't. Eric/Danielle got standby on the first flight with the other 3 teams, arriving at 100pm, but Oswald/ Danny settled for the 2nd flight, arriving at 145pm with the remaining teams.

The clue in cars directed teams to the Centro Acicultura y Ciencias del Mar of Universidad de Los Lagos in Metri about 20 km south of Puerto Montt. Uchenna/Joyce and Ian/Teri elected to follow a shared hired cab while Uchenna/Joyce got their own. They found a fish farming ROADBLOCK "Who can handle a slippery situation?" in Metri at the Centro Acuiculturas del Mar at the Universidad Los Lagos. The selected person empties all 80 fish out of a 1800 gallon tank into a holding tank. When completed the bottom of the tank revealed the clue (which team should copy down). Eric told Danielle: "Just pick 'em up and put your boobs on it. Use your boobs." Joe said "I'm the Fish Whisperer" for using his hands to calm them. There were differences in time to complete this task, but larger ones in coming transportation. Teams are sent about 50km to La Maquina by the river to a cluebox: "Find the sign for La Maquina along the river. Just before you enter Petrohue, search for your next clue." Joe/Bill missed the clue's second half. Driving to La Maquina was hazardous to many teams. Dustin/Kandice were unable to find

51

that cluebox but lucked into the actual location of a DETOUR. David/Mary, distracted while driving past the turnoff sign, went out and back for another 3 hours. Charla/Mirna were totally lost a long way from their target. They fortuitously spotted Joe/Bill, totally lost as well. They pooled resources to jointly get to the DETOUR point.

The DETOUR is Vertical Limit or Wild River. Vertical Limit is walk 200 yards to a cliff where a 40m rock climb by each team member retrieves 2 halves of the clue. Wild River is drive 2 miles to a launch point, don safety gear and paddle down the river for 2.5 miles through class 3 or 4 rapids. On finishing, change back to your clothes and drive to the pit stop at Playa Petrohue, a black volcanic sand beach. No team finished Vertical Limit; probably 2 teams tried.

Rob/Amber finished first. Several teams had problems. Dustin/Kandice arrived at the pit stop 4th, were sent back to find the DETOUR clue, found it and returned to still finish 4th. Joe/Bill ran over a post; Charla/ Mirna lost their car keys; David/Mary finally finished in order #7/#8/#9. David/Mary were eliminated.

AR11, Ep.4 "No Babies on the Race"

The release times were:
Rob/Amber   611am
Uchenna/Joyce 626am
Eric/Danielle   628am
Dustin/Kandice 640am
Danny/Oswald 651am
Ian/Teri   653am
Joe/Bill   805am
Charla/Mirna   811am

Teams flew 800 miles south to Punta Arenas and found Lord Lonsdale's Shipwreck, 15 miles from the airport by taxi. The top 6 teams for the first flight arrived at 1150am, but Joe/Bill and Charla/ Mirna took a second one that arrived 125pm. Uchenna requested written directions from a flight attendant; Rob intercepted them. The Shipwreck has a clue, although teams have to find Maria Jetty first. With the clue teams found DETOUR Navigate It or Sign It revisits Magellan's circumnavigation or uses the methods available in his time to get somewhere. They honor Magellan, discoverer of the Straits of Magellan offshore from Punta Arenas. Sign It has teams on an adjacent hill bringing a vertical pole, paint and supplies to make and hang signs from up the stairs to Magellan's map. The 14 signs should be the major places visited by Magellan in order on his trip, the names of places correctly spelled. In a tricky move, those include Seville as the start and again at the end of the voyage. The signs must point either west or east for their predominant direction they are relative to Punta Arenas, with no penalty for pointing them wrong. Navigate It teams used a map to the town square to receive a compass from a sailor to walk south to Nautilus Company.

Eric/Danielle, Danny/Oswald and Ian/Teri chose Navigate It and finish it quickly. Dustin/Kandice, Rob/Amber and Uchenna/Joyce chose Sign It, but Uchenna/Joyce were the only team to success-fully complete it. Rob/Amber, unable to complete it due to misspel-ling Philippines, were forced to switch to Navigate It. Dustin/Kandice followed Rob/Amber. Eric said of Danielle, "I treat her pretty much like a guy, except that she has nicer boobs", which is true but indicates what a boob he is!

After completion, teams must get to the Sky Airlines Counter to check in for 1 of 2 charter flights to Ushuaia which use LAN Chile equipment, the second 3 hours after the first. This put a high premium on the performance in Punta Arenas, because only teams on the second flight should be involved in the battle to avoid elimination. Rob/Amber earned next-to-last arriving to sign up for the charter, which put them on that second flight. Amber says of Rob "He's full of crap. He wants to finish first; I know he does. Because he's deeply upset that we're not on the first plane. It just makes me mad that he lies. Admit that you want to be in first." He was right to be afraid of being tied with 4 other teams. What if a luck-based task happens and he is unlucky?

Ushuaia, Argentina is the southernmost city with Cape Horn the southern tip of South America 120 miles away. On landing teams went by taxi (Rob/Amber steal Charla/Mirna's reserved one) to Playa Larga in Bahia Lapataia National Park to find a cluebox. Rob/Amber misdirected Charla/Mirna further down the shore. Amber: "They actually believed me telling them that the clue (which Rob/Amber had not found either or would not have been there) is down there. I didn't talk to you guys. I was talking to him." It was a move worthy of a Survivor veteran (Rob and Amber), but not of Amazing Racers, where there's typically only minor deceit. Charla/Mirna responded "Lying bitch".

Teams went to a dock at the end of the Pan American Highway for a boat which left every 20 minutes but shuttled only 2 teams each run over to Isla Redonda. Teams did this ahead of the arrival of Uchenna/Joyce, Charla/Mirna and Rob/Amber and finished Oswald/Danny #1, Eric/Danielle #2, Ian/Teri #3, Joe/Bill #4, Dustin/Kandice #5. The last 3 teams were on the last 2 boats not 20 minutes apart but maybe 5 minutes apart maybe due to low weight of Charla/Mirna or maybe a mistake in releasing the last boat. There was a ROADBLOCK "Who's good at sorting things out?" at the southernmost post office Unidad Postal Fin del Mundo in which a bag of 1600 letters is searched to find 1 of 2 addressed to them. All letters were written by other teams from their original season. It's Rob vs. Mirna with the loser eliminated soon thereafter. Rob got a letter from Patrick and Susan who have strong negative feelings toward him. This is a classic luck-based task and The Force is with Mirna, who found a suitable letter at least 10 minutes before Rob. The editors tried to create ephemeral drama. I believe by then Charla/Mirna had already reached the pit stop so Rob/Amber take their time and did not rush. They know what's coming, their elimination after 3 consecutive leg wins for near-perfect racing.

There was one more task left, walk around the island to find the Mastil de General Belgrano, location of the pit stop. On the way, Mirna had said for motivation "Let's beat the liars. Let's bite karma in the ass." Charla/Mirna were not very fast and took an inferior route, but they got there ahead. How the mighty are fallen! This ended the possibility of that rematch between Rob/Amber and Uchenna/Joyce in the Final 3. It also took two very colorful characters out of the race. Rob managed to state "I have an amazing wife, a great life, a great family. I'm a lucky guy. I'm already a winner." He is absolutely right!

AR11, Ep.5 "You Need to Watch Your Jokes, Guy"

Teams are released at:

Danny/Oswald 1202am
Eric/Danielle 1206am
Ian/Teri 104am
Joe/Bill 155am
Dustin/Kandice 158am
Uchenna/Joyce 238am
Charla/Mirna 241am

The clue sent teams to the Martial Glacier above Ushaia. The chairlift there had hours of operation starting at 8am, when teams go to the end of the line. There they found a backpack with an avalanche beacon and icepick in it. The beacon was to locate and dig up another similar beacon under the snow and ice. Dustin/Kandice failed to take a backpack, so they had to return down to the chairlift and then come back up. Oswald/Danny quipped: "If you get caught in an avalanche, never come looking for Danny and Oswald to get you out." The clue said fly to Maputo Mozambique 7000 miles away. The route is Ushuaia to Buenos Aires, Buenos Aires to Sao Paulo, Sao Paulo to Johannesburg and finally Johannesburg to Maputo. Everyone appeared to be on the same LAM flight as it arrived at 940am two days later.

Once landed in Maputo, teams navigated a marked car with driver for hours to Apopos training field. Ultraviolet detection technology is used to find land mines all over Mozambique. They missed the Hours of Operation and have to wait for the next morning. There was a serious verbal altercation between Joe/Bill and Eric/Danielle. A task was ROADBLOCK "Who smells a rat?" where the selected individual dons special gear, chooses a trainer and guides a rat through a maze until finding a marker above a deactivated mine. The area was searched by an Apopos technician to validate the marker. Teams then traveled to Trabalhadores dos Praca in Maputo. EN1 or EN4 was used. Team performance was determined by how well teams navigated in Maputo.

In Maputo teams faced the choice of DETOUR Pamper or Porter. In Pamper, teams chose a nail polish kit to sell applied colored nail polish to men and women at a Maputo Central Market, a job usually done by males. They must earn 30 meticals, equivalent to $1 U.S. In Porter teams go 2 miles to Market de Janet and load ten 45 pound bags with coal, sew them shut, then haul a bag to a specified address. The Pamper DETOUR was considerably faster. Teams then received a clue to Fortaleza de Maputo, the pit stop. The only race was between the bottom 3 teams, with Joe/Bill slightly ahead of Eric/Danielle, who beat Uchenna/Joyce by using a child guide (good for Eric/Danielle to trust a child with this critical role).

The finish order was:
1. Charla/Mirna
2. Dustin/Kandice
3. Ian/Teri
4. Oswald/Danny
5. Joe/Bill
6. Eric/Danielle
7. Uchenna/Joyce, who are Marked for Elimination

AR11, Ep.6 "We're Going to Trade You for Food Now"

Teams are released from the pit stop at:
Charla/Mirna   907pm
Dustin/Kandice 947pm
Ian/Teri   1013pm
Oswald/Danny 1018pm
Joe/Bill   1032pm
Eric/Danielle   1033pm
Uchenna/Joyce 1036pm and Marked for Elimination

So began the most unexpectedly difficult leg of any Amazing Race. WRP has detailed plans for each location, but missed on this one. It was Hajj. Holy Muslim pilgrimages in Africa made flight reservations very scarce. Teams at Maputo Airport can't find confirmed space on the normal route, 1400 mile nonstop from Maputo to DarEsSalaam, the destination specified in the clue, probably booked months in advance by the WRP staff other than the camera/sound crews. Maputo Airport opened at 5am; Ian/Teri claimed the first place in the line. Only Charla/Mirna got standby on a 800am flight to Johannesburg. All other teams got on the 1145am one hour flight.

The biggest problem was Johannesburg, where a huge overload of pilgrims is. Charla/Mirna immediately connected to reach DarEsSalaam mid-afternoon. The next wave of racers,

Danny/Oswald, Dustin/Kandice and Uchenna/Joyce made the standby cut for the next Air Tanzania/ South African Airways flight due to going "upstairs" to the Air Tanzania office and wangling the best standby positions while Joe/Bill and Ian/Teri did not. Eric said "still waiting for someone to run after us and tell us to stop." Is he prescient? The agent told Eric/Danielle they had mistakenly been given somebody else's seats; now they are asked to leave the plane. Eric offered $50 for any 2 passengers to trade places, but got no takers so they are bumped off this flight leaving at 1200pm and arriveing 530pm. The 955am flight the next morning puts Eric/ Danielle 1 day behind Charla/Mirna. Ian/Teri and Joe/Bill, the final teams to leave Johannesburg, had experienced "Waiting for Godot" in the line in Maputo, but hedged their bet by earlier getting standby on a flight to Johannesburg with the other teams. They got a later Air Malawi combination. They both seek to avoid last place.

Next was a dhow trip to Zanzibar Island on one of 4 dhows. High winds and bad weather in Zanzibar Channel gave producers a pretense to slow down the leading teams. They halted Charla/Mirna for approximately 12 hours (and the next group by about 9 hours). They plus Oswald/Danny took the 530am dhow. The 830am dhow had Dustin/Kandice and Uchenna/Joyce on it. Dhows are pulled by oars with no engine; transit time varied due to tides as well as winds, between 4 hours and 9 hours with the longest being Dustin/Kandice/Uchenna/Joyce. Eric said "Tanzania is where the Tanzanian Devil lives". Danielle, more knowledgeable in this subject, corrects him with Tasmania. He says he was kidding but body language indicates he wasn't and made a mistake.

Next was finding a cluebox for DETOUR Schlep It or Solve It. Schlep It required going 1 mile to the Kijangwani Lumber Yard, loading two 50 pound logs on a handcart and transporting them to a local shipyard. Solve It is walk 1/3 mile to the Beyt al Chai Hotel and put together a 62 piece puzzle involving local artwork known as tinga tinga. Teams then traveled to Kikungwe Masai village for ROADBLOCK "Who's on target?" The selected individual used a Masai wooden weapon the rungu to destroy clay targets 65 feet away to retrieve the next clue. Then they took a taxi 15 miles to the pit stop, Old Fort in Zanzibar's StoneTown.

The finish order for the first 5 teams to complete this difficult leg is:

Charla/Mirna
Oswald/Oswald
Uchenna/Joyce (even with the penalty of 30 minutes in their time)
Dustin/Kandice
Eric/Danielle

That left Ian/Teri and Joe/Bill to fight it out. They landed on Zanzibar and both chose Solve It. Joe/Bill earned a lead of a few minutes by discovering that the pieces also work on the back side. At the rungu toss task, they did OK and finished as Ian/Teri arrived. Ian broke the target on his second try. Both teams took a taxi 15 miles to the pit stop. Joe/Bill got lost trying to find the correct entrance into Old Fort. Joe/Bill won by 2 to 3 minutes and Ian/Teri were eliminated.

Many viewers knowledgeable about this leg believe WRP actually had the pit stop set up in Arusha, on the mainland of Tanzania near Kilimanjaro International Airport. However, difficulties and delays altered the plans for this leg; the pit stop moved to Zanzibar.

AR11, Ep.7 "If I Were In Town, I'd Ask for Your Number"

After trials and tribulations the previous leg and a 36 hour extended pit stop, teams are released from the pit stop in StoneTown:
Charla/Mirna   420am
Danny/Oswald   428am
Uchenna/Joyce 755am
Dustin/Kandice 800am
Eric/Danielle   315pm
Joe/Bill   701pm

Note that differentials between teams are after the first 4 teams were held for 9 to 12 hours. Also note that Joe/Bill arrived and left 15 hours behind the top two teams. I smell a Bunching coming!

Teams flew 5000 miles from the Zanzibar Airport to get to Warsaw Poland. Charla attempted to get a travel agent to not help her competitors. Eric in conversation with Danielle got the response "I'm surprised that Jeremy didn't kill you?" no doubt projecting what she wanted to do to him independent of finishing placement. There are interesting side issues. Dustin/Kandice were first to get tickets.

They connected in Arusha (Kilimanjaro International Airport mentioned earlier), Addis Ababa, and Frankfurt to get to Warsaw at 915am the next morning. Uchenna/Joyce connected in DarEsSalaam, Johannesburg, Frankfurt and are supposed to arrive Warsaw at 915am. Oswald/ Danny and Charla/Mirna connected in Nairobi and Amsterdam to reach Warsaw at 940am. That left Eric/Danielle and Joe/Bill booked to Kilimanjaro International Airport, but they missed the connection there as a KLM pilot rejected them for being 5 minutes late on 50 minute connect time. Joe went out on the runway to flag down the plane, but this didn't work. They stayed overnight and went to Frankfurt and on to Warsaw arriving at 1040pm about 13 hours after the first 4 teams. You know that one of these teams will be last as this leg ends. Uchenna/Joyce missed the connection in Frankfurt and had to arrive in Warsaw on a flight 2 hours later, just before the pre-booked WRP tickets arrival at 1125.

Arriving teams went to the Czapski Palace and found a DETOUR Perfect Angle or Perfect Pitch. In Perfect Angle teams walk 0.5 miles to an Escada Boutique and select a mannequin for transport 400 yards to a Panaramik laboratory where X-Rays at the exact correct angle will reveal the clue. In Perfect Pitch teams travel 3/4 mile to the Pilsudski Palace and on a selected grand piano with a hammer and other tools provided tune the one note way out of tune. Then they listen to a concert pianist check it playing some Chopin. Dustin played a fiddle solo winning the non-finalist talent competition in the 2006 Miss America contest. How long do you think it took them to tune one note? Charla/Mirna couldn't find Panoramik Lab until a 15 year old girl helped them.

Next teams must find Jan III Sobieski Lazienski monument, easy as the taxi drivers know where it is. The next task was a ROADBLOCK to paddle around in Lazienski Park Palace on the Water, but it was edited out of a busy TV episode. Finally teams arrive at that Palace for the pit stop. Dustin/Kandice arrived first. They found that due to Bunching, their bus won't leave for 14 hours (just enough for lagging teams to get there and have a 12 hour pit stop). The producers know what is ahead and have to get things more balanced. Oswald/Danny finished second. Despite a huge lead for Charla/Mirna, Uchenna/Joyce finished in third place and Charla/Mirna fourth. Joe/Bill and Eric/Danielle arrived and the former chose Perfect Angle, the latter Perfect Pitch. Joe/Bill had trouble getting the correct angle for the XRay viewing and finished an hour and a half behind Eric/Danielle. However, it was non-elimination and they got the Marked for Elimination penalty.

AR11. Ep.8 (no episode title due to TBC)

The first bus left at 1pm for the former Auschwitz-Birkenau Concentration Camp 180 miles away in southern Poland with Uchenna/Joyce, Danny/Oswald, and Dustin/ Kandice. Eric/Danielle made the second bus leaving at 5pm along with Charla/Mirna and Joe/Bill. Buses took maybe 5 hours to reach Auschwitz Museum and Memorial for a 'pay tribute and honor the dead' stop, with no Amazing Race tasks, just the celebration of the human spirit. Teams arrived in the evening and their tour sent them to an optional memorial candle lighting and mandatory reading out loud a passage about events there in World War 2 plus a moment of silence. Then they were off to Krakow 35 miles away.

Krakow brought an Intersection. Danny/Oswald teamed up with Uchenna/Joyce. Dustin/Kandice did not want to team with Charla/Mirna, so hid from them, but they don't want to fall behind either so they do pair with them. The last pairing was Eric/Danielle with Joe/Bill. This is unfair because Eric can (and does) maneuver to prevent Joe/Bill from getting 30 minutes ahead of them. Joe/Bill had essentially no chance to make up time. The first intersected group elected a FAST FORWARD walking up the tower of St. Mary's Basilica and tower of Town Hall, counting steps and totalling. The correct answer sent them directly to the pit stop at Pieskowa Skala.

The other 2 groups of intersected teams had to do a DETOUR, Roll It Out or Eat It Up. Roll It Out is to go 1.5 miles to J.Mazurek bakery, then produce 20 fresh bagels and deliver them to a restaurant 1/4 mile away. Eat It Up is to make a 3 inch length of Polish Kielbasa sausage, then all 4 in the group must eat 24 inches of that type of cooked sausage. When all are finished, they get their next clue. Joe/Bill and Eric/Danielle wanted to Roll It Out, but could not find the bakery and had to Eat It Up. There were some exciting verbal moments during the eating. Eric said "You have to eat 24 inches." Bill: "Put it on and just get it really long like he did. And just keep squeezing it off." But the topper came from Eric in response to barfing by Dustin: "Ladies and gentlemen, Miss California" (a line worthy of the prize of best quip for all of AR11; the visual impact of this is stunning). Eating that much sausage went quite slowly for almost every team but they did progress and finish.

At that point 3 teams are left besides Joe/Bill. The next clue sent them by self-drive car 20 miles to Pieskowa Skala. Charla/Mirna got a shady taxi driver. He wanted to extort a higher amount from them and stopped in the middle of nowhere as a negotiating tactic. Mirna cleverly lied in response: "You think I'm made of money. I'm a young girl. I don't have $100. I'm not a millionaire." Awaiting them on arrival was a ROADLBLOCK "Who's a knight in shining armor?" The selected member dons a suit of authentic medieval armor and walks a horse a half mile through a dark forest to the gates of Skala Castle. Then they give the horse to a groom, enter the courtyard and look for the pit stop. Dustin/Kandice did this without incident. Charla is a bit tiny for most suits of armor, but World Race Productions had thought of that and had an appropriate size for her. However, the incongruity of Charla acting like a knight was truly comic. Joe stated "She looked like a dressed up rat." Her horse led her in circles and she fell "flat on her face" twice but she finished. So it's now Eric/Danielle versus Joe/Bill. Bill moved rapidly and finished. Eric was relaxed because he knew he did not have to rush. He finished a few minutes behind Joe/Bill, so Joe/Bill were eliminated because of the 30 minute Marked for Elimination penalty. Given the structure of this leg, it wasn't possible for them to get first place and it would have been improbable if they had escaped elimination. Bill gallantly said "I've had a knight in shining armor for 20 years now." Tied for first were Uchenna/Joyce and Oswald/Danny.

AR11, Ep.9 "The Way You Look, Yeah"

This episode started with these releases from the pit stop:
Uchenna/Joyce 948pm
Danny/Oswald 948pm
Dustin/Kandice 252am
Charla/Mirna 316am
Eric/Danielle 322am

Teams flew from Krakow airport 5500 miles to Kuala Lumpur, Malaysia. Scarce flight reservations forced teams to get cutthroat. Eric asked Charla and Mirna, with a slight head start over Eric/Danielle, if they would relinquish 1 of the 2 personal computers they were using for flight research. Mirna refused. Later that day they requested of Eric to cut in line in front of him. He didn't get mad; he got even. Oswald/Danny considered connecting in Frankfurt but concluding the risk of missing the connection was high they booked via Paris to arrive Kuala Lumpur 725am the next morning. Dustin/Kandice booked the same, as does Eric/Danielle. Uchenna/Joyce took the Frankfurt connection, supposed to arrive Kuala Lumpur at 645am. Eric said "You guys are braver than me." Uchenna responded "I'm optimistic," which proved a bad decision.

Mirna/Charla used their research time to good advantage as they went through Warsaw and Vienna to arrive Kuala Lumpur at 445am. With that lead they should have a lock on first place. The agent in Krakow had computer problems and couldn't deliver a normal ticket. Uchenna/Joyce had 50 minutes, 5 more than the minimum to connect in Frankfurt, but ticket validity questions caused them to be stranded. They booked an alternate route via Hong Kong but it didn't arrive until 430pm, 9 hours behind and after all other teams had checked in. The only prior winners of an Amazing Race in AR11 are about to be eliminated. I guess this leg was originally meant to be non-elimination (NEL), but having Uchenna/Joyce so far behind would have caused severe logistical problems for Phil Keoghan and the production crew, so I believe an on-the-spot Bertram van Munster decision changed it to an elimination leg. Corroborating evidence will soon appear.

Back to the race! Teams are asked to go to Batu Caves, 7 miles north of Kuala Lumpur, and walk up its 272 steps to get their next clue. Charla says they definitely don't need a Stairmaster in this country. Charla/Mirna arrived 2 to 2 3/4 hours ahead of the next 3 teams. Next they went by taxi 10 miles to Kampung Baru Mosque where a Yield and DETOUR awaited. Dustin/Kandice elected to YIELD Eric/Danielle. Eric was upset and responded: "Those dirty, dirty pirate hookers" and told Danielle they got YIELDed because of "those dirty pirate hookers." The DETOUR is Artistic Impressions or Cookie Convection. Artistic Impression requires teams to travel on foot to Dewan Lama where they batik 1 of 3 available patterns onto a 45 square foot piece of cloth and then dye it. Cookie Convection is to walk 1/2 mile to Chow Kit Bomba and find a marked cookie stall set up by the street, then find the 1 cookie in 600 boxes of Malaysian festive cookies with a black licorice center, your classic random task. I think all teams chose cookies.

Next was ROADBLOCK "Who's ready for a part-time job?" in the Taman Sir Hartamas district. Danielle complained "Every ROADBLOCK that is designed for a guy, I am doing; everyone that is designed for a girl, Eric is doing. He's a woman." Teams traveled 6 miles by taxi to find a recycled newspaper truck. The selected individual uses a bicycle with side cart to purchase enough old newspapers to measure of 8 hands high. In some cases the buyers were bidding against each other and near the end Danny paid an exorbitant amount for the quantity he wanted.

The pit stop was at Caracosa Seri Negara. After arriving at Kuala Lumpur airport, it was time for the mercy finish for Uchenna/Joyce. Their first clue told them to travel by taxi to the next pit stop, where they were eliminated. Finish order is:

Dustin/Kandice
Charla/Mirna
Eric/Danielle
Danny/Oswald
Uchenna/Joyce, last and eliminated

How could Charla/Mirna lose a 2 ¾ hour lead and finish in 2nd one hour back? It had to be poor performance at each of the tasks, particularly Cookie convection, which was a random task. This will have to be one of the great mysteris of AR11.

AR11, Ep.10 "We Are Trying to Make Love, Not War"

The 4 remaining teams are released from the pit stop:
Dustin/Kandice 1228am
Charla/Mirna   129am
Eric/Danielle   150am
Danny/Oswald   219am

Teams flew 1500 miles to Hong Kong. All teams played games as a result of being on standby for the first flight. Only Danny/Oswald, getting ahead by intelligently going to airline offices and on standby before the other teams, got the 750am flight arriving Hong Kong 1155am. There was a lot of infighting between Dustin and Mirna. Dustin said of Mirna "she wins the pushy award of the year." Dustin/Kandice and Charla/ Mirna were on the 915am flight arriving 1255pm. Eric/Danielle were stuck with the 1005am flight via Ho Chi Minh City landing in Hong Kong at 320pm. Danielle said "the standby fairy doesn't like us, apparently, so we are absolutely dead last." Charla unveiled her secret weapon by putting her Wheelys into place at Hong Kong airport. Teams had to locate Sun Wah Kiu Dry Cleaning & Laundry in Kowloon to receive their next clue.

The clue packet had a FAST FORWARD, the last of AR11. A team goes for this at Kai Tak Airport (the old one), where an action movie scene is supposedly being filmed. Team members have to don safety gear before they get in with a professional stunt driver and are tilted up to almost 90 degrees. Oswald/Danny got there and finished it as the next 2 teams arrived at the airport. Oswald/Danny drove to Happy Valley Race Course and Hong Kong Jockey Club, the pit stop. They spent all their money on the $20 toll to get there.

The other teams have DETOUR Kung Fu Fighting or Lost in Translation. What both have in common is difficulty finding the starting point. Kung Fu fighting requires taking a taxi 5 miles to 5 Tonkin Street to locate the former Cheung Sha Wan Police Quarters. They must climb an 11 story building on bamboo scaffolding and avoid the ongoing battles of stunt Kung Fu experts to get to the clue at the top. This is a visually rich task but its difficulty rating for anybody that can climb is low. Dustin/Kandice selected this option. Teams finished this quickly.

Lost in Translation at 120 Nga Tsin Wai Road in Kowloon is exactly match a symbol in a photo with a symbol on hundreds of pages of similar symbols. Charla/Mirna started, but elected to switch to Kung Fu Fighting. Charla on scaffolding in the midst of battling swarming kung fu experts was comical. The line "We can make a beauty queen sandwich out of her (Mirna)" was stated by Dustin/Kandice.

Teams took the Star Ferry to Hong Kong Island and taxi 4 minutes to the abandoned Kennedytown/Block Police headquarters. There they found ROADBLOCK "Who's Ready to Break Down Barriers?" requiring the selected individual to kick down doors until finding a room with their clue. This is a classic luck-based task, with the strength needed to kick the doors relatively low. Kandice excelled.

Teams now took a marked car and drove it 5 miles to Victoria Park, Causeway Bay to find its boat pond, where they used a control to maneuver a toy boat with a Travelocity gnome on top to the other side. If the gnome fell off they have to redo it. This required patience but not a great deal of skill. No teams' gnomes got wet. Teams went to Happy Valley Race Course/Hong Kong Jockey Club for the pit stop. Charla/Mirna don't communicate well with their initial taxi driver going to Hong Kong Island and the Star Ferry Terminal. There they rode the Star Ferry back to Kowloon to take it from Kowloon to Hong Kong Island as required. This cost time; they fell behind Dustin/Kandice and eventually finished about 2 hours back. They finished in the order Oswald/Danny, Dustin/Kandice, Charla/Mirna. Eric/Danielle are lost near Happy Valley when Danielle intelligently insisted hiring a taxi to follow to the pit stop. They are last but non-eliminated, Marked for Elimination.

AR11, Ep.11 "Good Doing Business With You"

Teams left the pit stop in Hong Kong at:
Oswald/Danny 341am
Dustin/Kandice 523am
Charla/Mirna   706am
Eric/Danielle   931am, for 6 hours from leader to last team

The first clue is to Hong Kong/Macau Ferry Terminal where they get a turbojet ferry for the 40 mile trip to Macau. The ferry took 55 minutes and service is less in the wee hours when Danny/Oswald arrived. Teams took taxis 2 miles to Macau Tower which at 1109 feet towers over the city (I could not resist that one). The clue mentions a YIELD ahead. Teams find Macau Tower doesn't open until 10am, giving all teams but Eric/Danielle time to get there. Oswald/Danny ran out of money the prior leg, wanting to build a cushion selling the YIELD to Dustin/Kandice, who negotiated based on not being exactly rolling in money. They agreed on the price of

$45 and on Dustin/Kandice getting the right to specify which of the 2 lagging teams Oswald/Danny will use it on. "Now we are officially the YIELD Queens. We just bought a YIELD." At 10am they entered to find the Tower Hours of Operation are 11am to 10pm.

Oswald/Danny stepped aside to let Dustin/Kandice get to the pulled numbers first so they will have #1 then passed them on the way to the YIELD. They kept their bargain. Mirna stated "Oswald and Danny made a deal with the Beauty Queens. That's like making a deal with the Devil." Next was ROADBLOCK "Jump off Macau Tower" with a tethered system to allow jumpers flexibility but guarantee their safety after walking around the SkyWalk first. The jump is 660 feet, almost 60% of the available vertical space.

Next teams went to Lou Lim Ioc Gardens, where the clue introduces a DETOUR Noodles or Dragon. In Noodles, teams get to a pasta factory on the second floor of a commercial building, use traditional methods with two poles to flatten the dough, then cut it to make 2 bundles of noodles which if acceptable gets their next clue. In Dragon, teams go 1 mile to a warehouse for dragon heads and drums, then carry them 3/4 mile to Dam Van Lake where a number of dragon boats are moored. They match the head to the boat, which results in their next clue. Oswald/Danny elected Dragon and they had taxi troubles. After a late arrival, Oswald/Danny now faced navigation trouble finding a specific dock to match their dragonhead to the correct dragon boat and finish this DETOUR. The other 3 teams were Dustin/Kandice redoing it, Charla/Mirna redoing it twice and Eric/Danielle mastering it the first time.

Finally teams must travel to find a marked mini moke (tiny car) and drive that to the Island of Taipa and Coloane fishing village. They are redirected on that island to Trilho da Taipa Pequena 2000, the pit stop. The first team to arrive is Dustin/Kandice. Eric/Danielle arrived second and the clock starts on their 30 minute penalty. Charla/Mirna arrived before it is completed, so they are the official 2nd place finishers this leg. Since the clock runs out 90 minutes before the arrival of Oswald/Danny, Eric/Danielle got third. Oswald/Danny were now in last place, but it is a second consecutive non-elimination leg. They got a Marked for Elimination penalty to be applied on the next leg. Oswald/Danny saw their 6 hour lead over Eric/Danielle compressed down to about 30 minutes by the Hours of Operation, but they performed poorly from there through all transportation and tasks to the pit stop. It is lucky to be non-elimination, despite the Marked for Elimination penalty. Oswald/Danny were philosophical about it: "today was a day when karma bit Oswald and Danny in the ass." Oswald tells Phil "No regrets darling."

As it happened, there were 2 non-elimination legs in a row. That has happened very few times before but there is nothing prohibiting it. I believe the consecutive NELs were a byproduct of the previously mentioned change of Kuala Lumpur from non-elimination to elimination leg due to the huge delay that Uchenna/Joyce suffered.

AR11, Ep.12 "Oh My God, the Teletubbies Go To War"

Release times from the Macau pit stop were:
Dustin/Kandice 215am
Charla/Mirna   250am
Eric/Danielle   306am
Oswald/Danny 437am

Teams flew to Guam, 2100 miles to the southeast. Mirna asked a Hong Kong taxi driver "How you say airport?" His response: "Airport" since Hong Kong has English and Mandarin Chinese as its official languages. Oswald/Danny can't get the originating flight of the 3 other teams, but with a long layover in Tokyo they caught the others before the flight from Tokyo to Hong Kong. It's another Bunch. They arrived Guam 10pm and drove a marked car 9 miles to Anderson Air Force base, but found an Hours of Operation delay until the base opens at 7am. Then they got a military escort, and traveled with the escort to the control tower, which they climbed. There they found a DETOUR Care Package or Engine Care.

Care Package is neat. Teams selecting it got to ride a C-17 plane and participate in a training run for its Operation Christmas Drop, which sends essential suppliers to locals on neighboring islands. Charla/Mirna were the only team to sign up for this. They had to load 500 pounds of supplies in this huge box, which is sealed up and put on a pallet with a parachute attached, to the approval of the Load Master. The C-17 flew over the target island and dropped the box over a predetermined place, then the plane returned to base and the team gets the next clue. Later reporting of this indicated that the training run was actually over a remote part of Guam itself. However, the actual box packed by Charla/Mirna was dropped on an outlying island about a week later.

The 3 other teams thought Engine Care would be quicker. B-52 engines have to be cleaned. This was brute force grunt work, doubtless why these teams chose it because of its predictability. The cleaning job must pass the inspection of the Air Force Maintenance Officer before they get the next clue. Either Dustin or Kandice stated "There is no charming the sergeant. The sergeant is all about business. We weren't getting anywhere with a smile. We had to scrub." Danny said of another of those sergeants "I'm bringing you over to tell my maid how to clean, cause obviously I don't know what to tell her." Oswald incisively observed as Charla was suited with protective gear for her role in the airlift: "O my God, the Teletubbies go to War."

Teams drove to Asan Bay and the War of the Pacific Historical Park. Oswald/Danny were lost and not taking the most efficient route. They did it again on the next self-drive segment. There they got directions to the U.S. Naval Base-Guam, a further 21 miles, where a naval escort drives them to their next task. It's a ROADBLOCK "Who's ready to search far and wide?" The selected individuals used a hand-held GPS device to navigate around a jungle and locate 1 of 4 Search and Rescue Training Officers. That officer reprogrammed the device to the coordinates of a landing zone for a helicopter which returns them. I remember this in the original episode with the camouflage so good that a training officer less than 20 feet from Danielle was invisible. Oswald also found them very difficult to spot. Both teams lost critical time.

The next clue took them to the pit stop at Fort Soledad. Dustin/Kandice performed very well to take first place. Eric/Danielle were second. Charla/Mirna struggled at times but good enough for third place. Oswald/Danny were not able to make up the relatively small amount of time lost in self-driving and finished fourth, so they were eliminated before application of the penalty. Oswald referred to the sold YIELD as the turning point: "We know that karma was a particular bitch on the last leg of the race, and we got slapped hard for it."

AR11, Ep.13, Finale "Low to the Ground, That's My Technique

This episode started with a clue to fly to Hawaii (it's a long way to swim) and find Lanai's Shipwreck Beach. Due to the time of day and fit with the flight combinations, to fly to Hawaii (mostly east) was best accomplished by connecting in Tokyo-Narita for a 5,500 mile total flying distance. Charla/Mirna, either through planning based on careful study of the schedules or by dumb luck as they were rolling through Tokyo-Narita airport, discovered an earlier flight that had started boarding but they were able to talk their way onto it. They then took the first of the Sunshine Helicopters to get them close to the Lanai beach that is near the shipwreck. They had to wait over an hour for scheduled departure at 900am, Eric/Danielle got the 910am, and Dustin/Kandice lagged on the 920am.

Next was a DETOUR, Over Water or Under Water. Over Water means to paddle a surfboard to reach a buoy with the next clue attached. Under Water is to swim into an underwater cave which has the clue. You might ask "Where is the ROADBLOCK?" for this episode. It is likely that there was one, probably on Lanai, but it was unaired. It involved cliff-jumping similar to the cliff divers in Acapulco. Charla/Mirna did Over; Eric/Danielle started with that but switched after seeing the balance difficulties that Charla/Mirna had; Dustin/Kandice did Under. Next, teams had to walk fast for one mile along the rocky coast to Shipwreck Beach, where teams take kayaks out to the side of the World War 2 wreck to find the clue with their final destination city.

They discovered their next destination is 2300 miles away, Oakland International Airport (probably due to ease of having all three Final 3 teams on the same flight and because it positions the arrival into that early morning time that is desirable for Amazing Race Finale arrivals). The flip side of that was a wait of nearly 12 hours before flying. Teams flew Honolulu to Oakland International Airport and then find taxis. I have visions of Wil trying to cut the taxi line in AR2 and being prevented by a dispatcher from doing that, which probably cost them $1 million. Differential taxi performance was the determinant of the final placement with Eric/Danielle having a more competent driver. Dustin/Kandice were slightly behind them and Charla/Mirna back a bit. There was an unaired task, to visit the Grateful Dead House at 710 Ashbury one block from Haight St.

69

Eric/Danielle won the taxi race to there.

Next teams drove to San Francisco's Old Mint. A difficult task waited to test the insights team members have of what their partners believe. One from each team (Eric, Dustin and Charla) was chosen to set a code by answering 4 questions on teams in the race. The most interesting were "Who was the most annoying?" and "Who was the most overrated?" There was an array of the numbers 0 through 9 each representing one team so one had to be left out. The other partner punched in with numbers answers they expect the original person used. If a team didn't solve this in 10 minutes, they are released to taxi to the pit stop, which happened to both Dustin/Kandice and later Charla/Mirna. Danielle was able to crack the code and finish before time ran out by changing the answer on "most trustworthy" to Oswald/Danny while Dustin/ Kandice did not match on that question. Eric/Danielle now hopped into a taxi with the cumulative impact of first arrival and quickest time at the Old Mint going for them. The drive to Strybing Arboretum was relatively short and nothing happened to change the order of the finish. Eric/ Danielle won the $1 million and Danielle won redemption by doing for Eric what his buddy Jeremy could not. Dustin/Kandice finished about 10 minutes behind and Charla/Mirna were dropped on the wrong side of Strybing Arboretum and had to use Charla's Wheelys to get to the Finish Line. At the finish Line Phil Keoghan handed Eric a dialed phone and told him to talk to his family. He got Jeremy on the line and said this classic: "Yeah, yeah I'm rich, biotch. Dude, I'm going to give you some spankings when I get home."

This was the first time a composite team had been put together. This was the first time that 2 female/female teams had finished in the F3. It was the second time Rob/Amber were disappointed by their finish. No, they did not finish 2nd; they were 8th although I would have preferred to see them exit just before the F3. Viewership for AR11 should have been higher. I was pleased by this race's quality as well as the unexpected demise of the top 2 teams in the race; this left the Final 3 open for whoever could outlast the others and wanted it a little more. Eric and Danielle certainly wanted it and stayed in long enough to get their only win in the final episode.

AMAZING RACE 12

The teams for AR12 are:

Shana and Jennifer, Los Angeles, best friends, actress and legal assistant, Age 32/32

Azaria and Hendekea, New Orleans and Torrance CA, brother/sister, facilities engineer and aerospace engineer, age 27 and 23

Christina and Ronald, Tacoma WA and Washington DC, father/daughter, VP sales and policy analyst, age 58 and 26

Jason and Lorena, Sherman Oaks CA, dating, videographer and bartender, age 27/33

Ari and Staella, Long Beach and Fountain Valley CA, best friends, waiter and restaurant manager, age 21 and 24

Marianna and Julia, Los Angeles CA, sisters, art gallery manager and production assistant, age 25 and 26

TK and Rachel, Huntington Beach CA, dating, substitute teacher and florist, age 22/23

Kate and Pat, Thousand Oaks CA, married, ministers, age 49/65

Nicolas and Donald, Chicago and Elkhorn WI, grandfather/grandson, pilot and retired, age 23 and 69

Kynt and Vyxsin, Louisville KY, waiters/receptionists, age 31 and 29

Nathan and Jennifer, Fountain Valley and Huntington Beach CA, volleyball coach and student, age 24 and 23

What's special about this cast? 4 of them were at Huntington Beach CA high school at the same time. Casting maybe took recommendations on who a contestant could recommend. It is common in reality TV to cast the young and beautiful or those aspiring to be actors. AR12 has a heavy dose of models/actors. Where are the real people also not from California? I wish Amazing Race casting directors knew the answer. They did choose Kynt/Vyxsin. Kynt says "we're like little Energizer bunnies." What better philosophy to win this race! Let's see how energized those bunnies are after constant travel/tasks and little sleep.

Ep.1 "Donkeys Have Souls Too"

The actual start of the race is the Playboy mansion. Nicolas/Donald ask the gate attendant for directions to LAX and it takes a while during which time the other teams in a lineup all 10 vehicles behind have to wait and fume (I fumed watching this). The first clue sends teams to Shannon, Ireland. The first flight with 6 teams on British Airways connecting in London is supposed to land first at Shannon and the second flight on Aer Lingus is scheduled to land later. They both land about the same time. Teams get a taxi to the Rossaveal ferry dock and take the ferry to InishMore in the Aran Islands in Galway Bay. Then they walk up a big hill to find their next clue at an ancient site Tempall Bhean, the smallest church in Ireland. Then they pull numbers for 800am, 830am and 900am departures, eat and Rest, Relax and Mingle. The next morning they take the return ferry to the mainland.

The next morning teams are raring to go. After returning from Inishmore Island, they drive 42 miles to a ROADBLOCK "Who wants to pedal for their partner?" on the Cleggan Farm, County Galway. It sounds easy, doesn't it? Teams doing this find out one will take the lead and pedal the top half of a dual bicycle, their partner will ride on the bottom half of it on a wire 200 feet over Cleggan Bay. This is quick but scary, followed by pedaling real bicycles-built-for-two to dig peat. They need to dig up 15 proper sized blocks of peat and select a donkey the team directs to its tethering post to receive the clue. This is some of the best humor of all episodes of AR12. The donkey does not cooperate for Nathan/Jen and they lose 4 hours. Even worse, the donkey for Ari/Staella stopped cold and will not budge. After 7 hours of delays they get it moving and all the other teams are long gone with the clue to the pit stop. Ari says "Karma came back and bit us in the ass." His behavior toward other teams and the donkey did merit serious punishment.

Teams self-drove 13 miles to Connemara Heritage and History Center in Clifden, pit stop for this episode. The order of arrival at the pit stop:
1. Azaria/Hendekea
2. Kynt/Vyxsin
3. TK/Rachel
4. Lorena/Jason
5. Nicolas/Donald
6. Shana/Jennifer
7. Ronald/Christina
8. Kate/Pat

9. Marianna/Julia
10. Nathan/Jennifer
11. Ari/Staella, who are eliminated

AR12, Ep.2 "I've Become the Archie Bunker of the Home"
Teams fly 600 miles to Amsterdam after they leave the pit stop. The release times from the pit stop are:
1. Azaria/Hendekea 1200am
2. Kynt/Vyzsin   1205am
3. TK/Rachel   1215am
4. Lorena/Jason   115am
5. Nicolas/Donald   135am
6. Shana/Jennifer   157am
7. Christina/Ronald   246am
8. Kate/Pat   247am
9. Marianna/Julia   259am
10. Nathan/Jennifer   300am

All teams except Marianna/Julia, Ronald/Christina and Kate/Pat were flying 90 minutes ahead. Teams take a 20 minute train from Schiphol Airport to Centraal Station and find the Melkmeisjes Bridge. Azaria/ Hendekea were innovative in their approach paying "on the train." With no conductors to buy from and very occasional ticket inspectors they would either have to pay a large fine or nothing. Which do you think it was? A DETOUR awaits, Hoist It or Hunt It. Hoist It is use your strength to dead-lift items of furniture to a home where the entry is via a large window that opens. Getting the rope hoist just right is the key to success. The items are chair, table, lamp, stroller and TV. Hunt It involved finding two bicycles with identical colors on the tag out of thousands in a parking lot spanning several blocks and 3 levels. Once they get and match they must ride those bikes 5 miles to buiksloter meerplein. The selected individual doing Hoist It best was tiny Rachel. She had perfect leverage and did it quickly after TK had failed.

Next is a trip by #30 bus (except Kate and Pat after hours used the #44 bus after missing the last #30 by seconds) to the rural village of Ransdorp. ROADBLOCK "Which of you is the Acrobat?" is at the fierljeppen, muddy ditch. The task is ditch-vault over to get the clue and back. The ditch is not very wide, but with the awkward long pole the technique of the selected individuals had to be pretty good to get across. If they did not pay attention to principles of forward momentum, they likely got a dunking. For an unknown reason Nicolas listened to Donald about his ability to do ditch-vaulting and let him do this ROADBLOCK. Donald: "I had to strip down a little bit", removing all except large bikini briefs. Phil states "There have been complaints from the locals you got down to your underpants." Donald responds "I went further than that."

The final task was ride a bakfiets cargo bicycle on a specified route to Durgerdam Yacht Club on the edge of Lake Marker and find Phil at the pit stop. Lorena/Jason had trouble spotting the pit stop, as did others. You can see the order of finish here:

1. Lorena/Jason
2. Shannon/Jennifer
3. Nathan/Jennifer
4. Kynt/Vyxsin
5. Azaria/Hendekea
6. TK/Rachel
7. Marianna/Julia
8. Nicolas/Donald
9. Christina/Ronald
10. Kate/Pat

Last place Kate/Pat were eliminated. Kate says "the Amazing Race is a love letter to the planet." How true! Ronald is obnoxious this episode.

AR12, Ep.3 "Please Lord, Give Me Milk"

The pit stop release time for each team was:
1. Lorena/Jason   419am
2. Shannon/Jennifer 430am
3. Nathan/Jennifer   431am
4. Kynt/Vyxsin   521am
5. Azaria/Hendekea 522am
6. TK/Rachel   523am
7. Marianna/Julia   546am
8. Nicolas/Donald   547am
9. Ronald/Christina   626am

Ronald's ability to irritate included himself. He developed a hernia during the last leg. The clue directs teams to fly 3000 miles to Ouagadougou, Burkina Faso and take a taxi to the train station. Nathan/Jennifer got an early flight; other teams faced a delay causing a tight connection in Charles de Gaulle Airport. This is over-dramatized as all teams make it through CDG to Ouagadougou. When teams arrive at the train station it's closed and won't open until 6am the next morning. Teams buy tickets to Bingo, a special whistle or flag stop in the middle of nowhere 25 miles north of Ouagadougou, reached in 45 minutes.

At Bingo is ROADBLOCK "Who's ready to work up a thirst?" which is to do what the Tuareg nomads do, milk a camel. A bowl must be filled at or higher than a marked line and you drink it. If teams spill it, the level must be returned to above the line. Any camel that runs dry will result in the selected individual waiting until all other teams start before they can switch to another camel. Next the team must lead 4 camels provided by nomads along a marked path to the next route marker, which turns out to be next to the local school. Marianna/Julia had a difficult time with a dry camel. Then they provided route guidance to their friends Lorena/Jason, competing for last place, because Lorena had great difficulty in milking her camel and then spilled it. It was a good move for the friendship, but it led to the elimination of Marianna/Julia.

Next is DETOUR Teach It or Learn It. In Teach It, a child with no knowledge of English must be taught the correctly pronounced words for 10 common objects shown on flashcards. In Learn It, the team must learn from a child how to pronounce the names of 10 common objects in the local Moore language shown on flashcards. The English words include skyscraper, motorcycle, helicopter, baseball, bridge, camera and cowboy. The Moore words were car, hut, camel, bicycle, fish, train, girl, boy, tree and drum. After Learn It, Shana thanked the teacher but not her actual instructor, a young boy. Teams followed a marked path to the pit stop. Teams finishing 2 to 6 arrived in less than one minute of each other. Ronald wore a "Who's Your Daddy?" tee shirt. Once again in AR12 the winners of the humor prize are animals, this time camels.

The finish order was:

1. Azaria/Hendekea
2. TK/Rachel
3. Nathan/Jennifer
4. Kynt/Vyxsin
5. Christina/Ronald
6. Nicolas/Donald
7. Shana/Jennifer
8. Lorena/Jason
9. Marianna/Julia, eliminated

AR12, Ep.4 "Let's Name Our Chicken Phil"

Teams are released from the pit stop in Bingo, Burkina Faso as follows:

Azaria/Hendekea	758am
TK/Rachel	812am
Nathan/Jennifer	813am
Kynt/Vyxsin	814am
Christina/Ronald	815am
Nicolas/Donald	816am
Shana/Jennifer	838am
Lorena/Jason	1007am

The first clue directs teams to follow a marked path to find the tribal chief, who gives them a present plus the clue. That present is a live chicken which must be caught and kept for the entire leg. "No chicken, No check-in". Teams get into a van to go 100 miles west and a bit south to Bouda-Pelegtanga. Once there they find a DETOUR Shake Your Pans or Shake Your Booty. Shake Your Pans requires teams to mine for gold by panning for an ounce of gold. Shake Your Booty has teams learning a traditional local dance, from which they will innovate to bring something new and interesting. It will be performed in front of a large audience including 3 celebrities who will be the Judges. If they are judged OK, they get their clue. If not, then they get a 10 minute penalty. However, the main penalty is waiting in the line to perform as it takes at least 5 minutes for each performance and its judging. Teams receiving the 10 minute penalty were Nathan/Jennifer and Christina/ Ronald. Jason accurately stated that "I feel like we're on American Idol right now. In Africa. I wonder if that's Simon or that's Paula Abdul."

A U-Turn is a new innovation introduced in this episode. It is always found in conjunction with a DETOUR. When exercised by a team on any other team behind them, the trailing team has to perform the other DETOUR they did not elect the first time. This takes maybe 15 to 30 minutes. It effectively replaces the YIELD which had a predictable length of time (about 30 minutes) but was static and lacked the excitement of another DETOUR performed. Teams are next sent to the local Bouda-Pelegtanga market where a U-Turn precedes the next clue.

The only team that exercises its U-Turn rights is Shana/Jennifer who started 80 minutes in front of Lorena/Jason and a very small amount ahead of TK/Rachel. They U-Turned Jason/Lorena, forcing them to spend an extra 15 minutes at Shake Your Pans, gold mining before receiving the clue. That clue directs teams to taxis for a 2 hour journey to Tampouy goat market on the outskirts of Ouagadougou. It's ROADBLOCK "Who's Ready for a Juggling Act?" where a bicycle is used to deliver several items to specific places after the selected individual has packed them on a carrier on back of the bicycle. The items were 3 blankets printed with African patterns, 2 yellow jugs, a bundle of sticks, a plant, 2 teakettles, 2 loops of twine and, honoring where they were, a live goat.

After the ROADBLOCK is a clue for a taxi to pit stop Ouagadougou Hotel de Ville. Teams surrender their live chicken to check in.

The finishing order was:
1. Azaria/Hendekea
2. Nathan/Jennifer
3. Christina/Ronald
4. Nicolas/Donald
5. Kynt/Vyxsin
6. Shana/Jennifer
7. TK/Rachel
8. Lorena/Jason
Lorena/Jason never had a chance. Their ride to the Goat Market started 95 minutes behind; most teams had arrived when they started and had checked in before Lorena/Jason arrived at the Goat Market. This episode had no Bunching points, quite unusual but not unique. The episodes involving animals (chickens and goats this

time) are interesting. See the Animals chapter for details.

AR12, Ep.5 "We Really Burn Bridges, for Sure"

These are the release times from the Ouagadougou pit stop:

Azaria/Hendekeka	645am
Nathan/Jennifer	646am
Christina/Ronald	717am
Nicolas/Donald	718am
Kynt/Vyxsin	727am
Shana/Jennifer	744am
TK/Rachel	756am

The clue is fly to Vilnius, Lithuania. Once there they drove marked cars to St. Anne's Church. It is believed that there was a not-shown FAST FORWARD at Trakai Island Castle west of Vilnius, with no team electing it. The action ahead is fast and furious.

We now have a case of airline ticketing bingo. All teams found an Internet café before Air France's office at Ouagadougou airport opens but they cannot get ticketed by AR14 rules except at an authorized airline ticket office. All teams were departing Ouagadougou on a flight to Paris-CDG so all the jockeying was about how teams get from Charles de Gaulle to Vilnius. Christina/Ronald found one arriving Vilnius 210pm (connecting through Prague). Other teams know that the earliest arrival is 125pm so they fight to get seats on it. Nicolas boldly says right in front of those other teams as they arrive at Air France ticketing to "Everyone else? Give them later flights." I have seen many racers attempt to have flight ticketing personnel screw their opponents, but this was as raw as it gets. Besides that it has only worked once out of about a dozen attempts. What goes around comes around, at least the way AR12 is edited. Azaria/Hendekea's ticket agent give them the 125pm flight. Next, Nicolas is immediately told that the 125pm flight is full and booked to arrive at 535pm. Nicolas argued to no avail as that agent pretended to not understand. Nathan told Azaria "That was karma." So Nathan/Jennifer went to the same ticket agent and requested the 125pm flight and are ticketed for it. Shana/Jennifer also get the 125pm flight (connecting through Amsterdam). TK/Rachel find that there really are no more seats on the 125pm flight but they get a connection arriving at 135pm (connecting through Frankfurt). Kynt/Vyxsin get the 135pm and Nicolas/Donald also switch to that. Shana/Jennifer tried to block the entrance to that office to complete getting up front seats. Jennifer told Hendekea it's the turning point in the game and karma will bite the blondes in the ass.

TK now says "someone used the U-Turn and it's not a big group of happy campers anymore. The teams that stress out and waste too much energy are the ones who don't make it to the end."

Now 6 teams are maneuvering in the Vilnius area after landing at roughly the same time. There is a critical spot where if a team turns right they will reach the church without trouble and if they turn left they will have trouble. 4 teams go right but Shana/Jennifer and TK/Rachel go left. When they arrive about 45 minutes later, Christina/Ronald decided to hire a taxi and follow it to St. Anne's Church. If they could afford to do that, World Race Productions must be giving teams too much money or teams must be begging too much.

Nicolas/Donald reach St. Anne's Church first. They find ROADBLOCK "Who's a good listener?" The selected individual chooses a local Vilnius working woman they find outside and takes a package from her plus directions on who and where to deliver it to, but not how to get there. The individual must figure out how to get there, navigating the streets of Vilnius' Old Town. Once at the destination, they receive a second package for delivery to a hotel, a café, a restaurant, or hair salon. Nicolas finds Weinius at the Vilnius University courtyard, who gives him a package for Olga at the hair salon. Hendekea and Kynt are both directed to find people at that same courtyard. Lost, TK/Rachel were directed correctly but Nathan/Jennifer were directed badly and stayed lost. Ronald arrived and was sent to deliver to Milde in the Courtyard. Hendekea found her target and is sent to Olga at the hair salon. Kynt had to deliver his second package to the Gabi Café. Nicolas can't find the Sydabrynus hair salon. Kynt got first place by finishing the ROADBLOCK first and was directed to Rumsiskes to the Lithuanian Outdoor Museum to find Dzukija Village for their next clue.

TK/Rachel finally reached St. Anne's Church and TK took the

ROADBLOCK. Nathan/Jennifer finally arrived and she took the ROADBLOCK. Shana/Jennifer were still lost. TK had to go to the Courtyard first and then the St. Germain Restaurant to deliver his second package, finding a local to lead him there. Although I despise following taxis, following a live local is quite OK with me. It provides enough cross-cultural interaction to satisfy me. How about you? Jennifer and Ronald both made their first deliveries. Ronald was on his way with his second package to the Shakespeare Viesbutis hotel. TK with a fabulous example of catch-up took second place as he finishes. Jennifer found a local to take her to Gabi's Café. Ronald finished third. Jennifer found Gabi's Café with that help and was fourth. Hendekea found a local to take her to the hair salon. Hendekea finished in fifth. It is now Nicolas vs. Shana's Jennifer, who has just started the first package. Nicolas finally finds a local to guide him to the hair salon. He should be sixth, but the curse of karma has bit him big time. Shana's Jennifer has to get to the Shakespeare Hotel with the second package but finds a local to guide her. She actually reaches the church ahead of Nicolas but Shana/Jennifer ask locals for directions and Nicolas does not, so he retook sixth place after 2 hours on the course.

At the museum the next task was to find a Travelocity gnome among many Lithuanian gnomes. Kynt/Vyxsin found a Travelocity gnome and did the DETOUR, Count Down or Step Up. In Count Down there is a picket fence with 717 pickets. Teams must get the correct Count for the marked segment of the fence. In Step Up, stilts are used. Both team members must navigate to an end point and then return on stilts the whole way and without falling (if you do you have to start over). TK/Rachel and Christina/Ronald both find gnomes. Kynt had trouble with the stilts. Nathan/Jennifer and Azaria/Hendekea arrived and Nathan/Jennifer found a correct gnome. Kynt/Vyxsin decided to switch. TK finished but Rachel was still out on the course. Christina/Ronald had trouble on stilts. Nathan/Jennifer decided to Count because Jennifer thinks "I can do this fast." Azaria/Hendeka finally found a gnome (there are declining numbers available as other teams have taken them) and chose stilts. Kynt/Vyxsin had to recount. Christina finished stilts, but Ronald cannot even stay up. Rachel finished and she and TK walked to the pit stop nearby at the Aukstaitija Windmill, finishing as team #1 barely ahead of Kynt/Vyxsin who finished Count quickly the second time. Azaria/Hendekea found stilts too demanding so they switched to Count. Nathan/Jennifer finished their first pass at counting, but wrong. Ronald suddenly found his second wind and finished in third place. Nicolas/Donald and Shana/Jennifer arrived and both teams found their gnomes. Azaria/Hendekea Count successfully and finished 4th. Nathan/Jennifer had to recount again. Shana/Jennifer chose Count. Nathan/Jennifer switched and Nathan finished, then Jennifer did for 5th place.

That leaves the same two teams, no surprise since they arrived much later than the others. Nicolas got the wrong Count, but then sees that he double counted some pickets. When he adjusted, his Count was correct. They went to the pit stop in 6th. Shana/Jennifer finally finished hoping for a non-elimination leg, but this isn't it. They are eliminated.

The finish order was:
TK/Rachel
Kynt/Vyxsin
Christina/Ronald
Azaria/Hendekea
Nathan/Jennifer
Nicolas/Donald
Shana/Jennifer (eliminated)

AR12, Ep.6 "Cherry on Top of the Sundae That's Already Melted"

Release times from the Windmill were reported on the telecast, but are not reliable enough (if so the pit stop would be 6 hours at most). So I will just tell you that the range of times shown for TK/Rachel through Nicolas/Donald was 42 minutes from earliest to latest. Teams fly 900 miles to Dubrovnik, Croatia to find Fort St. Lawrence.

Christina/Ronald pursued their own path with a trip to a travel agent as all other teams head for the airport. They reserved a 625am flight arriving Dubrovnik 1120am but still had to ticket it at the airport. The CSA ticket office opens at 430am and there were seats available. Azaria/Hendekea attempted to book it over the phone without success. There is a line that had formed for CSA. Christina/Ronald left the CSA line to get their tickets at LOT. TK/Rachel finished their ticketing at 510am for a CSA flight leaving at 600am. Kynt/Vyxsin booked the same LOT flight as

Christina/Ronald. Nicolas/Donald booked the same CSA flight as TK/Rachel at 530am but how can that happen if check-in closes at 530am? Nathan/Jennifer tried to get tickets on the 625am LOT flight and succeeded. Azaria/Hendekea asked the travel agency for the same thing and economy class seats were available, but the travel agency screwed up and gave them business class instead. Azaria/Hendekea did not check them at this time and proceeded to check in. They returned to the travel agent when they find out, but it's too late for economy on that flight now. However, the 600am CSA flight is delayed and will miss its connection. The original flight combination was to Prague, connecting to Vienna, then connecting to Dubrovnik to arrive 11:20am. That became an undesired 3.5 hour layover in Vienna and arrival at 240pm for TK/Rachel and for Nicolas/Donald from Prague to Zagreb and finally connecting to Dubrovnik arriving 245pm. For Azarla/Hendekea it was a "you can't get there from here" experience with the best alternative connecting in Amsterdam and then Frankfurt to Dubrovnik arriving at 415pm. At that point there should be no chance to get back into the race. Most revised flight combinations landed on time but Nicolas/Donald were 1 hour later at 345pm than planned. They start at Dubrovnik with a 30 minute lead over Azaria/Hendekea.

Teams arrived in the harbor and locate the cluebox. It led them to ROADBLOCK "Who has a builder's eye?" finding the 8 blocks that fit into an under-repair section of the walls out of 150 blocks available. Next teams scale the wall of Fort St. Lawrence to get to a tandem zip line on top that goes over the water to Fort Bokar. That brings them to DETOUR Short & Long or Long & Short. In Short & Long teams rappel down the wall of that fort, scale another section with a rope ladder and then find a path to Old Town and navigate through Old Town to find the cluebox. Long & Short involves the use of a second tandem zip line to a platform in the harbor, choose a rowboat and then row it to the other side of Dubrovnik, then find that same plaza from that angle.

Rowing appeals to 4 teams, including Nicolas/Donald and Azaria/Hendekea in the last two places. Nicolas/Donald was substantially ahead of Azaria/Hendekea but still in sight when Azaria/Hendekea started. Azaria, having a tough day, no longer had good observation skills. He didn't notice his rowboat was moored to an anchor for about 30 minutes while he rowed to nowhere. By then the edge

Nicolas/Donald built was too large and good rowing by Azaria couldn't catch up.

Teams must now travel by taxi to the Stone Cross Overlook, the pit stop for this leg. Christina/Ronald performed well throughout and won first place. Nathan/Jennifer were ready to take second place, but a taxi refused them due to their wet bathing suits. They ended up third behind Kynt/Vyxsin. TK/Rachel were fourth and Nicolas/ Donald fifth. Azaria/Hendekea, after a very difficult day, were eliminated. Since the race has 5 legs left to eliminate only 2 teams to establish the Final 3, I think having a non-elimination leg next is very likely. Even though the producers had publicly stated that there would be no NELs, the sheer mathematics of 5 legs to reach a total of 3 teams dictates that there will be a total of 3 NELs or TBCs or combination of the two equaling 3.

AR12, Ep.7 "This is Forever, Now"

Teams are released from the Dubrovnik pit stop as follows:
1. Christina/Ronald   219am
2. Kynt/Vyxsin   255am
3. Nathan/Jennifer   345am
4. TK/Rachel   537am
5. Nicolas/Donald   706am

The clue directs teams to the Dubrovnik bus station where they will get a bus to Split, Croatia. Arriving there they will take the SNAV high-speed ferry across the Adriatic Sea to Ancona, Italy. Ronald/ Christina, Kynt/Vyxsin and Nathan/Jennifer all take the 500am bus. TK/Rachel take the 600am bus and Nicolas/Donald get the 730am bus. The daily ferry departure in the summer was at 5pm, arriving Ancona at 930pm. Teams must on arrival self-drive to Tuscany, over 300 km away to the north and west. The main route to get to Tuscany is the Autostrada toll highway, but the key decision for teams is where to get off and which roads to take to the west once you did that. They must drive at night on no sleep and some facing a complete closure of the autostrada one exit south of where they wanted to go. TK/Rachel lost their clue at a rest stop and had to go hours more to retrieve it so they could continue. Teams get to Empoli, southwest of Florence and the Campo di Volo Silvano Poli in Comune di Courtenova. I have to consult an Italian to English dictionary to discover the several meanings of the word "volo" but the most relevant is "low level flight." At Empoli there is a ROADBLOCK "Who's feeling ultra light of heart?" This requires the selected individual to obtain some instruction in how to operate a small ultralight aircraft. The individual and an instructor will go into the air for not more than 30 minutes (refueling if needed with time lost) and search for 6 miles in all directions the ground for the next clue, which will be a name of an Italian town. It is Vinci and that is the next destination of the teams. Teams arrived at that small plane airport in this order and pull numbers for the order of doing the ROADBLOCK:

Nathan/Jennifer, who were there hours in advance of the 7am opening
TK/Rachel, there before 7am
Christina/Ronald arrive after 7am after driving all night
Nicolas/Donald, who waited until the autostrada reopened at 6am and arrived after 7am
Kynt/Vyxsin, who were totally lost all night and arrived maybe 60 to 90 minutes after opening

The cluebox offers both the ROADBLOCK and a FAST FORWARD that is billed as a local seafaring tradition but is really each getting a permanent tattoo somewhere on their body. For the FAST FORWARD, Nicolas/Donald went to FABIO Studios to obtain the tattoos as a small "FF" on their upper arm. They are directed to the pit stop at Boboli Gardens in Florence. They finish 2 to 5 hours ahead of the other teams.

Back at the ROADBLOCK, Nathan/Jennifer, Christina/Ronald and even Kynt/Vyxsin find the name VINCI and direct the instructor back to the ground where they receive the next clue for a correct identification. Poor TK is up for 4 tries before he finds VINCI. Teams go to Vinci and find out that it is the birthplace of the legendary Leonardo da Vinci, which is pretty easy to understand. Teams face a DETOUR Invention or Tradition. Invention is to choose a replica of a centuries old crane, then assemble such a crane, hoist a rock at least 1 foot up, and insert then look at a mirror underneath to get the next clue. This is one of the best Amazing Race tasks ever although flying an ultralight is pretty excellent too. In Tradition, teams must go to Piazza Guido Masi and learn a traditional local flag routine involving tossing and catching the flags. Teams receive instruction and observe the right way to do it. They must demonstrate their routine to receive the name of their destination on a flag. TK/Rachel were the only team to try Invention but TK appears to be expert in physics and got that clue quickly. Kynt/Vyxsin switched DETOURs. Driving from one parking area to another their car's transmission died. They were extremely lucky for it to happen just before doing Tradition because by the time they finished a replacement vehicle was available. TK/Rachel blew a tire on the way to the pit stop, so they lost 2 places in the finish order.

That finish order is:
1. Nicolas and Donald
2. Nathan/Jennifer
3. Christina/Ronald
4. TK/Rachel
5. Kynt/Vyxsin, who Phil tells it's a non-elimination leg mandating the new concept of SpeedBump the next leg, a task only they do

AR12, Ep. 8 "Honestly, They Have Witch Powers or Something"

The release from the pit stop in Florence is as follows:
1. Nicolas/Donald   1012pm
2. Nathan/Jennifer 1155pm
3. Christina/Ronald 106am
4. TK/Rachel   211am
5. Kynt/Vyxsin   323am, with a SpeedBump to do

Teams travel 4000 miles to Mumbai, India (formerly known as Bombay). Teams jockey for aircraft flights, Nicolas and Donald by telephone for reservations and the other teams by actually going to the Florence International Airport. The favorite is the Air France flight from Paris to Mumbai arriving 1035pm but only 3 teams are able to get seats for the entire itinerary. That combination actually arrives at 1105pm. Kynt/Vyxsin had a different combination than the Air France combination and arrived on-time at 1050pm. TK/Rachel went through Frankfurt and arrived at 105am. All teams take an auto-rickshaw to Mr. Naik's Newspaper stall in Khar Danda, purchase the Times of India and look for ads with the next clue.

What they find is "travel by auto-rickshaw to Chauhan Alteration Tailors, St.Joseph Church, A.B.Nair Road corner, Juhu."

Kynt/Vyxsin were required to do the SpeedBump, which is travel to/from yoga exercises. I believe that took about 30 minutes. Next is DETOUR Paste 'em or Thread 'em. In Paste 'em teams go to an under-pass at Dadar Bridge West and paste a 6 panel Bollywood movie poster up. In Thread 'em teams find a marked flower market at the Dadar Flower Market where they thread 108 flower petals in an alternating pattern into a traditional wedding garland and deliver it to the groom for the next clue. Nicolas/Donald and Christina/Ronald elect to Paste while TK/Rachel (she is a florist), Nathan/Jennifer and Kynt/Vyxsin Thread. Nicolas/Donald, TK/Rachel and Kynt/Vyxsin all work fast. Christina/Ronald must do a second 6-panel because of alignment issues with their first. Nathan/Jennifer just acted typically, with a lot of conflict.

Teams must now find the Kabutar Khana traffic island where there is a U-Turn. Three teams go by without activating it, but Kynt/Vyxsin elect to U-Turn Nicolas/Donald, who were well ahead of that place then. The only team Kynt/Vyxsin could U-Turn was 5th-place Nathan/Jennifer, who were given a reprieve from almost-certain elimination. They got to the U-Turn just after Kynt/Vyxsin and can see that they are still alive.

They take a taxi to Bharatgas Colabras Propane Gas Service. There the clue is for a ROADBLOCK "Who's got a strong back and good sense of navigation?" They load 6 propane tanks onto a cart which they must use to deliver 3 each to two different addresses, bringing back the order slips and signed delivery receipts. The men are selected to do this physical task except for Jennifer. TK, Nicolas, and Ronald all performed well. Jennifer did a really good job but did not get the 1st delivery receipt, forcing her to go back. She did finish ahead of Kynt/Vyxsin. The pit stop was at Bandra Fort 14 miles away by taxi. The teams finish in the same order:

1. TK/Rachel
2. Nicolas/Donald
3. Christina/Ronald
4. Nathan/Jennifer
5. Kynt/Vyxsin were eliminated; Phil rates them the most

fashionable couple ever on the Amazing Race, putting them ahead of Oswald/Danny and Joe/Bill in sartorial excellence. Since then they wear pink/black.

AR12, Ep.9 "I Just Hope He Doesn't Croak On Us"

Release times are as follows:
TK/Rachel   125pm
Nicolas/Donald   133pm
Christina/Ronald 144pm
Nathan/Jennifer 238pm

This looks like a 24 hour pit stop to me. Teams get the clue to fly 4000 miles to Osaka Japan and take a taxi to Kishawada Castle, where the next clue is available on the grounds. In spite of being the first team to reserve, TK/Rachel got the worst flight combinations and arrived last in Osaka. They are about 3 hours behind the 3 other teams. I guess they must be too trusting of inferior travel agency or airline reservations services. The hours for the museum at the castle are 10am to 4pm but that's a red herring because the clue says to search the grounds (and by inference not the castle). Nicolas/Donald went up to the castle so that they can see the grounds better. Nathan/Jennifer did as instructed. Christina/Ronald tried to search the Museum without success.

Next they get a clue to the Japan Railways Kanjoson Noda Station to search for the cleaning man. At this point Jennifer has stated "There are like no signs in English here"; Nathan responds "That's why we aren't driving, Babe." Christina says "I'm never driving in Japan." Now the World Race Productions staff had to be laughing uncontrollably, as the next task is a ROADBLOCK "Who's a backseat driver?" subtitled Drive a Taxi. The selected individual must wear a hat and gloves like the local cabbies and transport a Japanese couple 5 miles through a maze of confusing and one-way streets. They may not receive any help from the locals, who will give them their next clue when reaching their destination (Osaka Central Post Office). Then pseudo-taxi driver must navigate back to his/her starting point to open the clue with their teammate. First to arrive back is Jennifer. Christina knows a little Japanese so she is doing well on this, finishing 10 minutes in front of Nicolas, who has some trouble returning after reaching the destination easily. Rachel tries to regain that lost time but only gets small amounts. Christina: "I don't think Japanese helps that much. Driving skill helps more." Jennifer: "By the way, nobody here speaks English. At all."

The next clue sends them to Kita-Mido Buddhist Temple, which is just a place to get their next clue. It is a DETOUR, Sense of Touch or Sense of Smell. Sense of Touch is find the Shimojima Building and use miniature robots controlled by cell phones to play table soccer against 2 robotic defenders. Each team member must score a goal. Sense of Smell sends them to the Saera Flower Shop to pick out the one real flower among many thousands of artificial flowers in a 2-story business. Although TK/Rachel need to make up time, this is a bit unfair because Rachel is a florist in real life. The structure of DETOURs, usually completed in less than 30 minutes, does not allow them to catch up much. Nicolas/Donald were the only team to chose Sense of Touch. The same task finishing order was maintained throughout the entire day. Although Rachel makes up time there is still a healthy gap when she is done on this task. Phil gets the best lines of the day: "teams without a delicate sense of touch may end up kicking themselves instead of goals" and "teams that can put their olfactories to use may surprise themselves by quickly sniffing out a winner."

Teams go by taxi to Tempozan Park for the pit stop. The finish order there was:
1. Nathan/Jennifer
2. Christina/Ronald
3. Nicolas/ Donald
4. TK/Rachel, who find that there are NELs in AR12, despite propaganda that said there would not be any NELs. TK/Rachel survived due to a NEL. The penalty for last in a NEL is a SpeedBump exclusively next leg.

AR12, Ep.10 "Sorry Guys, I'm Not Happy to See You"

The pit stop release times are:
Nathan/Jennifer   702 am
Christina/Ronald 715am
Nicolas/Donald   721am

TK/Rachel   1018am

Teams must take taxis to the Umeda Sky Tower and find the "floating gardens" there. The building is closed until 10am, which means that TK/Rachel's deficit could be in the range of a half hour. However, they have trouble finding the cluebox and then more locating the observatory at the top level that is the "floating gardens". Nathan may be serious or not, it's impossible to tell with this gem: "Jen and I know absolutely nothing about Taiwan except we think Thai food's pretty good" even though they were in Taipei, that hotbed of Thai food (NOT).

Teams flew1000 miles to Taipei Taiwan and took a taxi to the main train station in Taipei to find the next clue. Christina/Ronald arrived ahead of the other 3 teams. They speak Mandarin Chinese so there is little chance anyone is going to catch them on this leg. TK/Rachel were spotted by 2 teams going through customs so they have caught up. The clue sent teams by high speed rail to Taichung, transferring to a taxi to the small town of Jiji. It is likely Christina/Ronald got the 430pm train arriving Taichung at 530pm. The others probably got the 500pm train that arrived at 552pm for a 22 minute deficit. In Jiji they found Acrobatics Jeep and ROADBLOCK "Who's ready for a tricky ride?" which is enter a special vehicle with a professional stunt driver, who will get the car onto a raised platform and have it approximate a 3-dimensional pinball machine. Then the other team member replaces the driver, the car becomes amphibious for 17 feet and passengers use goggles and hold their breath. Then they exit that vehicle for the next clue.

TK/Rachel preceded the ROADBLOCK with their SpeedBump, to don protective clothing and run through fireworks exploding around them and then follow a local custom by being doused with water. This is pretty simple and probably costs them less than 30 minutes.

The clue from Acrobatics Jeep sends teams back on the high-speed train to Taipei and to GK Tea House where they must order and drink one cup of tea to get the next clue, which is printed in Chinese on the bottom of the cup. They must get help from a local to translate it and direct them to Gong Guan Night Market. There they must find a clown to get their next clue. It sends them on a DETOUR, Fire or Earth. Fire is to write messages of Good or Bad luck on lanterns. They burn spirit money under lanterns to fill them with hot air and lift them into the air. They must do so for 20 lanterns, which sounds slow enough to teams that none elect it. In Earth, go to Youth Park and find the marked stone path. Both team members have to walk each way on the 220 foot path over the sometimes painful rocks. All chose Earth.

Nathan/Jennifer gambled on locals' advice to reach Youth Park quicker on subway and bus. That proved misguided, since the other 3 teams took taxis directly there to arrive ahead of Nathan/Jennifer. TK/Rachel took 2nd place out of that DETOUR. The final clue was to take a taxi to Chiang Kai-Shek Memorial Hall Plaza, the pit stop. The finishing order was:

Christina/Ronald—how lucky they were to be in Taiwan where they were the only team to speak the language
TK/Rachel—how lucky to erase a 3 hour deficit; no longer last
Nicolas/Donald—they had a low profile but moved along
Nathan/Jennifer—losing due to decision to take different transportation mode; they might have been 1st but instead they were eliminated

We now have our Final 3, all decent teams with different strengths and weaknesses. Where will the finale be and who will win?

AR12, Ep.11, Finale "The Final Push"

The release times to start the final leg were:
Christina/Ronald 947am
TK/Rachel   1030am
Nicolas/Donald   1037am

One thing students of the Amazing Race know is that in the final leg the producers are careful to Bunch the Final 3 for a large part of this leg. So it's no surprise that there is only one flight which makes any sense to get to Anchorage Alaska, which is where they must fly. It's a China Air nonstop flight leaving late afternoon and arriving early morning of the same day, through the magic of crossing the International Date Line west to east so that a day is recovered.

The first clue in Anchorage sends teams by taxi to 6th Avenue Outfitters, which has important gear for them. Next they must take a taxi to the Ship Creek Boat launch. Nicolas and Donald on arrival discovered that they had left 6th Avenue Outfitters without the gear, so they had to return. TK/Rachel got a bad taxi driver who did not know the way; after delay a local gave directions so they could get to the launch area. There a DETOUR awaits, Cut the Cod or Grab the Crab. What alliteration! Cut the Cod involves filleting 50 pound ling cod until you find a clue hidden inside one of the fish. Grab the Crab is icky. Get into a boat with 500 crabs that are using their claws to discourage people from getting close and find the one with the Amazing Race colors. Phil: "Teams without fast hands could find themselves in a pinch." Christina/Ronald and Nicolas/ Donald selected Cut the Cod. TK/Rachel selected Grab the Crab. All did pretty well, with Christina/Ronald enjoying a 20 to 25 minute lead leaving there.

Teams took a taxi, then a Jet Boat to 20 Mile Glacier to do an Ice Climb to the top of it. Climbing is hard. Ronald managed. Christina lagged but finished. Next teams took a helicopter to Merrill Field to walk to an adjacent field and take a taxi to Goose Lake Park.

At Goose Lake Park is ROADBLOCK "Who wants to relive your experience on the race?" to determine the winner of AR12. I recall observing Rachel in taxis and elsewhere with a notebook writing down the significant events and places of the race. This ROADBLOCK is a memory challenge, so it looks like she will have an edge even though starting minutes behind Christina. There are 10 items that match a specific leg of the race: 3 animals or animal byproducts; 1 U-Turn; 2 transportation methods with wheels, 1 being on a DETOUR and another shaped like a stick; 2 items at or brought to the pit stop. Only 1 specific group of 10 items out of a larger group can be put on the scale and weighed to see if it is correct (there being a unique weight for those 10 items). If it weighs right, the selected individual receives the next clue. The winning items are tandem bikes from Ireland, detour bike in Amsterdam, milk in a gourd and chicken from Burkina Faso's 2 episodes, DETOUR stilts in Lithuania, a gun like the one used in a pit stop arrival salute in Croatia, a Blackberry from Italy, a U-Turn sign in Mumbai, cleaning man from Japan and tea cups from Taiwan. She had to figure out these items are extra and did not fit: donkey from

Ireland, vault pole from Netherlands, row boat from Croatia, gas cylinders India, flowers from Japan. This is one of the BEST ROADBLOCKS EVER.

Rachel finishes the ROADBLOCK, is approved by the judge and gets a clue to the Captain Cook Statue. TK/Rachel left with an insurmountable lead. The clue there sent them to find the Salmon Hooker, which is a statue of a fisherman. They found out from a local it's at 5th and G Streets. The clue there directed them to take a taxi to the tiny Girdwood Airport and run for the Finish Line. They have first place, the $1,000,000, and "10 cities, 4 continents and 30,000 miles" according to Phil. With 11 legs, that may leave out Anchorage. TK stated "Nice guys finish first" and he's right for AR12 (but not always).

Christina and Ronald finished second. They have reconciled somewhat as he has learned to better appreciate her and modified his behavior accordingly. Nicolas and Donald were third, with Donald achieving the distinction of being the oldest person to ever be in an Amazing Race Final 3 at age 68. That is a record that may not be broken any time soon. AR12 was interesting throughout. The cast had some live wires like Kynt and Vyxsin and plenty of the conflict Amazing Race viewers have come to expect and depend on. For the "nice" couple to win based solely on their intelligence was appropriate. They had some poor flight decisions throughout the race, but they overcame them.

AMAZING RACE 13

11 teams gather at Los Angeles Memorial Coliseum to race around the world for a $1,000,000 first-place reward. Phil Keoghan introduces the stadium as the only one to have hosted an Olympics twice. Teams are:

Toni/Dallas, Mother/Son, California, accounting consultant and student, age 51 and 22
Nick/Starr, brother/sister, New York, actor and former NFL cheerleader, age 22 and 21
Ken/Tina, separated husband/wife, San Diego/Tampa; an ex NFL player; homebuilder and entrepreneur, age 51 and 48
Aja/Ty, dating long distance Los Angeles/Detroit, actress and banker, age 25 and 25
Marissa/Brooke, southern belles/friends from South Carolina, student and graphic designer, age 22 and 24
Andrew/Dan, fraternity brothers, Phoenix, student and hotel manager trainee, age 22 and 23
Anthony/Stephanie, dating 4 years, Los Angeles, mortgage broker and financial saleswoman, age 32 and 32
Anita/Arthur, married beekeepers doubling as old hippies from Oregon, retired paralegal and playground maintenance, age 63/61
Kelly/Christy, recently divorced, Texas, sales rep and business development, age 26 and 26
Terence/Sarah, newly dating, New York City, running coach and investment analyst, age 35 and 31
Mark/Bill, best friends/geeks, San Diego, Treasurer of Comic-Con and student aid administrator, age 42 and 42

AR13, Ep.1 "Bees Are Much Calmer Than This"

Phil tells teams there will be 8 elimination points; it is known that there are 11 total legs with one for the finish line so only 2 legs will be To Be Continued (TBC) or Non Elimination Leg (NEL) status. A U.S. Amazing Race course set down by WRP has no NELs or TBCs for early legs to eliminate several teams so presumably fewer camera/sound crews are needed. The first clue is fly to Salvador de Bahia, a 3 million population city on the east coast of Brazil.

It's the usual mad scramble to the Los Angeles International Airport. Ken distinguishes himself as the mad racecar driver passing everyone else. Aja knows the city where she lives even better and she tells Ty to go into the Carpool Lane, which results in them being a close first to the designated airport parking area. Anthony/Stephanie are also from Los Angeles and they take a direct route to the airport, not using the longer one, the Interstate which all other teams took. Arrival in an airport parking lot was not enough for success, as teams had to find the correct Amazing Race check-in lane for American Airlines 252 to Miami, connecting there to Rio de Janeiro and from there to Salvador. Teams taking this combination of flights were Mark/Bill (a surprise to me), Ken/Tina, Anthony/Stephanie, Nick/Starr, Aja/Ty and Kelly/Christy. For United flight 843 to Chicago and on to Sao Paulo, connecting from there to Salvador. That left with Andrew/Dan, Arthur/Anita, Anthony/Stephanie, Toni/Dallas and Marissa/Brooke. I have the "American" route scheduled to arrive Salvador at 1220 pm and the "United" route at 240 pm. However, a weather delay affecting the "American" route reduced their advantage but it's still significant.

The race after later arrival of "United" route teams is essentially between them for avoiding last place reaching 19 Batalhao de Cacadores military base, a pseudo-pit-stop. Teams arrive in downtown Salvador looking for sandwich shop O Rei Pernil. They receive instructions to maneuver a traditional vending cart overfilled with food items and candy for sale up the Funicular Goncalves. At the top they find the Praca de Se and next clue to the 19 Military Base where they will sleep in tents. First, they have to sign in for a release time the next morning. Signing for 900 am are Terence/Sarah, Nick/Starr, Mark/Bill and Ken/Tina. For the 930 am release time are Aja/Ty and Kelly/Christy. Later when they arrive first in the second group, Andrew/Dan became the final team in the 930 group. That leaves Arthur/Anita (already lagging behind), Anthony/Stephanie, Toni/Dallas and Marissa/Brooke for the 945 am release.

On release the next morning teams are directed to a DETOUR, choice of "Hard Way Up" or "Soft Way Down". Both of these tasks are situated in the Pelourinho area with a specific geographic purpose in mind. "Hard Way Up" is to crawl on hands and knees up the step leading to the Igreja San Francisco and then answer a mystery question. The only team out of 10 that chooses this was

94

Andrew/Dan, who did well at it. They crawl up, get the mystery question ("How many steps have you just done?"), which they can't answer and have to go around and down to repeat it. The second time they count and get the right answer of 53. The other teams went to the Elevator Lacerda, 240 feet above the bottom, where cargo netting was draped to the ground and extensive safety equipment was mandatory. I did not see any teams trying to go fast. They all were careful and cautious. This task did not change the order of anyone. All of the 0900 group got down the netting; the 0930 group did so as well. That left the last 4 teams in the 0945 group to battle to avoid last place. Arthur and Anita continued to move at a leisurely pace and so they were last off the cargo netting by a bit.

First team off the cargo netting was Nick/Starr and the clue sent them locally to walk to the dock for Forte Sao Marcelo. They get a small passenger boat apparently dedicated to Amazing Race teams and arrive at the pit stop first to win a prize of 5 night trip for 2 to Belize. All behind them do the same walk and boat ride. Order of finish is:

1. Nick/Starr
2. Ken/Tina
3. Terence/Sarah
4. Mark/Bill
5. Kelly/Christy
6. Toni/Dallas
7. Andrew/Dan
8. Aja/Ty
9. Anthony/Stephanie
10. Marisa/Brooke
11. Arthur/Anita

Arthur and Anita are eliminated and go to Casa Legouia in Acapulco for about 3 weeks of Sequesterville.

AR13, Ep.2 "Do You Like American Candy?"

From Salvador Brazil, the first clue sends teams to Fortaleza, 2 hours by plane north along the east coast. Teams leave the pit stop:

Nick/Starr	407am
Ken/Tina	413am
Terence/Sarah	418am
Mark/Bill	424am
Kelly/Christy	444am
Toni/Dallas	457am
Andrew/Dan	503am
Aja/Ty	505am
Anthony/Stephanie	511am
Marisa/Brooke	513am

World Race Productions decided to have teams enjoy a longer period of time at the pit stop, specifically 18 hours instead of the normal 12, 24 or 36 hours. They released teams so that even the last team could get on the same plane with the others. All teams race to the Salvador airport. The first team to arrive finds that the first airline visible, TAM Aereas Lineas, doesn't have a flight until 1130am. That won't do so teams go on to GOL. GOL's next flight is at 645am but there is only one seat available. Think about it for a moment. There are 10 teams X 2 + 10 sound/camera crews x 2 = 40 individuals who want to take that 645am flight to Fortaleza. How can they be accommodated?; only if GOL just happened to have a larger plane waiting idle for just such an eventuality. This was all stage managed for maximum effect, but I believe WRP and GOL were in cahoots long before any teams reached Salvador Airport. That means GOL and WRP were just acting out a charade so they could appear to be "good guys" by accommodating the request of the 40 who wanted to go at that time. Tina believed that she had personally negotiated that larger plane, but that made little sense.

All 10 teams landed at the same time and sprint for taxis. Anthony/ Stephanie made a bad choice and their taxi can't function. It took several minutes of trying jump starts before they give up and get another one. The clue sends all to the Cumbuco Village Market. Somehow Ken/Tina wound up even behind Anthony/Stephanie. Teams have to ride dune buggies to get to the next clue on the beach. They look like they are having fun for a change, particularly Terence and Sarah kissing. The DETOUR is Beach It (move a jangada large sailboat on wooden rollers for 100 meters with the help of a crew of 2) or Dock It (take a serial number for container in the container port, look it up in a database to find its general location - SUBU, then go that location and find the actual container among many that look similar). Only Mark/ Bill elected Dock It although Marisa/Brooke expected to get there but found themselves on the beach instead. Mark/Bill made steady progress and ended up in second place at the end of this episode, so Dock It appears to have been the better choice for geeks at least.

The rest of the teams struggled with the displacement of rollers from the back after exposed to the front to keep the operation moving. Even a team I expected to have trouble, Marisa/Brooke, seemed to get through it with ease. Nick told Starr to kiss their crew to motivate their best performance and that appeared to work. Kelly/Christy were at the front of the pack but moved way back when they misunderstood the nature of DETOURs and think they have to do both parts; they searched needlessly then finally decide to go ahead, the correct decision.

The ROADBLOCK "In Plain Sight" sent teams to a 600 foot section of painted wall. There were many things on the wall, only one of them the name of a place that is the pit stop. Teams found at the far end of the wall a group of 11 place names. Several correctly assumed that writing down all 11 on a list and repetitively naming them to the painter would get the job done. That method worked best. Ken/Tina finished first and were off to the Cidade do Crianca, the pit stop at a park back in downtown Fortaleza. Kelly/Christy made a huge mistake by not asking their taxi to stay. They searched in vain for another taxi before they stumble on their own taxi which had waited for them. This cost them several places. Nick seemed out of it for a long time, but finally used the "list" technique. Dan (or maybe Andrew) had a very difficult figuring it out. The last three were Andrew/Dan, Marisa/Brooke and Anthony/Stephanie. Ken/Tina walked fast to the pit stop for first place, besting Mark/Bill who had a luggage problem. The total finish order was:

Ken/Tina
Mark/Bill
Terence/Sarah
Aja/Ty
Tony/Dallas
Nick/Starr

Kelly/Christy
Andrew/Dan
Marisa/Brooke
Anthony/Stephanie

It's too soon in AR13 for a NEL, so Anthony/Stephanie were eliminated. I attribute that to their bad luck and stubbornness with the initial taxi.

AR13, Ep.3 "Did You Push My Sports Bra Off the Ledge"

This is one of the most exciting Amazing Race episodes I have seen (which is all of 14 U.S. AR seasons times an average of 12.36 episodes, a total of 173 episodes). Episode 3 starts in Fortaleza with pit stop release at the following times:

Ken/Tina	1251 am
Mark/Bill	1253 am
Terence/Sarah	113 am
Aja/Ty	114 am
Toni/Dallas	115 am
Nick/Starr	117 am
Kelly/Christy	118 am
Andrew/Dan	122 am
Marisa/Brooke	122 am

Although not shown on the broadcast, my research indicates teams flew to Sao Paulo first and arrived late morning, switched to a flight to Santa Cruz, Bolivia, then connected to a Bolivian national airline Aerosur flight to arrive at destination LaPaz at 8pm, well after dark. After they went to the Statue Simon Bolivar (named for the liberator of much of South America from the Spanish), they were given blankets and sleep on what appears to be sidewalk next to a street which is not busy when they try to sleep but the next morning it is busy and noisy. Teams wait for something to happen and it does; a newspaper delivery truck comes by with a bundle of newspapers for them. Based on past Amazing Race experiences which all would know if they looked at several recent Amazing Races as preparation for AR13, teams had no problem figuring out that there is an advertisement hidden in the paper giving their next clue. That clue sends them to the Marvaez Hat Store for a Cholita hat used by the fighting cholitas, women who are adept professional wrestlers. Anybody want to guess what will be ahead?

Before that, there was a DETOUR first. Teams choose between Musical March and Bumpy Ride. Musical March sounds hokey. Teams walked to one of 3 plazas and peeled off two drummers to form the core of their band. They then went to other plazas where they pick up some trumpets and other performers. Somewhere on the Plaza Abaroa was the Band Master, who provides their next clue. Dan/Andrew and Toni/Dallas chose this. The other DETOUR, which 7 teams chose, involved walking to the Market de las Brusas to pick up a wooden bike with no brakes, then maneuvering it downhill to Plaza Abaroa. As I watched Nick/Starr doing this, I observed a car coming through the intersection perpendicular, a huge safety issue because Nick/Starr could not stop on that steep section. Later in their ride I saw a motorcyclist (presumably a policeman) blocking traffic from a side street. Teams completed this DETOUR is this order:

Mark/Bill
Marissa/Brooke
Andrew/Dan
Terence/Sarah
Ken/Tina
Nick/Starr
Aja/Ty
Kelly/Christy
Toni/Dallas

All teams except the last are given the opportunity to U-Turn a following team. All decide not to, although Kelly/Christy may have regretted that decision, not aware that Toni/Dallas were behind them. The teams take taxis to the Multifunctional Arena in El Alto, several thousand feet higher than LaPaz at above 13,000 feet. This causes respiratory problems for Bill. Taxi performance is highly variable. Teams arrive to interact with the cholitas. I know what you're thinking and you're close, as fighting professional women wrestlers would be interesting but bloody and short. However, give WRP credit for concluding that fighting wrestlers of any sort either will usually be faked or one-sided. They instead devised tests the slowest and weakest can do as long as they keep their wits.

ROADBLOCK "Who's Ready to Pick a Fight?" is work in a practice ring to learn 6 standard easy pro wrestler moves. They then demonstrate them in the main ring with a male pro wrestler. If they miss any, they return to the practice ring repetitively. Much low-brow entertainment ensues. Many Amazing Racers get it right the first time. The moves are:
Chest Kick
Taunting
Re-Entry
Duck & Flip
Kicked
Slapshot

Teams head next for Mirador El Monticulo, the pit stop. Initial finishing order was almost the same at both places with exceptions noted:
1. Ken/Tina for their second win
2. Toni/Dallas, who made a spectacular recovery in last 2 taxi rides
3. Terence/Sarah, who made a mistake by not reading the clue carefully, took a cab instead of walking and going back to fix it
4. Marisa/Brooke, who are out of last place
5. Aja/Ty
6. Nick/Starr, who have been disappointing the last 2 legs
7. Anthony/Dan
8. Mark/Bill, who also did not read that clue properly, took a cab, gained an advantage and did not discover until the pit stop that a penalty of 30 minutes applies; Bill was in the ring 3 times, but they persevered; now it's out of their control as they wait for Kelly/Christy
9. Kelly/Christy, eliminating Mark/Bill by arriving soon after them

The irony Mark/Bill point out is due to their limited speed and agility they were a team who had to excel (and expected to do so) at reading clues, but they missed key information and paid the price.

AR13, Ep.4 "I Wonder if They Like Blondes in New Zealand

This episode started in LaPaz Bolivia and ended in New Zealand. That is covering a lot of the Southern Hemisphere in a giant leap. Teams are released from the pit stop as follows:

Ken/Tina	1233am
Toni/Dallas	1259am
Terence/Sarah	104am
Marissa/Brooke	105am
Aja/Ty	106am
Nick/Starr	107am
Anthony/Dan	108am
Kelly/Christy	121am
Andrew/Dan	108am
Kelly/Christy	121am

Teams fly east to west on the Trans-South Pacific crossing to Auckland New Zealand after positioning from LaPaz to Santa Cruz, Bolivia to Buenos Aires Argentina to Santiago Chile, where the 13 hour flight departs late evening. It arrived Auckland around 4am second day due to crossing the International Date Line east to west. Needless to say, all teams have been Bunched since they were all on the same flight.

From the Auckland airport teams are sent to the North Shore community of Gulf Harbour on the Whangaparoa Peninsula in marked cars. They drive there to unwind a Gordian knot to get their next clue. That includes a FAST FORWARD opportunity at the Sky Tower in downtown Auckland. Ken/Tina beat Andrew/Dan there. This FAST FORWARD was not for the faint of heart as it was climbing up the outside of the top segment of Auckland Sky Tower to almost the top to find a gnome. Ken/Tina were then taken directly to the pit stop by helicopter. If not winning that, teams have to drive up Mt. Eden in Auckland, the site of an extinct volcano. Andrew/Dan and other teams do a Maori ROADBLOCK. A fierce-looking group of about 44 New Zealand aborigine Maoris (as best I could count them on PAUSE) awaited at ROADBLOCK "Who has an eye for detail?". One teammate is selected to match a pattern against the face tattoos of the Maoris until they find the match. I only saw 2 teams go back for a second pattern, so it appeared to be easy. Time to match could be in a 5 to 30 minute range.

The next task is blatant product placement, but I will watch Travelocity product placement within reason because Travelocity as a major sponsor several seasons back kept the Amazing Race alive. Teams had to drive to the City Life Hotel in downtown Auckland, go onto a balcony on a high floor and use binoculars to spot Roving Gnomes on or outside of buildings in the immediate vicinity. The next clue sent teams to a DETOUR 2.5 hours away in the Bay of Plenty Region. Matter of Time at Kiwi360 in Te Puke involves both teammates stomping kiwis in a vat until they produce 12 quarts of juice; then they have to drink one maybe 16 ounce glass each (even with clean feet who would want to do that?). The trick was to find and use a lever on the side bottom that releases the juice flow. This shows contestants will do almost anything for a shot at the $1 million prize. Matter of Skill involved going to a Blokart race track in Papamoa, assembling a sailcart for each teammate and navigating them 3 laps around a figure 8 course.

Several teams chose to abandon the juice DETOUR because the stones on the bottom of the vat hurt their feet. Terence/Sarah and Nick/Starr and Aja/Ty switched DETOURs. Marissa and Brooke appeared to progress, but they were running last all day and had to do it faster to stay in the race. The next clues directed teams to the pit stop at Summerhill Recreational Farm in the hills above Tauranga. Finish order there is:

Ken/Tina - ran an excellent leg, were ahead of the other teams; could not get in the Sky Tower until 0830, so pit stop arrival was about 10am
Terence/Sarah - very good leg, no mistakes except a minor wrong turn; their decision to switch DETOURs was good
Kelly/Christy - they rose throughout the day, finishing after an excellent performance at Kiwi360
Toni/Dallas - a good sound leg
Nick/Starr - she had trouble controlling her sailcart; injured her arm as it tipped over and she failed to remember "keep your arms in"; then she was shown driving their car to the pit stop with only one good arm
Andrew/Dan - made several mistakes including trying to compete for the FAST FORWARD, costing them 15 minutes after abandoning it when they knew Ken/Tina were parked ahead of them
Aja/Ty - he called her Fidel Castro (code for "dictator") but the footage shows him being a jerk, not her; they finished after dark, maybe 645pm
Marissa/Brooke - despite a good kiwi fruit stomping they failed to overtake Aja/Ty, finished maybe around 7pm and were eliminated

AR13, Ep.5 "Do It Like a Madman"

The pit stop is on a farm 2.5 hours away from Auckland
International Airport. Teams fly to Siem Reap, Cambodia. Release
from the pit stop:
Ken/Tina   603am
Terence/Sarah 819am
Kelly/Christy   932am
Toni/Dallas   1015am
Nick/Starr   1130am
Andrew/Dan   1204pm
Aja/Ty   304pm

Since Aja/Ty arrived at that pit stop after dark, say around 7pm, it
appears that it was a 20 hour pit stop. Ken states that it is 220km
and he estimates it will take 3 hours (a bit more than I do) to self-
drive. With the first reasonable flight departing at 1225 pm to
Sydney (and then connecting to Singapore and Siem Reap), only
Ken/Tina can make it easily. Terence/Sarah should make it, but
they are delayed by Terence getting a ticket from Highway Patrol
officers for going 117 km/hr in a 100 km/hr zone. It is not clear how
much the ticket was. Terence/Sarah made the flight after being told
that they can't. Starr also gets a speeding ticket that is not shown in
the episode.

Kelly/Christy, Toni/Dallas and Nick/Starr had no trouble being there
for the next suitable flight, a 455pm flight to Brisbane that continued
to Singapore and then connects to Siem Reap. Kelly/Christy in a
private conservation overheard by the microphone compared
Dallas' hair to "Teen Wolf". They did it in such a snarky way
they encouraged negative reactions. Andrew/Dan should make the
airport in ample time to be on this flight but for an unknown reason
they were not allowed on initially. After pleading, the airline
reconsidered and they got on this flight. Any drama with respect to
which team will finish last was over; it will be Aja/Ty. They are on a
flight scheduled to miss connection with the one from Singapore to
Siem Reap only the other teams got and arrived hours later.

WRP and CBS are using editing tricks to make you think Aja/Ty have a chance. All the other teams are Bunched and get an even start in Siem Reap. The first task was a truck fuel stop reached by taxi. The taxi for Kelly/Christy went awry and cost them time. Teams had to hand-crank a pump for diesel fuel oil used by trucks, which Andrew/Dan couldn't figure out (Ken got in a good quip with "It's like pulling a zipper down and letting it flow, boys.") and maybe lost a half hour there. Next was a ride in the back of the truck they had just fueled to Siem Reap Dock. Nick, in the lead, stated that he wanted to pull a large branch into the road to hold up other teams "maybe 30 seconds", as bad an action as anything any other team has suggested. Teams take captained motorboats for a ride on Tonle Sap Lake. All the boats would be carefully regulated to make sure they go the same speed. Terence/Sarah's boat engine died in sight of their destination. Terence and a crew member poled the boat in while the captain fixed the engine. They lost enough time to lose a few places from 1st they had been in.

The next task was DETOUR of Village Life (navigate your boat to get a set of teeth from the dentist, an item from the seamstress and then at the basketball court on the water make one basket by each team member, getting a basketball as a prize) or Village Work (take your boat to fishing grounds, find 2 traps with fish in them, bring them back and empty them into baskets). Nick/Starr, Toni/Dallas, Andrew/Dan, and Aja/Ty each did Village Work. Ken/Tina, Terence/Sarah, and Kelly/Christy did Village Life. I didn't see an advantage to either one.

Next, a tuk tuk drove teams to Angkor Wat, where there was a ROADBLOCK "Who has the better sense of Direction?" for the selected team member to find the Echo Chamber. Either Andrew or Dan distinguished himself there and Tina had poor performance locating it. The task was to beat your chest to create an audible echo, then take a stone tablet with the next clue. That clue directed them to the Bayon Temple, which was the pit stop for episode. The finishing order was:

Nick/Starr
Toni/Dallas
Terence/Sarah, who were told the 30 minute speeding penalty would apply on release (a questionable practice in my opinion, because it should have been applied at the mat in New Zealand)

Ken/Tina
Kelly/Christie
Andrew/Dan
Aja/Ty, eliminated
Clips show that Starr and Dallas have a relationship developing.

A13, Ep.6 "Please Hold While I Singe My Skull"

Teams were released from the Bayon temple after a 12 hour pit stop at:

Nick/Starr	1122pm
Toni/Dallas	1134pm
Ken/Tina	1153pm
Kelly/Christy	1159pm
Terence/Sarah	1205am
Andrew/Dan	1229am

All of the time differences and relative positions shown above are equalized as teams get to a travel agency (it looks like all teams used the only one open in the middle of the night) and are booked on the same flights to Delhi, India. Starr and Dallas get to know each other in the airport, with Dallas getting in this quip: "My mom's the worst wingman ever." The first is an in-the-daylight flight on Bangkok Airways to Bangkok, connecting to a flight to Delhi from there. The time of arrival in Delhi is 415pm. Sunset was at 700pm. By the time teams got through customs, in a taxi and across town in very heavy rush hour traffic commensurate with a combined population of 13.8 million for Old Delhi and New Delhi, it was after dark. In addition to the huge number of cars on the road, there were honking horns typical of all of India and cows allowed to wander wherever they choose; the median strip in motorways and the sides of the road appear to have many cows. The first clue sends teams to Moonlight Motors in India AutoMall complex. There is a Roadblock there; one team member chosen for "Who's got an artistic flair?" has to tape newspaper to cover the non-black painted sections of an auto-rickshaw so they won't be painted over when that individual uses a spray gun to paint the black green. Ken/Tina in particular had a difficult time finding this business. The usual "tax driver roulette" prevailed; those teams which had a competent, knowledgeable taxi driver did better.

First to complete this task was Andrew/Dan, with Nick/Starr right behind them, followed by Toni/Dallas, Ken/Tina, Kelly/Christy and Terence/Sarah in last place. During this roadblock the stress in the Terence/Sarah relationship was so thick that you could cut it with a knife. Sarah was putting them in last place and Terence was understandably critical, but Sarah insisted that he confine his comments to only positive ones. He did but he was upset in a big way over that. The difficulty navigating with a well-meaning but not knowledgeable taxi driver put great strain on Ken/Tina. A quip by Dan: "Andrew's a Da Vinci, Michelangelo, David just rolled into one right now."

The next clue sent teams to the Ambassador Hotel for another clue. This was a DETOUR option of Launder Money (obtain at Prakash Banquet Hall by exchange with locals exactly 780 rupees from ten pieces of currency combined, then use them to modify an intricate necklace and finally find the groom at a major wedding full of dancing locals to get their next clue) or Launder Clothes (use a traditional Indian iron heated by charcoal inside to press 20 items of clothing to receive their next clue). Nick/Starr, Toni/Dallas, Andrew/Dan and Kelly/Christy chose Launder Clothes, as it was more or less predictable depending on a team's efficiency. Ken/Tina and Terence/Sarah both chose Launder Money. Launder Clothes worked out as planned. Nick/Starr finished first and got their clue to the pit stop at Bahai House. Kelly/Christy worked very hard and efficiently to move into second place. Toni/Dallas got it done next. Then Terence/Sarah made a great progress after getting the money exchanged with locals. For those interested it would take one 500 note, two 100 notes, one 20, and six 10s to reach 780 exactly. Teams had to figure out this one exact combination was the solution. They fought their way through throngs of revelers and finally located the groom at the far end of a large room. Ken/Tina were behind in finishing the same steps. Terence/Sarah came in 4th and the major problems that Dan/Andrew had with the ironing caused them to be in 5th. Ken/Tina departed behind Terence/Sarah from the wedding and finished in last place.

The Baha'i House pit stop finish mirrored departure from the DETOUR:
Nick/Starr

Kelly/Christy
Toni/Dallas
Terence/Sarah
Andrew/Dan
Ken/Tina, non-eliminated and next leg will have a SpeedBump task

Nick/Starr and Toni/Dallas at this point are the only solid teams at this point. Each of the other teams has demonstrated major flaws that prevent them from getting consistent performance.

AR13, Ep.7 "My Nose is On Fire"

This episode stayed in the cities of New Delhi and Old Delhi, India area. Being transported around with a variety of taxis, pedicabs, and auto-rickshaws provided plenty of drama and difficulties for the teams. As in other Asian countries, transportation suppliers have a tendency to accept your fare even if he doesn't know where it is. They assume that by asking someone along the way they will get there. It's true, they do get here but sometimes at a cost of precious time versus someone who really does know where it is. The problem is that it is impossible to tell the difference between the two types. Such is the central problem of navigating around major Asian cities. The real winner of this episode was Delhi area transportation systems.

Teams were released from the Baha'l House pit stop at these times:
Nick/Starr   855am
Kelly/Christy   902am
Toni/Dallas   910am
Terence/Sarah 931am
Andrew/Dan   944am
Ken/Tina   951am

The first clue sent teams to an apartment complex central park area where some wild activities are underway, the celebration of Holi, the festival of colors and a major Hindu holiday really celebrated in February or March. Amazing Race 13 is actually staging this event in May for the benefit of a more interesting episode, achieved because in my opinion it is the most memorable task of all Amazing

Race 13. Brilliant dry colors create raining and inescapable clouds of color, often thrown directly at passersby. Bright colored waters and water balloons are used. This is one fabulous roadblock, staged for our benefit!

This clue is ROADBLOCK "who's ready for a colorful experience?" for one team member to enter the compound, walk (or run) to a rotating set of holders reachable only by climbing a ladder. The holders have one good clue and all the rest TRY AGAIN. There are only 6 clues in total at 6 stations. The filming does not indicate whether there were more than one at any station. I think not, implying that this is a task where the probability of all teams doing well is the same if they do not get sidetracked. Starr took it and did fine. Kelly took it and had major problems, so serious that she claimed she would "seriously die" if she had to continue. Of course after the commercial break she does continue as you know she must. She does not finish until her 5th try, which puts them in last place by that time. Dallas took it and did fine. Terence had minor problems with colors in his mouth and nasal passages, but it does not appear to slow him up much. Dan took it and did OK. Tina was slowed up a bit, but she got it done.

The next clue sent teams to a bird hospital in a Jain temple in Old Delhi. It was only a task to extend the episode by sending team elsewhere. All teams appeared to find the next clue quickly, except Terence/Sarah search under the litter box when that wasn't necessary (but they did not know that). Ken/Tina received their SpeedBump first, which takes them to a nearby temple to give out glasses of Holy Water (for drinking) to anyone who wants one, which is maybe around 200 (the editing only showed one individual refusing it). My guess is that it took about 30 minutes to get to the temple, complete that task and then from the temple to the next task. As a result of time at the SpeedBump, Ken and Tina were last leaving the bird hospital.

Next was the DETOUR Teary-Eyed or Blurred-Eyed. Terence/Sarah were the only team to select Teary-Eyed, transporting two 40 pound chili pepper bags on foot for 1/4 mile, then pounding chilies as finely as possible. This resulted in severe respiratory problems for Terence in particular, as forecast by Phil who had first-hand experience with those peppers. They persevered after being instructed to keep grinding to make the pepper segments finer and demonstrated the wisdom of a predictable task. The alternate was Blurry-Eyed, which is a partially luck-based task involving walking down a street Nai Sarak and spotting then recording the numbers of small numbered tags on the complex of electric wiring (a total mess unthinkable with American standards). The trick was to spot each and every number, which was quite difficult. Nick/Starr took a pass, but didn't succeed. As they were about to try again, Toni/Dallas arrived. The two teams agreed to work together, a successful short-term alliance. Those teams finished together and received the clue for the pit stop.

Andrew/Dan arrived next and were fairly clueless. Kelly/Christy arrived. Both teams had messed up 3 passes when Andrew/Dan made an offer of a short-term alliance to finish this task. Christy said no although it appeared that Kelly favored it. So, it's back to the drawing boards with both teams ready to make another pass. While that was happening, Ken/Tina's first pass was successful; then they ran into Andrew/Dan. They offered the secrets (look for the small tags) of how to do it right, with Tina telling Andrew/Dan they owed them if they survived this leg. Kelly/Christy got no such advice but solved it themselves. All teams now had the final clue to the pit stop at Humuyan's Tomb.

The arrival at the pit stop mirrored the finish of the DETOURs. Nick/Starr beat Toni/Dallas in the taxi ride competition for first place. They won a vacation for 2 from Travelocity to Kauai, including a Na Pali Coast trip and some additional inclusions. Terence/Sarah easily got third. Ken/Tina demonstrated what a good team they are by not only recovering from essentially a 30 minute penalty but also by getting IOUs from helping Andrew/Dan. Andrew/Dan proved inept and feeble once more. This is going to catch up with them, but they have squeaked through multiple times. Kelly/Christy were last and eliminated. Those women were tough competitors, but I just didn't care for their style. I am glad they will confine their future impact on this race to maybe a decoy role during the final leg and maybe talking to the other eliminees by phone on an Elimination Station segment.

The final finish was:
Nick and Starr

Toni/Dallas
Terence/Sarah
Ken/Tina
Andrew/Dan
Kelly/Christy, eliminated

AR13, Ep.8 "I'm Like An Angry Cow"
Teams release from the pit stop in Delhi India to fly to Almaty (Alma
Ata in the era of 1960s Russian missile program) Kazakhstan at:
Nick/Starr   1014pm
Toni/Dallas   1024pm
Terence/Sarah 1043pm
Ken/Tina   1118pm
Andrew/Dan   1200am

CBS played up Borat in its commercials for this episode, but used
the real Almaty, former capital of Kazakhstan and one of two largest
cities (which the movie Borat did not). Amazing Race
producers went for questionable slapstick comedy and splashy
scenes. This episode was centered in Kazakhstan. Teams took
late-night flights from Delhi to Dubai, Frankfurt or Moscow and
transferred from there to Almaty. Nick/Starr, Toni/Dallas and
Ken/Tina chose Frankfurt, with the earliest arrival at 1155pm.
Terence/Sarah elected Moscow and arrived at 110am on the
following day. Andrew/Dan did not arrive through Dubai until about
6am the next day. Their taxi drive to the Chicken Farm, Almaty
episode Roadblock, was just in time for its opening at 0730.

All teams sprinted to a cluebox inside the Chicken Farm gate. Dan
was first, but Nick inches behind grabbed it from him. It offered a
ROADBLOCK and the final FAST FORWARD of AR13.
ROADBLOCK "Who's feeling puckish?" was for a selected team
member to Find a Golden Egg among 7 dispersed among 30,000
chickens in a huge henhouse. Toni, Andrew and Tina all tried this
luck-based task. The skills needed were good eyesight and ability
to clear chickens out of your path. They completed this
ROADBLOCK without incident.

The FAST FORWARD was for each team member to eat a
traditional Kazahh dish based on the rear end of a sheep. What

110

was strange was before 8am there were several other diners (at least 2 of which were also eating a traditional Kazakh meal), no doubt to provide encouragement and tips to the AR13 teams. It did look incongruous. How often do you see people eating dinner at 8am? Although theoretically possible, it is completely unlikely. Nick/Starr and Terence/Sarah went for it. Both teams need to know that the odds are against the loser in a 2-way battle for FAST FORWARD surviving.

I can understand why Terence/Sarah in Terence's desperate move to get in first attempted it, but it made no sense to me that Nick/Starr did. Apparently they are big-time risk-takers. Nick moved along, but Starr finished in half the time it took him. Terence is a vegetarian and had not eaten meat in 15 years. I have no idea why, when arriving and finding out the details, he did not just jump back into the taxi and return to the ROADBLOCK. Sarah was not far along when he decided to abandon the FAST FORWARD attempt (which they were not going to win anyway based on the eating patterns I observed). They returned to the ROADBLOCK far behind. Was this one hour? Probably but for sure it was significant time. Nick/Starr proceeded to Old Square park, the pit stop for this Kazakhstan leg. They won a 180hp WaveRunner each.

The other 3 teams were struggling with the task. The clue sent them to Koktobe Mountain in a crane vehicle. The trick was that provided drivers were instructed only to follow the instructions of the teams to get there. Navigating in the Cyrillic language must have been interesting. Many people on the side of the road didn't know or wouldn't say how to get there. Eventually they all did get there. The task there was absurd and ridiculous. Walk up a mountain road so that 2 Mongol warriors can escort you to a site whether there are 2 falcon handlers and one falcon. Handler #1 releases the bird, which flies maybe 100 feet to Handler #2, who presents the clue to the teammates. Why go through all that rigamarole just to do what a cluebox normally does? What a waste of talent just to highlight falcons and Mongol warriors for seconds! These 3 teams did this without incident, although Andrew/Dan were behind and later Terence/Sarah were far behind them.

The next task was DETOUR, Play Like Mad (go to the Museum of Instruments, pick two specific ones, and learn how to play a simple tune on them, then perform it to win $1.50 change in Kazakh money on the street) or Act Like Bulls (get a 2 person cow costume at the Marionette theatre, put it on and navigate the streets to find a specific milk vendor, then drink a glass of milk and use the clue in the glass at the bottom to get directions to a meat vendor in a special Meat Market which you had to walk to). No team chose Play Like Mad, probably due to the uncertainty of learning to play an instrument (which is quite easy if you have almost any music training). All went for Act Like Bulls and it was truly a comedy of errors. Navigation was the problem, then following the clue was the problem. Toni/Dallas started out with some minor navigational problems but continued on through. Ken/Tina were right behind them and even got ahead slightly at one point, but they had more serious navigational issues. They drank the milk but did not look at all on the bottom where the prior clue said the new clue would be. Later they abandoned their cow costume too soon even though Ken had questioned that. They reached the Meat Market and found out they would not receive the clue unless than were in cow costume. They easily fixed that but at the cost of precious time. Andrew/Dan were haphazard all the way, with many navigational errors. They were portrayed as a team with Terence/Sarah right behind them. Andrew/Dan took a taxi to the pit stop; the clue directed them to walk. They had to take a taxi back and walk to the pit stop. Editing shows Terence/Sarah were shown flying through tasks.

If you look at the probabilities for a team looking for 1 of 5 Golden Eggs vs. that for 1 of 4 Golden Eggs on the ROADBLOCK, on average Andrew/ Dan would be quicker doing it than Terence/ Sarah. On the DETOUR I expect Terence/Sarah were faster than Andrew/Dan, but not enough to overcome their late start on that ROADBLOCK. Terence/Sarah were eliminated; when questioned afterward they said they lost by 7 minutes.

The order of the finish was:
1. Nick/Starr—zipping through with the FAST FORWARD
2. Toni/Dallas
3. Ken/Tina
4. Andrew/Dan
5. Terence/Sarah—eliminated as a result of Terence's macho

Phil asked: "Why couldn't you eat meat for $1 million?" Terence took responsibility for his decision to go for the Fast Forward over Sarah's objections, resulting ultimately in elimination. He said that he didn't want a future without Sarah, who says their relationship is very good.

The Golden Egg search was fabulous! I did not understand why the falcons and Mongol warriors in the next task. Act Like Bulls was totally comical and provided some insight into the difficulties of reading clues properly (note that both Andrew/Dan and Ken/Tina made big mistakes on this) and cross-cultural communications. The people of Almaty come across as able to enjoy a good laugh with the teams and of being variable in their helpfulness to provide English directions locally.

AR13, Ep9 "That is Studly"

Teams are released from the pit stop in Almaty at these times:
Nick/Starr   921pm
Toni/Dallas   1047pm
Ken/Tina   1117pm
Andrew/Dan 1241am

Nick and Starr's FAST FORWARD victory had won them a 1.5 hour advantage over the next team, but all are leveled by a Bunching at Almaty Airport. Dan and Andrew have no shoes and come there in slippers, so they elect to spend $300 to get the least expensive sneakers for each of them at that Airport. All teams get a 605am nonstop flight from Almaty to Moscow. Then taxi driver roulette takes over for the rest of this episode because all rides were long. Moscow is a huge metropolitan area. Teams that are lucky enough to get a competent and knowledgeable driver move ahead while teams with bad luck fall back; if they have a GPS even better. Minimum taxi fare in the Moscow area was $17, but long trips meant much higher fares.

On the first taxi segment, driving to a Monastery, both Ken/Tina and Andrew/Dan were victims. All teams lit a candle, got their clue and were off to the Kolosok decommissioned military base. They found a DETOUR but on the way Nick/Starr are delayed by taxi driver inability to find the destination quickly. Either way they had to change to military garb, including a cloth wrapping over the feet. Doing that wrapping takes a huge amount of time for Andrew/Dan. Boots is selecting a drill group, learning how to march, then doing a tour of the grounds using the distinct goosestep with swinging arms. Nobody has any problem with this except Dan. Andrew was in marching band so he knows how to do it, but Dan is hopeless and hapless. The "soldiers" (they might actually be that) got great laughs from Dan's style because he has no rhythm and cannot match the needed precision. So while the other teams have left Andrew/Dan decided to switch to the other DETOUR of Borscht service for 75 soldiers. Dan almost immediately think this was a mistake after they started the preparations, so they went back to Boots but Dan has made no progress and still can't do the required marching well enough and they are rejected one more time. So they go back to Borscht again, did this well and finished. Andrew says "Dan and I have made more dumb mistakes." He's is so right. The taxi driver for Nick/Starr was hopeless on the next segment to Zhukovsky where they must locate a specific bakery. They replaced him but the next one isn't much better. By the time they get there, they were far back in 3rd place. It is ROADBLOCK "Who has a strong back?" with the task being carrying 50 55-pound sacks of flour from a truck into the bakery and stacking it neatly. Dallas has a head start and manages to finish first, but he went out of the blocks too hard by carrying 2 bags each load. Ken with his NFL strength was able to do that and he and Tina made up most of the time deficit against Toni/Dallas. Nick was clearly slower but he progressed steadily and left to chase the others to the pit stop. Andrew/Dan showed up soon after; Dan plowed through the flour bags, making up time on Nick/Starr.

Getting to the pit stop required another long taxi ride to find Neskuchniy Park at a specific address, #14 on Leninsky Prospekt. There teams locate a hard-to-find gate to reach the garden where the finish mat is. Toni/Dallas maintained their lead, finished first and won a Travelocity trip to the Punta Cana resort area of Dominican Republic. Ken/Tina were a close second and happy with that performance. Nick/Starr had more taxi troubles and finally arrive in third place. Andrew/Dan continue with the same taxi driver, but the length of the trips and total taxi expense of several hundred dollars for the day have wiped out their funds and leave them $200 short as best I can tell. They got their taxi driver to accept something (it's not clear to me what) for the shortage. They finished last but are saved by a non-elimination point. They will face a SpeedBump on leg 10. The finish order is:

Toni/Dallas
Ken/Tina
Nick/Starr
Andrew/Dan, non-eliminated

This was a hilarious episode. The "soldiers" laughed hard at Dan's feeble attempts to march and AR13 viewers also had fun with it. The can-do attitude of all doing the ROADBLOCK was a positive statement. Ken did best, Dallas second, Dan third and the less muscular Nick last. The setup of this leg to focus on differential taxi driver performance was fun to watch, but it had to be hard with all teams except Toni/Dallas with a good taxi driver gritting their teeth.

AR13, Ep.10 "You're Gonna Get Me Killed"
This was a wild and woolly episode of Amazing Race 13. Nick/Starr were in front almost the entire way, so their first-place finish was never in doubt. What every Amazing Race fan wanted to know was "who lost their passports and money?" due to CBS promotion of that question. Would it be Ken/Tina, Toni/Dallas or Andrew/Dan? I was expecting it to be Andrew and Dan. Let's see how it turned out.

The CBS telecast didn't provide the pit stop release times for any teams. Was this designed to heighten the uncertainty on the above question or to obscure the duration for that pit stop was approximately 18 hours? We already knew that Toni/Dallas then Ken/Tina then Nick/Starr had up to 1.5 hours between them. We also had Andrew/Dan starting probably quite a bit behind, say 3 hours. The first clue was available at the diesel submarine B-396 Novosibirsky Kosomolets museum near the Skhodnenskaya metro station. Andrew/Dan were lucky to get an English speaking taxi driver but he took them to the wrong park. Both leading teams arrived there about the same time hours before the 8am opening hour of the museum. Nick/Starr followed; Andrew/Dan arrived after opening.

They all received their clues and headed off to Park Iskusst, where the Monument of Fallen Heroes ROADBLOCK "Who's good at solving mysteries. Literally." awaited. This was complicated. The non-active team member had to go ahead to Bulgakov House. The active team member had to count statues which were labeled in Cyrillic to find the number of Lenin statues (6 was correct) and the number of Stalin statues (2 was correct), then they had to go to a designated bookshop, cite those results as consecutive digits (62 was the winner) to receive a book which had the address for the next clue on page 62 (a 6 story building on Sadayev St.). Any team that failed to get this right would wait 10 minutes until they could submit another number. Once the selected individuals collect their teammate, they go to Sokol'niki Park to the lady with a Shetland pony for the next clue.

Here is where it got really interesting, as this was certainly the best ROADBLOCK of AR13 and competitive with the best one of any Amazing Race. Nick took his time and carefully noted 62 as his result. He went to the bookstore, was correct, went to join Starr and they never looked back for the rest of the episode. Tina had the next shot; she was uncertain but chose 52 and had to wait 10 minutes. While that was happening, Dallas (who had been picked by Toni to do this) came and gave number 36 which meant he had reversed Lenin and Stalin in the count order. It was wrong, so he had to wait. Tina then picked 62 as her next try and was rewarded. As she left, she took pity on Dallas (resulting in major and valid criticism when she reunited with Ken due to going against their decision to not help other teams) and gave him her insights about his reversing the numbers and being too high on the smaller one. Dallas had one more incorrect guess, then a correct one.

So now with Andrew doing the Roadblock Dan went to the waiting area where he met Dallas reaching there from the bookstore. However, Dallas had left his pack in the back of the taxi so he and Toni now had no money and no passports. He asked Dan for a loan, but Andrew had all their money so he had nothing to lend. After Dallas was out of earshot, Dan said to the camera that he would not have given it if he had it. So now Toni decided their only alternative was begging. They successfully got enough rubles for bus fares and they arrived at the Rizhki tram stop close to the clue in Sokol'niki Park. They found the woman with the Shetland pony prominent inside the entrance, but she refused to give them the clue. They presumed that it means that they had to travel by taxi to get the clue (but how would she know?; obviously someone from World Race Productions is on top of this and giving her guidance out of the camera's view). So they raised more money by begging because they need the small fare back to Bulgakov House but also 400 rubles for the taxi fare. Before they can do this Andrew finished by trying first 61 and then 62(a lucky guess) and is out of there with only one 10 minute penalty. Dan/Andrew get to Sokol'niki Park by taxi and find a sign for the SpeedBump, which for only them was dancing with a young Russian dance troupe and finishing only when the dancing master determined that they were good enough. They went through one and then a second try to complete it in what they later reported was about 15 minutes. They weren't very good (Dan being his uncoordinated self) but the dancing master took pity on them. The really good news for them is that this activity was adjacent to the Shetland pony lady, so they lost little time in trans-portation. They were about the same time frame as Toni/Dallas' rejection when they got their clue from the Shetland pony lady.

Next was DETOUR of RIDE THE RAILS (take the underground metro from Sokol'niki Station to a specific stop after changing once to get to 1905 Street Station and then go to a marked samsa sandwich stand and the wrapper will have the clue, which sends them to Kitai-Gordo Station where they find a statue and babushka, then trade her the samsa for a postcard with the name of the next place and instructions to find a cluebox near its metro station) or RIDE THE LINES (actually trolley bus which you have to take to another tram to Karnosel'skaya Station where you get a key from a specific keymaker and go to Rizhskaya Station to a locker where the postcard is found). Nick when he got this clue says "Being a New Yorker has finally paid off." He and Starr RIDE THE RAILS without trouble and went to VDNKh Park, found the clue and entered the park where the pit stop is in an unusually busy area (for Amazing Race pit stops). They finished first and won one 5 night vacation for 2 in Anguilla compliments of Travelocity. All other teams chose RIDE THE LINES. Toni/Dallas were now last and they had to keep begging to get anywhere. Ken/Tina did RIDE THE LINES and made it to the VDNKh metro station but could not find the clue box. Who knows how long this took, probably more than an hour, edited to make it appear that they are only slightly ahead of Toni/Dallas. Andrew/ Dan passed them at Sokol'niki Park just after their SpeedBump while Toni and Dallas had to redo using a taxi. For Andrew/Dan finishing second in spite of their start time, taxi to wrong park delay, and requirement to do the SpeedBump was a huge achievement. That was some really fine racing. Ken/Tina finally finished 3rd after their simultaneous arrival at VDNKh metro with Andrew/Dan was negated by their inability to find the cluebox with the clue to the pit stop location.

Phil went out onto the course to do the elimination "in-the-field" for Toni/Dallas. Both of them say they were very proud of each other and had improved an already-good relationship. Toni stated she would have done nothing different the whole race. If so, she is kidding herself. If elected to do that ROADBLOCK, I know she would have been quicker and more accurate in counting Lenins and Stalins and it is highly unlikely that she would have lost the bag with money/passports.

AR13, Ep11, Finale "You Look Like Peter Pan"

We are now ready for the Finale. It's Nick/Starr, Andrew/Dan (who nobody thought would be here except maybe themselves), and Ken/Tina. They still have several relationship issues to work out. Tina feels under-supported by Ken, but he really appeared to be trying. It became a two team race soon after the teams landed in Portland Oregon. The check-in time for Nick/Starr I am guessing to be around 4pm, which if true means that it was a 7 hour pit stop to get to a 1056pm release time. They go to the Domodedovo airport (almost certainly directed by the clue) and book a 705am departure connecting at Frankfurt to Portland Oregon. Once there a clue directed them to driving to Newberg Oregon to the Tilikum Adventure Center.

Andrew/Dan released at 228am and Ken/Tina at 330am. It's amazing Ken/Tina were lost more than an hour the prior episode after crossing paths with Andrew/Dan. Nick/Starr and Ken/Tina went directly by taxi to Tilikum, but Andrew/Dan had a poor taxi driver and fall behind. From that point the race for the $1,000,000 was between just Nick/Starr and Ken/Tina. A DETOUR awaited at Tilikum, High and Dry or Low and Wet.

Teams chose between climbing a tree, then walking out a fairly low circumference log to jump for a metal triangular bar (which has the next clue) or walking along a long log in the water. Nobody chose Low and Wet. Starr competed against Tina; Starr finished first because Tina is afraid of heights. Nick/Starr were ahead by several minutes, but by the time teams got to the next competition site they missed a simple turn as their taxi driver was not familiar with this area and had to go ahead and come back. Ken/Tina slid into first place. They climbed stairs onto the Bridge of the Gods east of Portland on Interstate 84 at exit 44. They went to the middle and got attached to a 2000 foot zipline onto Thunder Island adjacent to the Cascade Locks. On that island were 150 clue-boxes each with a picture. There was a game board with 10 slots, one for each prior episode of AR13. Teams must be together (no double-dipping) as they find a DETOUR or ROADBLOCK or task or pit stop requested for each episode. The correct pictures were:

leg 1 moving cart with many items on it in Salvador
leg 2 moving boats on log rollers for Beach-It DETOUR near Fortaleza
leg 3 fighting the cholitas in El Alto near La Paz
leg 4 sheep at pit stop, Summerhill Farms near Tauranga, New Zealand
leg 5 not shown (why not?)
leg 6 Ambassador Hotel in Delhi
leg 7 not shown (again, why not?)
leg 8 a gentleman from whom clue received in Almaty, Kazakhstan
leg 9 Monastery interior, Moscow
leg 10 Lenin/Stalin roadblock in Moscow

Nick/Starr finished slightly ahead of Ken/Tina but the taxi ride was even except at the end when Nick/Starr's taxi driver took a different route and got them there first. The next clue took them to the Portland building in downtown Portland, but the following clue is at a green dinosaur in the Standard Plaza across the street. The next clue took them on foot to find a food stand on Alder Street Cart Pod between 9th and 10th for the cart of the last country they were in (Russia). The clue there took them to "magic is in the hole", a reference to Voodoo Doughnuts, a local specialty that they must ask locals to figure out. The last clue sent them to the Finish Line at Pittoch Mansion. Both teams could not find a taxi, but Nick/Starr succeeded first. Nick/Starr offered their taxi driver $70 to get them there first. Ken/Tina finished 5 to 11 minutes behind for quite a close finish. Host Phil Keoghan on the mat says "after 23 days, 5 continents and almost 40,000 miles, Nick and Starr you are the official winners of the Amazing Race." They won $1,000,000. As Ken/Tina finished 2nd he pulled out the wedding rings they haven't been wearing and puts them on Tina's and his own left ring fingers. Tina acknowledged that the race had brought them back together. Andrew/Dan were not shown doing anything in downtown Portland, but finished third over one hour later.

I want to comment on the physical fitness levels needed to win this race. It appeared to be neck-and-neck in downtown Portland, where the tasks were on foot after they arrived at the Standard Plaza to get a clue. Both Nick and Ken appeared to be effortless and able to run all day. Starr in particular was shown dragging many times, which I am sure was done to fake us out. I will bet that Tina was dragging even more. They just didn't show it.

AR13 will rank in the top half of my ranking of Amazing Races. After bumbling in AR12's casting, AR13 casting did a much better job selecting the teams. Mark/Bill, Sarah/Terence and Toni/Dallas were all first-class competitors to join teams in the Final 3 to make this an interesting and exciting season.

AMAZING RACE 14

This race begins with Phil on a peninsula in Southern California and 11 teams approaching the Los Alamitos Joint Forces Training base in one of two military helicopters. Their origination point is not revealed, but a good guess would be that they drove to Los Alamitos, boarded a helicopter, were flown out to the nearby coast and then back. The teams:

LaKisha and Jennifer Hoffman, New York and Kentucky, program coordinator and Marketing assistant, age 28 and 24
Preston McCamy and Jennifer Hopka, South Carolina, dating, software engineer and student, age 28 and 26
Mark and Michael Munoz, Hawaii and Los Angeles, stuntman/actor and jockey/stuntman, age 51 and 48
Tammy and Victor Jih, Los Angeles, sister/brother, lawyers, age 26 and 35
Christie Vollmer and Jodi Wincheski, Oklahoma and Houston, flight attendants, age 37 and 40
Brad and Victoria Hunt, Columbus OH, married, dispatcher and tax manager, age 52 and 47
Steve and Linda Cole, Martinsville WV, married, carpenter and customer service rep, age 43 and 52
Amanda Blackledge and Kris Klicka, San Diego, dating, student and sales rep, age 23 and 24
Cara Rosenthal and Jaime Edmonson, Boca Raton and Ft. Lauderdale, best friends, law student and former police officer and also former Miami Dolphins cheerleaders, age 26 and 29
Luke and Margie Adams, Denver, son/mother, college graduate and research assistant, age 22 and 50
Mel and Mike White, Virginia and Santa Monica CA, father/son, writer and writer/producer/director, age 68 and 38

Ep.1 "Don't Let the Cheese hit Me"

On to the action! Phil gives his usual pre-race summary, raised his arm and got out of the way as the teams stampede to their luggage, the clue and a waiting car. They must drive to LAX and get to Locarno Switzerland. They are restricted to flying either Lufthansa, which leaves at 335pm (in U.S. daylight savings time) to Frankfurt, where they connect to Zurich and arrive (in continental Europe's standard time) at 1255pm if on schedule, or Air France, which leaves at 4pm, connects in Paris to arrive Milan-Malpensa at 105pm, only 10 minutes after the other one. However, what teams would not know unless they did research on the Internet at LAX was that Zurich airport is on a train line and Milan is not. The standard way to get from Malpensa to the train line was to take a bus to the Italy/Switzerland border, how I believe the Italy-landing teams did it. That means that at an intermediate point teams got trains that had left Milan after about 230pm.

Train schedules from Milan indicated that a train leaving at 310pm through Lugano and Bellinzona arriving Locarno 1715 was the best they could do. From Zurich the most logical train was the 207pm arriving Locarno at 457pm, about 18 minutes ahead of the other one (that is logically the way World Race Productions would have tried to maintain parity, by choosing the flights that kept the train connections the closest possible). All teams arrived as expected except that Preston/Jennifer missed the train from Milan and had to wait for the next one. Christie/Jodi actually arrived first by following a local woman onto another train that left 13 minutes earlier. In Locarno teams were directed to the San Antonio Church where they signed the register for their departure time the next day and received from the priest (or actor impersonating a priest) directions to the splendid outdoor sleeping accommodations (it's November) nearby. Leaving at 715am will be Christie/Jodi, Margie/Luke, Tammy/Victor and Mark/Michael. In the 730am group are Brad/Victoria, Cara/Jaime and Mel/Michael. In the 745am group are Kisha/Jen, Kris/Amanda, Steve/Linda and Preston/Jennifer. The clue sent them 10km to Verzasca Dam where the second highest commercial bungee jump in the world at 622 feet awaits. Christie/Jodi went to a proper taxi area, but none are there and it takes them a while before they get into the street to hail a taxi. Linda got the prize for the quote of the episode by telling her taxi driver "Go fast, but follow the speed limit," an inherently contradictory instruction.

Next is ROADBLOCK "Who has nerves of steel?" requiring a risk-tolerant individual to bungee jump. The first 3 teams arrive there about the same time. Jumps require about 9 minutes before the next team can go. Based on the distance and the time to get there, Victor did the first jump around 750am; the last jump was at 914am. Tammy/Victor received the next clue to go to Interlaken Switzerland by train and search there for Kleine Rugen Wiese where they would pass a field and find antique cheese carriers to transport 200 pounds of cheese. They are followed closely by Mark/Michael and Margie/Luke. Christie/Jodi and Brad/Victoria are neck and neck at the train station, but take different train routes. Even though they leave 71 minutes later, the schedule indicates Brad/Victoria will get there first due to good research on the train schedules and taking the Simplon Tunnel route. The longer route is through the St. Gotthard Tunnel and Lucerne. Victor told Tammy to feign ignorance of where the next (correct) train is going. The other teams followed them and one of the stunt-brothers told them that they are not credible and will be carefully watched. Brad/Victoria tried a similar maneuver by feigning taking the same train as Christie/Jodi but not doing so, which had them taking a 1050am train rather than Christie/Jodi's 939am train and getting there earlier. The final group of five is where the eliminated team will come from. All teams chose routes using the Simplon Tunnel or the St. Gotthard Tunnel to get to Interlaken, a route some had already taken from Zurich in reverse.

Teams go to Interlaken, find Kleine Rugen Wiese and find the field on a mountainside with a steep slippery slope. A group of bell-ringers at the bottom performed, observed and are convulsed with laughter. Each person was given access to the 200 pounds of cheese (4 50 pound rounds) and a cheese carrier, which are so antique (read junky) that they fall apart under stress and they receive lots of stress. Walking up the hill with an empty carrier is not easy, but walking down with a loaded one was much worse. Many of the women had trouble carrying a 50 pound wheel. Many different approaches were used. Some tried the direct approach of putting the cheese in the carrier, others carry the block of cheese down without it, others slid the carrier along the ground and others slid down on their butts carrying the cheese. There was some separation due to rail arrival schedules (151pm, 155pm and 223pm are the possibilities). It looks to me that World Race Productions found a time frame that equalized the teams to the maximum extent. Several teams stated they were never going to eat cheese again after this. Margie/Luke finished this in the lead. Margie is both strong and quick and Luke even more so. This team should do well in this race. Tammy/Victor were right behind them, followed by Mark/Michael and Mel/Michael. Amanda/Kris and Brad/Victoria do well. Christie/Jodi appeared to have minimal race smarts as they make mistakes, but they persevered. The hill took a toll on Linda, moving particularly slowly, but they had done better than expected in their finish. Preston/Jennifer finally got out of last place by finishing the cheese task in 10th place. Jaime/Cara were last. Teams had to take taxis to Stechelberg's last postal bus stop. Teams listened for the sounds of yodeling and followed it to the pit stop. Some teams had directional difficulty while others went right to it. Preston/Jennifer went the wrong way and were eliminated. They had potential but failed to best some weak teams at the end. Margie/Luke and Brad/Victoria completed tasks and transportation ahead of my expectations.

The finish order was:
1. Margie/Luke
2. Tammy/Victor
3. Mark/Michael
4. Mel/Michael
5. Amanda/Kris
6. Brad/Victoria
7. Cara/Jaime
8. Kisha/Jennifer
9. Steve/Linda
10.Christie/Jodi
11.Preston/Jennifer - eliminated

AR14, Ep.2 "Your Target Is Your Partner's Face"

This starts in Stechelberg with release from the pit stop as follows:
Margie/Luke   256am
Tammy/Victor 257am
Mark/Michael 259am
Mel/Michael   318am
Amanda/Kris   342am
Brad/Victoria 356am
Cara/Jaime   359am
Kisha/Jen   402am
Steve/Linda   404am
Christie/Jodi   412am

The clue directed teams to get to Ruhpolding, Germany via flying from Zurich to Munich. The first flight was at 710am arriving 815am with a second flight at 845am arriving 945am. All teams except Margie/Luke, Mark/Michael and Linda/Steve called ahead by borrowing cell phones from their taxi drivers and made the 710am flight. Mark/Michael and Linda/Steve are left behind for the second flight. From Munich airport teams drove east into the Bavarian countryside to get to Ruhpolding.

At Ruhpolding teams found a ROADBLOCK "Who's ready to fly like an eagle?" They took a cablecar to Raushberg Mountain and found a paragliding task. The paraglider chooses an instructor, then waits for good wind conditions to make the 6000 foot glide down, or they can elect to walk/run down the mountain in an estimated time of one hour. All doing this task except Mel (who did not think he could safely walk down) elected to walk or run down as the winds were strong. Margie and Victor made it quickly. Everyone else did OK, except that Linda missed a route marker and went off course. She got a local driver to take her back to the point where she left the course so there would be no penalty. Not surprisingly, Steve/Linda finished in last place on this task. Mel finally got the desired lower winds and paraglided to earn a middle position among the teams.

Teams now drove 25 miles south to Schonau am Konigsee, a quaint Bavarian village on the beautiful Konigsee. There they faced a DETOUR of Balancing Dolly or Austrian Folly. Balancing Dolly is a 2 mile obstacle course that has to be done by each team member on a Segway electric scooter. Austrian Folly required locating a Bavarian beer tent with oom-pah brass band and plenty of drinkers dressed as if it was summer when it was really November. Rows of many pies were there, the winning ones having a cherry filling. Teams did this task by throwing pies into the face of their partner until the cherry filling is located. Luke wanted to do the Segway option and is highly frustrated with their apparent difficulty, but it should not take long at an estimated 15 seconds per pie to locate the winners. How many would Luke have to do to find cherry? The surprising answer revealed by Luke after AR14 was telecast is maybe 100 pies, for less than 25 minutes. The mess this created on the clothes and face of the contestants was very funny. The onlookers were having a wonderful time laughing at the human folly exhibit. There were some fine pies wasted in this exercise. Maybe they should have had team members eat a whole pie instead.

After the DETOUR teams had to find the Holzsager mechanical Tyrolean woodcutters, a cute exhibit of local culture. A thin slice of wood is stamped with the final clue, which is drive to Hellbrunn Palace in Salzburg Austria, maybe 25 miles away, for the pit stop. This did not cause any significant dislocations except Kisha/Jen continue navigational errors typical of them this day and Christie/Jodi were confused about what type of woodcutter they were looking for and where it was. The last 2 teams were newly-competitive Steve/Linda and Christie/Jodi who have dropped down during another mistake-filled day. Christie/Jodi finished ahead after "I've never felt like such a dumb blonde in my entire life". Steve/Linda were eliminated after great catch-up efforts.

The final finish order for episode 2 was:
1. Tammy/Victor
2. Mel/Michael
3. Amanda/Kris
4. Margie/Luke
5. Brad/Victoria
6. Cara/Jaime
7. Kisha/Jen
8. Mark/Michael
9. Christie/Jodi
10. Linda/Steve, eliminated

AR14, Ep.3 "I'm Not Wearing That Girl's Leotard"

This is an excellent Amazing Race episode, probably one of the best ever. The pit stop release times were:

Tammy/Victor 1013pm
Mel/Michael   1201am
Amanda/Kris   1212am
Margie/Luke   1230am
Brad/Victoria 1253am
Cara/Jaime   117am
Kisha/Jen   152am
Mark/Michael 200am

Christie/Jodi   242am

Teams discovered they must reach Bucharest Romania. They drove their marked cars to the Salzburg train station, got a fast train to Munich and transfered to a train direct to Munich Airport. The first flight available was a Lufthansa flight at 325pm and Tammy Victor were the only team that got on it. It proved to be a curse, as the flight had mechanical problems in flight and returned to Munich. By that time Tammy/Victor were too late to book the second flight, Tarom at 445pm, but Amanda/Kris, Margie/Luke and Mel/Michael got on it and arrived Bucharest 745pm. Brad/Victoria just missed that when they reach Munich airport, assess their risks and decide to take a 730pm flight to Amsterdam connecting to arrive in Bucharest at 1210am. This was only a slight advantage over the other teams who took the 930pm flight direct to Bucharest, arriving 1225am. Brad/Victoria made the initial risky decision, compounded by KLM Airlines' bad arrival performance. When Brad/Victoria reached Amsterdam after a flight delay, their flight to Bucharest was gone; they are stuck until next afternoon arrival.

The first 3 teams arrived and got a clue to the National Sports Palace for gymnastics. That was a challenge for Tammy/Victor, who appeared to be dropped a long way off by their taxi driver, then found the way in the dark since it was well after midnight. They found ROABDLOCK "Who's ready to access their inner Nadia?" It is a set of tasks on the Balance Beam, Parallel Bars, and Floor Exercise elements of gymnastics competition. The selected individual had to don a leotard, train with real Romanian pixie gymnasts and be judged by real Romanian gymnastics coaches, who were quite lenient in judging. The parallel bars looked difficult to me, but all selected racers got through it so the judging standards may have been lowered just a bit. The Balance Beam took them to their limits, but nobody had an injury. Floor Exercises looked pretty easy. Racers finish with their next clue 30 to 60 minutes later:

Amanda finished first
Margie finished second
Michael (of Mel/Michael) finished third
Cara finished fourth
Michael (of Mark/Michael) finished fifth
Christie finished sixth

127

Kisha was seventh
Tammy was eighth
Victoria (alone since all other teams had already checked in) last

The clue sent them to Brasov train station to Bunch for the 630am first train. All teams except Brad/Victoria arrived in Brasov, a major city of Transylvania, at 930am. They went to the Black Church to find a cluebox outside with a DETOUR, Gypsy Moves or Vampire Remains, taking them by taxi 24 km south to the property of Bran Castle. Gypsy Moves required a team to get to a created gypsy village to load all possessions of a "gypsy family" onto a horse-drawn cart, an old car body, truck tire, seat and assorted junk. Vampire Remains required the teams to go up a hill on a marked path to find a slightly buried coffin, then drag or carry that coffin down to a set of stakes. The first key unlocked the first lock. On the coffin itself had the second key, which unlocked the second lock. Then the teams opened the coffin and took out square wood frames and impale them on the stake until they find one with a flag inside. That won the clue to the pit stop. Vampire Remains was created to summon the Spirit of Vlad the Impaler, a notorious owner of Bran Castle also known as Count Dracula.

Amanda/Kris were in first place reaching the gypsy village (which was created and populated by World Race Productions expressly for this DETOUR), but they lost their fannypack with passports and money while unloading the contents of the cart they had moved. They were fortunate to find it after a brief search that cost them only a short duration of time and one place at the finish. Tammy/Victor had huge problems on this DETOUR. He did not see the red/yellow route marker directing him to the right so they went left and far up the mountain following a red and white marker. Tammy argued with Victor multiple times but he kept going until he finally had to admit that his stubbornness was killing them. He promised to not do "Big Brother makes all important decisions" again. Yeah, fat chance!

The pit stop is Villa Panoramic 2km from Bran Castle. Finish order was:
Mel/Michael (really a tribute to them that they can do this well)
Amanda/Kris
Kisha/Jen (where did they come from?)
Margie/Luke

Mark/Michael
Christie/Jodi
Cara/Jaime
Tammy/Victor
Brad/Victoria, who are eliminated when they arrive well after dark

AR14, Ep.4 "It Was Like a Caravan of Idiots"

The Romania pit stop release times were:
Mel/Michael   1049pm
Amanda/Kris   1053pm
Kisha/Jennifer 1055pm
Margie/Luke   1106pm
Mark/Michael   1107pm
Christie/Jodi   1108pm
Jaime/Cara   1129pm
Tammy/Victor 125am

Note that Tammy/Victor were 155 minutes behind the leader and
two hours behind the next closest team. The clue sent teams to the
place on the back of the 10-ruble note in Krasnojarsk, Siberia,
Russia. Teams got to the airport as some reserve flights by phone
in the car. Sometimes that practice works well and sometimes it
doesn't. In this case Mel/Michael got a booking that did not get
them to Krasnojarsk with the first wave. Teams booked in
succession and reaching Krasnojarsk first the only winners were
Mark/Michael, Kisha/Jennifer (connecting through Sofia) and
Christie/Jodi (connecting through Istanbul) who either got to
Moscow first or had higher priority reservations. There were routes
through Frankfurt or Munich to Moscow used by 5 teams. In
addition, there are 3 different airports in Moscow and 2 of them had
flights to Krasnojarsk at the appropriate time. Teams flew to
Frankfurt, Munich, Sofia and Istanbul. From there they are all
scheduled to Moscow-Sheremetyevo airport to be on Aeroflot flight
779 leaving at 855pm and arriving Krasnojarsk at 540am before
sunup the next morning. However, the 5 less fortunate teams for
reasons not identified in the telecast (but later identified as slow
customs clearance) did not make that flight. The 3 leading teams
departed on Aeroflot 779. That meant the ones missing it had to
wait for the 1245am flight which arrived Krasnojarsk at 910am, 3.5

hours behind the leaders.

3 teams got to Krasnojarsk that far ahead. They found out from taxi drivers that the back of the 10 ruble note is the Hydroelectric Dam across the Yenisei River, a major Siberian river. It did not open until 830am, allowing some catch-up. The clue there sent teams to Church of Innokenty in Osvyanka. There they found a DETOUR Stack or Construct. In Stack teams matched the style of a huge woodpile 6 feet high and 10 feet wide. Logs that were quartered or smaller are set into place carefully so that the pile is stable. This is a difficult DETOUR and several piles tumble down. Once a team has lost its pile, almost all elect to switch to the Construct DETOUR. Construct meant build from pieces and with provided tools one of the fancy shutters common on Krasnojarsk houses, then locate a house with a REPAIRS NEEDED sign. Mark/Michael lost their pile and switched to Construct but walk all over town (well maybe not as Krasnoyarsk is a city of 900,000 people and has a large land area) without finding it. Later when the second wave of teams had arrived they found it. Kisha/Jennifer and Christie/Jodi completed their Stacks and go on to the ROADBLOCK.

The ROADBLOCK "Who's ready to speed read?" uses a bobsled track at the Bobrovy Log Park, like a luge going down a fixed track at 55 mph. The selected individual had to navigate the 3.5 mile track in 4 minutes 0 seconds or less. They noted going by each of 7 letters displayed on the side of the track. They must show what the 7 letters are and then receive square letters of those 7 to organize them into a name of a Russian author. The answer is Chekhov and some individuals got this immediately. Luke when he arrived needs 5 tries to get it. However, first up is Kisha who beat the limit at 3:55 but got only 6 letters. She had to go again after Jodi made it down in 4:00 and spells Chekhov. Both teams went on to the pit stop at the Musical Comedy Theatre, Christie/Jodi finishing in first place, Kisha/Jennifer in second.

The second flight had landed while this was happening and they confronted the same tasks. Margie/Luke did well on Stack and found a new Blind U-Turn available to them based on the activator team not identifying who they are. The activated team can only guess from who is ahead of them. Luke wouldn't expose himself in the open, but the producers have found a way for the chaos of the

U-Turn to be used early in a season rather than only in late episodes by taking the stigma out of it. They do not need to help themselves, but Luke stated that he wants to help Jaime/Cara stay in the race. I bet he also wanted to eliminate Amanda/Kris as competition. He U-Turned Amanda/Kris. Then he had to solve the Chekhov name puzzle, which looked like he will be unable to do. Margie can't help but even if she could she did not know the answer. On a 5th try Luke got it. Tammy/Victor did Stack quickly and Victor was fastest of all in getting Chekhov. The word Chekhov does tend to favor the well-educated professional. Mark/Michael were joined by Mel/Mike and Amanda/Kris on the shutters. They all finished about the same time and then went looking for the elusive REPAIRS NEEDED house. All finished at close to the same time.

They all go to the Blind U-Turn area and there Amanda/Kris found out that they have to go back to Stack, which they had abandoned when they lost their pile. They redid it reasonably quickly but just going back took time and they were maybe 10 minutes behind when they finish. All the other teams have made finished ahead of them, so Amanda and Kris are eliminated. The finish order was:

Christie/Jodi
Margie/Luke
Tammy/Victor
Jaime/Cara
Kisha/Jennifer
Mel/Michael
Mark/Michael
Amanda/Kris, last and eliminated

I feel that Mark/Michael squandered a 3.5 hour lead with their inept-ness. I feel that Tammy/Victor, Margie/Luke and Jaime/Cara all did particularly well this leg. Since the identity of which team used the Blind U-Turn is bound to leak out (I expect Luke to do so to solidify his relationship with Jaime and Cara) the limitations of trying to use an early U-Turn and not suffer a reputation loss will be clearer.

AR14, Ep.5 "She's A Little Scared of Stick, but I Think She'll Be OK"

Pit stop release times from Krasnoyarsk after a 24 hour pit stop are:

1. Christie/Jodi   1234pm
2. Margie/Luke   1236pm
3. Tammy/Victor not shown
4. Jaime/Cara
5. Kisha/Jennifer
6. Mel/Michael
7. Mark/Michael

The fact that CBS is not displaying pit stop release times for the bottom 5 active teams is not good, but we will survive because all teams head for the Central Railway Station to get tickets for the same train to Novosibirsk, 400 miles away. It appears that the producers wanted all teams Bunched on the same train, the 10:26pm train. I first believed no such train exists in the Trans Siberian Railway schedule until discovering listings are Moscow time (626pm locally in Krasnojarsk) and arrived 1047am after a 12 hour 21 minute run. On the train it was clear that Margie/Luke have caved to the group pressure and admitted that they were the perpetrators of the Blind U-Turn on Amanda/Kris. The train ride was mostly in the dark, hindering video of the Siberan countryside.

Teams arrive at Novosibirsk and found Punkt Tehnicheskogo Osmotra, to get the clue for the DETOUR Russian Bride or Russian Snowplow. Russian Bride required self-driving a Lada regular transmission auto to find a "bride" (read actress) at the address #4 of a major apartment block and in apartment #14 there. They must give the "bride" a bouquet and transport her to a specific church to some men in Russian army jackets, one of whom is her "groom". After a photo of the teammates in it with the bride and groom, the groom released the next clue. This task required navigation skills in an unfamiliar city with Cyrillic language. I would not have picked it if I were racing. Victor pulled a fast one on Jaime/Cara and Margie/Luke by instantly abandoning an alliance when he expected he and Tammy could do better alone getting directions first. Jaime commented "They'll follow you until they can find something on their own and then they'll ditch you." Russian Snowplow required going to Spartak Stadium and looking for the snowplow obstacle course. Each team selecting this DETOUR drove around the course without bumping into the tire piles which were the edge of the course. None of the teams doing this seemed to have any difficulty with it. Christie/Jodi were directed by a local to the wrong church, so that cost them precious time. Jennifer was not the world's best stickshift driver and stalled out the Lada multiple times.

Teams are next directed to the Biblioteka. I don't know Russian but in French Bibliotheque is Library. I guess this destination is a Library (it's Gosudarstvennaya Publichnaya Nauchnaya Tekhnicheskaya Biblioteka). Teams find a ROADBLOCK which requires them to strip to their underwear and run a 1.4 mile course in 25 degrees Fahrenheit temperature after doing a 10 minute warm-up. They each have 2 fully clad local students running with them as escorts. For the voyeur, the views of Christie, Jennifer, Tammy and especially Cara were interesting. I guess women might say the same of Luke, Michael (of Mel/Michael) and Mark but maybe not. WRP minimized casting alpha male teams years ago. This was not a difficult run and each runner finished in the order they started. The order did not change with the clue to go inside the State Academy Opera and Ballet Theatre where Phil waited in the balcony. Only the first and last teams had a tiny prima ballerina dance briefly for them and greet them "Welcome to Novosibirsk."

The finish order was:
Luke
Tammy
Cara
Michael
Mark
Jennifer
Christie, non-eliminated

Christie/Jodi were fortunate this was a non-elimination leg. Phil Keoghan said next leg they will have an extra task that no other team will have. This SpeedBump will be difficult because they typically cost about 30 minutes. Tammy/Victor, Margie/Luke and Jaime/Cara did well.

AR14, Ep.6 "Alright Guys, We're At War"

This episode started as always with the pit stop releases at:
1. Margie/Luke   1218am
2. Tammy/Victor 1224am

3. Jaime/Cara   1230am
4. Mel/Michael   101am
5. Mark/Michael   102am
6. Kisha/Jennifer 128am
7. Christie/Jodi   309am, plus SpeedBump penalty

Note that Christie/Jodi were almost 2 hours back of the next closest team and almost 3 hours back from the leaders. However, what have we learned about Amazing Races and Bunching? It happened once again at Novosibirsk airport and all teams were effectively Bunched there, making the SpeedBump the length of time Christie/Jodi will have to make up to stay in the race. All teams are ultimately flying from Moscow-Sheremetyevo Airport to Delhi, then to Jaipur. The biggest variation in routing was to Moscow as some teams flew to Sheremetyevo and others to Moscow's Domodedovo airport. That transition earlier cost 5 teams the later flight into Krasnoyarsk due to slow customs processing but that shouldn't apply leaving Russia. From CBS video extras we know that at least Tammy/Victor went to Domodedovo airport and then had 4.5 hours to get on the plane at Sheremetyevo; they took the Moscow subway system and navigated poorly. We do not know why but CBS may not have gotten that footage; one guess is they did not have permits for the unexpected situation of subway travel. Tammy/Victor made the connection; so did all teams as there was sufficient slack.

Teams fly to Jaipur India, the Pink City with a 4 million population. Its range of sights along the roads provides a feast (frequently a revolting one) for the eyes, but those scenes were quintessential India. Teams saw cows (sacred in India) wandering anywhere they chose and other stray animals, children eating garbage, fires in the streets and garbage strewn everywhere. However, the most annoying thing was the honking of vehicle horns, which is loud, incessant and for no apparent purpose most of the time. The first clue was to go to Dhula village and find the sacred Peepli Ka Pedh tree. Two teams have to wait for their taxis to be refueled in route. Christie/Jodi also got way behind as a result of the taxi driver mistakenly thinking Pushkar was their destination. Mel/Michael got less behind and miraculously caught up. Teams dialed a phone and listened to an accented message "go to Amber Fort parking". Amber Fort is a famous landmark on top of a hill. Finding Amber Fort parking was easy.

All teams arrived at different times, with Tammy/Victor there first. It is a brutal physical challenge, to carry buckets of water and baskets of feed across a field to a ROADBLOCK "Care for Camels". Teams were to use a "native tool" to help them. Victor tried the smaller metal water bucket for the feed, but then he spotted a pile of baskets just the right size for this task. He finished quickly and left the field as other teams arrived. Mel for unknown reasons elected this physical task; Michael was second-guessing watching him, but once Mel figured out the basket he was OK and finished this task in second place. Way to go, Mel! The next 4 teams arrived close to each other. The sight of Kisha trying to stuff feed inside her shirt was pretty funny before she figured out the basket. Christie/Jodi arrived well after the others and Jodi gave it a go, did super and shaved some time off their deficit. Observing Margie on this ROADBLOCK, Luke stated the other teams now call her "the Bionic Woman." That nickname stuck throughout AR14 in tribute.

The next clue says to go to a Rajasthani puppet store at Johri Bazar, Ramniwas Rampogal shop #131. The clue is a DETOUR, Mover or Shakers. Movers required teams to select a wagon loaded with barrels containing straw and transport it 1.5 miles to Zorawar Singh Gate, where they must then empty barrels of straw to find a small elephant charm. Only Mark/Michael elected this task. Shakers required dancing skills once makeup and a costume are donned, with a traditional Rajasthani troupe to earn rupees from the onlookers. When they reach 100 rupees (approximately $2 U.S.), they receive their next clue. The 6 teams doing this were enthusiastic and finished quickly. Jaime/Cara freaked out when their taxi driver could not be found; he was not ready to go.

Before doing the DETOUR, Christie/Jodi had to do a SpeedBump, to Kalahaduman (that's as close as I can translate from Phil-speak into English) Temple to an elephant, filling marked areas on its trunk in with powdered colors (the type used in AR13 for Holi). They did this well and rapidly. When they finished the SpeedBump, they did Shakers and left for the pit stop, Jaigarh Fort 15 km from Jaipur.

Tammy/Victor were out front from the taxis at Jaipur Airport and finished well ahead of the other teams. Mel/Michael continued their good performance for 2nd. 3 teams all arrived simultaneously.

Elimination was a contest between Christie/Jodi, who left their DETOUR ahead of Mark/Michael, and Mark/Michael, whose Movers DETOUR was 1.5 miles closer to the pit stop. It was a very close ending, but Christie/Jodi were eliminated by about 2 minutes. They worked so hard and deserved better.

Finishing order was:
Tammy/Victor
Mel/Michael
Kisha/Jennifer
Margie/Luke
Jaime/Cara
Mark/Michael
Christie/Jodi, who are eliminated

One racer labels Luke a "sinister deaf kid". He is also shown in previews of the Phuket leg highly emotional over his mother's collapse. Which is the real Luke? He is complex; I think I don't see a conflict.

AR14, Ep.7 "Gorilla? Gorilla?? Gorilla???"

I consider the first 6 episodes of AR14 to be among the best ever. Episode 7 was an aberration with respect to that trend. The mix of tasks was fairly pedestrian. Also, the use of a tiger and an elephant as show animals to be exploited is unfortunate. I know that that it is the policy of the Phuket Zoo to benefit from that exploitation, but World Race Productions did not have to use that footage. The old adage that you can never fail with animals and children in a show is at most half right. I don't like to see the Amazing Race exploiting a tiger and elephant for photos or poses and I urge them to reconsider what they think are appropriate activities involving animals. There is an entire chapter titled "Animals" in this book.

Here are the times for release from the Jaipur pit stop:
Tammy/Victor 1021am
Mel/Michael   1102am
Kisha/Jen   1103am
Margie/Luke   NOT SHOWN, but it has to be 1103 or 1104
Jaime/Cara   1104am

Mark/Michael   1111am

In the introduction of the show, another preview of Margie fainting at the finish mat was shown, so we know that's coming near the end of this episode. Teams went directly to a local Jaipur area travel agency for their bookings, except for Jaime/Cara who booked at the airport. All teams are Bunched once again and on the same set of flights departing Jaipur at 520pm and connecting in Bombay and Bangkok to arrive Phuket, Thailand at 850am. The on-screen information says that they arrived in Phuket 14 hours later. When I calculate it they are close as it is 13 hours in transit. Off the plane all the teams except Mel/Michael easily got taxis to downtown Phuket to search for people who know where the gorilla statue shown in a picture can be found. It turns out to be at the Phuket Zoo. Mark/Michael reached there first and found the tiger's lair where pictures are taken with this Esso the Tiger, maybe friendly in spite of the chains keeping him in his place. The keeper for the tiger had only one arm, so you were left to wonder if maybe this tiger had taken the other one. Next, they went to the elephant area where a skilled professional elephant pretends to step on their backs. You may believe that this was OK as the first task in Phuket, but I think it's shameful as enumerated above.

The clue given by the zoo keeper gets teams to the Nguan Choon Tuan Herb Shops. The ride there was notable for the slurs that Jaime makes with regard to Mark/Michael. She says "they're like characters from a cartoon." Maybe so, but watch what happens. The storekeeper has an array of 99 drawers and I guess 6 to 10 of them contained clues. This is your typical random luck-based task where better teams can do poorly. Jaime/Cara got there first and left in 4th place. The first team to finish there was Mark/Michael.

They got the clue to DETOUR 100 Barrels or 2 Miles. In 100 Barrels, teams had to find the Pae Yod ship in Phuket harbor, fill 53 barrels with water and move the other 47 of them to an upper deck and arrange them neatly. In 2 Miles teams had to get to a place where rickshaws were available, then a team member (and the one selected can be switched at any time) can pull the rickshaw over a 2 mile course ending in Rama IX Park. No assistance from trailing or leading taxi drivers was allowed. When Mark/Michael arrived first to the 2 Miles DETOUR starting location, they discovered several

137

bicycle pumps on the ground and used one to put air in one strategically deflated tire. They then put all the pumps in a box to make it less obvious that teams were supposed to use them. Then they went off through the course and arrived first at the Wat Thepnimit pit stop. Phil would not check them in because they had incurred two 30 minutes penalties, one for maliciously depriving other teams of the pumps and the other for using a leading taxi while on most of the course. I thought both of these penalties were eminently fair and reasonable. The first was promoting fair play, the second was explicitly prohibited in the clue.

A 60 minute clock started counting down to the time when Mark/Michael would check in. Second to arrive were Tammy/Victor, who hit the mat with about 4 minutes left on the penalty clock. Then Jaime/Cara checked in and by that time there were about 30 seconds left on the penalty clock. So Mark/Michael took 3rd place. Finishing 4th were Margie/Luke and she collapsed from something like heat stroke at the finish mat. Luke really reacted in a big way to his mother's difficulties. She is his rock and vice-versa but while she functions in the world by herself, he is not capable of doing that.
The final finish order was:
Tammy/Victor
Jaime/Cara
Mark/Michael
Margie/Luke
Kish/Jen
Mel/Michael - eliminated

Mel appreciated the time with his son. He says that they didn't lose, they won just by being part of the race.

AR14, Ep.8 "Rooting Around in People's Mouths Could Be Unpleasant"

Teams started in Phuket Thailand, with release at the following times which I have modified from what was shown on the telecast to make them real. The reason this is necessary is that Tammy/Victor were checked into the Phuket pit stop 3 minutes of ahead of Margie/Luke and 4 minutes ahead of the expiration of the Mark/Michael penalty. There is no way Tammy/Victor could have

138

gotten 3 hours ahead, although it is totally moot given that the last flight on most nights out of Phuket to Bangkok leaves at 930pm, impossible to get with the shown 927pm pit stop release time. So release times are:

Tammy/Victor 1227am (adjusted as indicate above)
Margie/Luke   1231am
Mark/Michael 1232am
Jaime/Cara   1246am
Jen/Kisha   105am

All teams got the 720am flight to Bangkok, arriving 850am. Thus began a madcap series of tasks in the Bangkok area. They started with a boatyard on the outskirts of Bangkok. There Kisha/Jen and Mark/Michael left their backpacks behind with money and passports, either on the property or in the taxis. All teams competed for the ROADBLOCK "Who's ready to propel their team forward?" putting together the critical parts for a long-tailed boat propeller. This required some mechanical aptitude. Margie arrived and finished first. Jaime also blitzed this for second. Victor apparently finishes this third, but it does not work in the ultimate test of propelling a long-tailed boat. Tammy/Victor are going nowhere until he got it right, which means last place. Mark passed them and so does Kisha. Shortly after teams left the boatyard and are being maneuvered through Bangkok's canal system, there is some debate within by Mark/Michael and Kisha/Jen about whether to turn around and get the backpacks (and in Kisha's case shoes, fanny pack, money and passports), but they elected to wait and do it later. What they found was continuing to get farther and farther from the boatyard and will then have to go back through Bangkok's con-gested streets, taking much more time and money. What a mess! Victor anticipated this and took his and Tammy's gear with them.

After a brief stop at Peninsula Pier to get a clue, the next task was a DETOUR, Broken Teeth or Broken Record. Broken Teeth is to fit 5 people for dentures. Each one takes time but Margie later reports task completion in 5 minutes. Broken Record is to sing karaoke in a "party taxi" with 3 Thai transvestites, but it also involves the taxi traversing 5 miles in central Bangkok during a busy time of day. Margie/Luke found the right location on The Street of Happy Smiles, do the dentures quickly and get the clue for the pit stop at Phya

Thai Palace. All teams doing karaoke appear to have a fine time. Before arriving, Mark/Michael elected to go back to the boatyard but have only 500 baths to cover the 785 baht cost of the taxi from the boatyard to near the BROKEN RECORD Detour. They offered a flashlight to make up the difference, which is accepted by the taxi driver. To get back, they asked another taxi driver essentially to trust them as when they have their backpacks they will be able to pay. He accepted that offer and then brought them all the way back to the BROKEN RECORD Detour. They presumably paid for that with all the money they had, as these dislocations had consumed all their money. Kisha/Jen did not go back until finishing BROKEN RECORD. They asked a taxi driver to take them back for free, but he presumably got paid once they retrieved their money.

All teams now go to the Phya Thai Palace, Margie/Luke from BROKEN TEETH and the next 3 teams from BROKEN RECORD. Margie/Luke are #1, Jaime/Cara #2, and Tammy/Victor #3, arriving at same time as Kisha/Jen. Phil Keoghan refused to check in Kisha/Jen without their travel documents to exit Thailand. They now had to pay the piper and go all the way back to the boatyard and return. They asked a taxi driver to take them back for free, but he presumably got paid once their retrieved their money. That was a long way and took a long time. In the interim, Mark/Michael finished BROKEN RECORD and took a taxi with a 300 baht meter reading arriving at the pit stop; they had 200 baht and offered another personal possession. However, Phil told them that they had violated the rules by bartering personal possessions and were getting 2 two hour penalties as a result. That penalty clock had 3 hours 10 minutes left when Kisha/Jen arrived to be checked in at #4. So then Mark/Michael were checked in for last place. Phil told them the good news was it is a non–elimination leg (NEL). Other bad news is the SpeedBump they will incur the next leg. Jaime says "The language barrier really aggravates me and frustrates me, and I become a lunatic. And there's nothing I can do to stop it. It's like Dr. Jekyll and Mr. Hyde."

It is rare that Amazing Races had such bad judgment in action by the racers. What were the two teams that had to go back thinking? It will mean absolutely nothing for Kisha/Jen as their late finish will be washed out by an airport Bunching dead ahead. However, for Mark/ Michael it is likely to cause them to miss the first morning flight combination out of Bangkok. That could be fatal on top of the Speed Bump penalty workoff once they get to Guilin.

AR14, Ep.9 "Our Parents Will Cry Themselves to Death"

Release times after a 22 hour pit stop were:

Margie/Luke 936am
Jaime/Cara 1030am
Tammy/Victor 1040am
Kisha/Jen 1243pm
Mark/Michael 408pm

The clue specified that teams must connect in Guangzhou. Again, I have no idea why. The next thing you need to know is that If you study the flight combinations Bangkok to Guilin you know immediately that Mark/Michael are toast and essentially have no chance in this episode except a major flight delay for their competition or another non-elimination leg (NEL). The flights out of Bangkok to Guangzhou for the other 4 teams were Margie/Luke on the 1120am flight, Jaime/Cara and Tammy/Victor on the 115pm flight and Kisha/Jen on the 320pm flight. The first 3 teams were supposed to connect in Guanzhou to the 830pm flight to Guilin but it is delayed and actually left after the 910pm flight of Kisha/Jen. It must have departed before the 1030pm arrival of Mark/Michael or they would have gotten on it. Since they did not, there were no more flights until 940am the next morning, which Mark/Michael were on seen landing in Guilin in daylight on the first flight in.

There was a critical gap of the hours between about 1130pm and the first televised task, for which the 4 teams arrived at different times. That strongly implies that there was a task with Hours of Operation which did not start until early (9am or earlier) the next morning. The next step was an unaired task which had hours of operation delay until sometime the next morning. I have heard it was climbing 500 steps up Folding Brocade Mountain/Hill (take your pick) along the narrow stone path passing the Face-the-Cloud Pavilion and Over-the-River Pavilion, on the way to the top of the Bright Moon Peak. The Bright Moon Peak is the summit of the hill, where the Catch-the-Cloud Pavilion stands. Teams stopped for what appears to be an 8 hour faux-pit-stop and slept in the open somewhere on the mountain. This occupied teams until maybe 10am when they were allowed to go to the cluebox next to Qing Xiu Lu hair salon where the SpeedBump takes place later.

The clue there sends teams to the #24 bridge over the Li River. They find another cluebox with a ROADBLOCK "Who's ready for some fowl play?" Teams went out together in a boat, then one of each team transfered to a fishing vessel with the fisherman and his cormorant, a fishing bird whose neck is restricted so that it cannot swallow the large fish involved, plus a basket of 15 fish. The racer tossed fish into the water to attract the attention of the cormorant and then takes them out of its mouth, places them into a second basket until 10 are counted. This is an ancient Chinese fishing technique. The teams vary in their effectiveness on this. Luke competed with Tammy, Jaime and Kisha. He does well, but was bitten by a duck in the area. Jaime and Kisha did OK but Tammy is lagging behind here; her cormorant flies away temporarily and she finished in fourth place. Teams then went to the Ancient South Gate for a DETOUR of Choreography or Calligraphy.

In Choreography, teams took a path to Central Island, observed dozens of dancing couples, got instruction from a pair of instructors, and performed among the many dancing couples and in front of 2 judges. Jaime/Cara were the only team to elect this and judges rejected them twice for their dance performance. Jaime wanted to know why. As is frequently the case in China nobody can speak English (or if they can they won't, which makes it hard for teams competing here). Jaime/Cara found out that the reason for their rejection was not continuing dancing to the end of that dance. Their female dance instructor was shown twice in televised laughter at the hilarity of their dancing. The 3rd time they got it right but are behind the 3 teams headed to the pit stop.

In Calligraphy there were 4 stations and teams copied intricate Chinese characters (representing 1 to 3 words at each station) closely. When they succeeded they got the clue for the next station until finishing all 4 to get the pit stop clue. Victor said he and Tammy don't know enough Mandarin; that had nothing to do with essentially a copying exercise that even Americans who know no Chinese can do well.

The pit stop was on Banyan Lake with a view of the Sun and Moon Pagodas. Tammy/Victor started slightly ahead but Kisha/Jen passed them easily. Margie/Luke also passed them but by arrival at the pit stop Tammy/Victor were in second place. The first team to finish was Kisha/Jen. Second by a minor amount was Tammy/Victor. Third was Margie/Luke and fourth was Jaime/Cara. There were two serious shoving matches at earlier clueboxes between Jen and Luke, both of whom were highly competitive and itching for a battle. The word "bitch" was used by Jen against Luke and he overreacted. She stated that "he gave me an elbow and I called him a bitch because it was a bitch move." Actually, the way I saw it Luke gave her an elbow and a hip in response to the minor provocation of Jen's light shove. When they get to the pit stop Margie recounted at Phil's request what happened. Margie stated Luke would "like to go to a country where are the people are deaf and all the people sign so he would have the advantage." She is a highly biased observer and appeared a bit petty in her accusations but how can you expect objectivity from the mother of a deaf son? Luke said "All hearing people put deaf people down. They think we're stupid". Then Kisha and Jen acted like they are trying to goad Luke into a rash act while all 3 teams were at the pit stop. They succeeded; Luke overreacted and Margie again came to his defense: "Don't laugh at my son when he signs. I'm sorry, but that's rude." Kisha said, "I'm smiling because that's what we do, we smile." And then Margie just lost it: "If you laugh at my son again…. He's signing and they're laughing at him. Yes they are. I'm not going to put up with this." This wasn't the battle of the century hyped in CBS publicity, but is riveting television.

While this is happening Mark/Michael landed and attempted to catch-up. They first have to do a SpeedBump of washing and drying the hair of two old ladies. This looked like it took about 15 minutes with no extra transportation needed. They next fished with a cormorant, then elect Choreography, finishing that quickly (with the dance judges probably told there was no reason to be objective since their team would finish last). They got to the pit stop and did finish last. They waited to hear the magic words, non-elimination leg, but it isn't happening as they are eliminated. They finished about 2 hours behind Jaime/Cara as best I can estimate.

AR14, Ep.10

Starting at Sun and Moon Pagodas in Guilin after what appears a
24 hour pit stop or slightly more, teams are released from it at:
Kisha/Jen   148pm
Tammy/victor 149pm
Margie/Luke   150pm
Jaime/Cara   212pm

Their target in Beijing was a specific foot massage parlor. All teams
raced to the airport and got the same 510pm China Southern flight
to Beijing. There was jockeying for position in taxis, both to the
Guilin airport and from the Beijing airport, but relative positions of
the racers changed little. After hearing that a reservations person
could not (due to no English) help them, Kisha said "It's patented in
China, the dumb look. They should be able to say 'Me no speak
English or something!' " They have no idea how much they act as
Ugly Americans. Victor attempted to use his Chinese language
skills to get 2 opposing teams seated near the back of the plane.
Jaime/Cara were stuck there, costing them valuable time in getting
off. The flight arrived at 805pm.

The taxi ride to Jian Guo Men outer street's foot massage parlor
brought us ROADBLOCK "Who's feeling manipulative?" It is a 10
minute foot massage with lots of visible pain (highlighted on
television by editors' pathetic attempt to heighten the drama)
starting with drinking a cup of Chinese herbal tea. There were lots
of grimaces, but no cries of UNCLE (which triggers an end to that
session and restart of another 10 minute session, making it a
foolish option to elect). Jen, Cara, Tammy and Luke elected this
ROADBLOCK and teams finished with the same time differentials
as they entered. How absurd if designed to have time differentials
stay the same! In the middle of this, Victor told Margie "They'll be all
right. No one has died from this foot massage."

The next task is a DETOUR at the natatorium (basically indoor
water sports center with 2 pools) found at the north gate of (get this
name) "Guang Cai Ti Yu Guan Bei Men Yi You Yong Quan". Next
time you're in Beijing you find it if you can remember how to spell all
of it. The DETOUR was a choice of Sync or Swim. Sync was the

more interesting, teams putting on regular swim trunks and ascending the 3 meter (10 foot) diving board for a synchronized jump into the pool. No effort was made to force teams to attempt even a swan dive. Both divers had to enter the water together in good form to receive a score of 5 from each of 2 judges. Only 5s from each judge would earn them the next clue. Swim was to put on a spandex SPEEDO LASER full-body suit like the one worn by Michael Phelps at the 2008 Beijing Summer Olympics and each teammate had to alternate 2 sets of 2 laps in what appeared to be a modified relay format. I saw the freestyle, some backstrokes, and some using the lane markers to pull themselves along. Teams were encouraged to match Michael Phelps' gold medal time of 4 minutes 3 seconds (what a farce to even suggest that despite the teams having the edge of not having to swim the slower breaststroke).

This was where the excitement took place. Tammy/Victor arrived first, considering swimming but went to the board to dive. Unfortunately the best they ever scored was 4 and 3, not good enough to get the clue. They finally decided that swimming wasn't so bad and switched, finishing with 10:29 (10 minutes 29 seconds) well after Jaime/Cara and Margie/Luke. Kisha/Jen arrived second; Jen said she is scared of the pool and cannot do the swim: "The thought of water makes me extremely nervous." So they try diving but are poor at it; after the other 3 teams are finished they start the swimming and finish in 18:19. Jaime/Cara arrived third (with the clock at the entrance gate showing 9:31pm) and they swam quite well at 9:30. Margie/Luke arrived fourth and they set a blistering 8:05 pace, double that of Phelps. They were rightly very pleased.

So the departures from the natatorium were in the order Jaime/Cara, Margie/Luke, Tammy/Victor and Kisha/Jen, with I am guessing about a 30 minute spread from Jaime/Cara to Kisha/Jen. Victor had what looked like a severe cramp that had to die down before he could get his leg into the waiting taxi. They went to the expected pit stop at the north gate of the Drum Tower. Phil was there with a mat and no greeter in sight. Amazing Race veteran viewers know exactly what that means. Jaime/Cara, expecting their first victory, got a clue instead and a directive to KEEP RACING. The not-often-seen-on-Amazing-Races To Be Continued (TBC) had just been invoked. Since it was now approximately 1030pm, teams can now expect hours of racing in the middle of the night unless they hit an Hours of Operation restriction.

AR14, Ep.11

The start of this episode continues the action from Leg 10 in Beijing. Jaime/Cara thought they had earned a first place finish, but discovered that they must Keep On Racing. Since it wasn't a pit stop Phil handed them their next clue. The same logic followed for Margie/Luke, Tammy/Victor, and Kisha/Jen based primarily on the order they ended the DETOUR at the natatorium. I estimate from the Ep.10 tasks that the TBC meetings with Phil occured around 1030pm for Jaime/Cara and Margie/Luke, around 1050pm for Tammy/Victor and maybe 1115pm for Kisha/Jen. There is no indication of how we get to the next task at sunrise in Beijing (705am for that day of the year). Since team arrived to find a clue for getting a Travelocity Roaming Gnome at different times, that means Hours of Operation were not involved. I think there was an 8 hour faux-pit-stop for each team in a hotel.

Finding the Roaming Gnomes takes place at Bei Hai Dong Men shopping mall. It is not too difficult, but since this is a random task the first team to find one of presumably 4 gnomes can do so much easier than the fourth of the teams. Next was a trip to Gu Gong Xi Bei Jiao. There teams must get an electric bicycle and ride it past Tiananmen Square to Dong Dan Di Tie Zhou, the Dong Dan subway to search outside it for the next cluebox. That provides a clue for a DETOUR of Beijing Opera or Chinese Waiter. Beijing Opera was at Hu Guang Hui Guan where teams get into appropriate costumes, one for the gentleman and one for the princess, and the other team member applied makeup to them. One of the most poignant statements of any Amazing Race is when Kisha told Jen "I think you should be the gentleman and I should be the princess. I've never been a princess my whole life, so maybe this is my opportunity to be a princess." Then it was checked by the master who has the clues. Beijing Opera gave a significant advantage to Jamie/Cara since in their former Dallas Cowboys cheerleader job they learned a lot about professional makeup. Margie/Luke, Jamie/Cara and Kisha/Jen all elected this option since the other one will be difficult for them. The Chinese Waiter option was tailor-made for Tammy/Victor. They have to get to the Hu

Guang Hui Guan restaurant (which must be very close to the Opera House) to take single menu selections from each of 5 diners in Mandarin Chinese and repeat them back to the chef in understandable and correct Mandarin. Those orders were for good luck fish, vegetarian noodles, fried chicken, new taste beef, and golden pork spare ribs. With their understanding of Mandarin Chinese, they will breeze through this one, right? Wrong. They did very well, but their first attempt was rejected by the chef for one minor error. The chef held them to an extremely high standard of Mandarin pronunciation which was appropriate for a Chinese/American team that really does speak Mandarin. They had to do it again, which happened without difficulty.

Back at Beijing Opera it was taking longer until Kisha/Jen, Margie/Luke and Jaime/Cara finished. All teams had to find the U-Turn cluebox, in a different part of the same building as the Beijing Opera. It was here in finding that building that Tammy/Victor excelled. They had to go on foot to Wen Change Ge to locate the Opera House part where the U-Turn cluebox is. They did so very rapidly and are first there. They have already decided that if this is available they will U-Turn Kisha/Jen because of concern about beating them in a footrace. One of them left a note below the posted photo of Kisha/Jen saying "Sorry, but I can't outrun you" in a footrace. All the other teams had a difficult time finding the U-Turn box, which has their next clue. Jaime even exclaimed they had been doing so for 3 hours before they found it. It was in another part of the building they started from. There is no question that Tammy/Victor's knowledge of Mandarin was helpful for finishing Chinese Waiter DETOUR quickly and getting to the U-Turn station.

Margie/Luke found the U-Turn box next and they went on to the ROADBLOCK and Margie eats for the team. She did OK and they went to the pit stop to finish 2nd. Kisha/Jen finally found the U-Turn box and saw the nice note left for them. They now have to do Chinese Waiter, which is very difficult since they speak no Chinese. I am certain that the chef applied different standards for them than for Tammy/Victor or they would still be there now attempting to finish this. They are given the clue after their 3rd attempt and they head for the ROADBLOCK.

Jaime/Cara, lagging behind as a result of having the most difficulty in finding the U-Turn box, spoke no Chinese. Jaime in her typical Ugly American style said "Surely they know the name 'taxi' and they're playing dumb" as taxis will not stop for them or drivers do not know where they want to go. The taxi curse will descend upon them, but not this episode; let's wait to see what retributions the worldwide taxi drivers union has for Jaime (and the innocent Cara who rides with her). Jaime's attitude is personified by: "This is why I did not want to go to China. It sucks." They arrived after Jen started eating and Cara took it. Jen had to drink a lot of water to get the food down. Kisha comments on this and asks her to minimize it, but Jen rightly told her that it is necessary. A highly motivated Cara plowed through and they left minutes behind.

At Niao Chao Bird's Nest Stadium (a site of the 2008 Beijing Olympic Games), Kisha/Jen arrived and cannot quickly find the pit stop. Jen really needed to pee and they took a minute or two at a convenient porta potty. Jaime/Cara were more effective at finding the pit stop and they finished minutes before Kisha/Jen. Kisha/Jen accepted that they are out of AR14 with more equanimity than I would have expected. So the Final 3 are Tammy/Victor, Margie/Luke and Jaime/Cara. Anyone can win, although I think Tammy/Victor and Margie/Luke had a slightly better chance than Jaime/Cara. One thing you can count on in a finale is Bunching so all teams are in the race for the beginning of the critical task or tasks. I will admit to a preference for Tammy/Victor to win.

AR14, Ep.12, Finale

Teams wake up in Beijing and know that this is the leg for all those 1 million dollars and that they must be at the peak of their game on this fateful day. Only one team can win that money, except that all 3 teams are winners by virtue of having raced around the world and seen and done marvelous things. The release times from the pit stop are:
Tammy/Victor 915pm
Margie/Luke   1124pm
Jaime/Cara   204am

That's a huge range, rivaling the 6 hour lead of Kris/Jon starting the AR6 finale vs. Adam/Rebecca and more than Nick/Starr's 5.5 hours over Ken/Tina. However, all Amazing Race fans know that Bunching will erase it early in this episode. Teams learn they are headed for Kahului airport on Maui, Hawaiian Islands. There were no late-night flights so all teams can take the same morning flight to Tokyo and then an evening flight to Honolulu to reach Maui around 630am the same day (due to crossing the International Date Line west to east). Teams exited the plane at high speed and tried to impart urgency to their taxi driver.

The first task was at Fleming Beach (Maui Beach Access point 118), where they handled the key chores of preparation for a Hawaii luau. They started rubbing oil and seasonings on the dead pig and attached it to bamboo poles and then carried it 200 yards down the beach to the luau pits, a bed of very hot coals. They set it down on a bed of palm fronds and seasoned it, using more palm fronds. Then they close the pit with sand and let it bake. That earned them the next clue. Margie/Luke started last, but Jaime/Cara and Tammy/Victor faltered. It was Cara and Tammy that lacked arm strength, but Margie was a trooper, able to hold the pole on her shoulders to transport it. She is the Bionic Woman indeed. Margie/Luke take the lead leaving, with Tammy/Victor next and Jaime/Cara last. While Jaime stated multiple times that Tammy is a weakling and can be beaten they can't manage to do it and Jaime utters "This is how we lose $1 million." She's wrong, as there was worse to come. Both teams remaining at the pits discovered they had put palm fronds over the pig that did not belong, so those are dug out.

Next was pilot a personal watercraft along the coast of Maalaea Bay (Maui Shoreline Access point #36, the one nearest to the cross-island north/south road) to a marked area where 4 clues can be found attached to a total of 100 buoys. Margie/Luke kept their lead and finished before the other 2 teams arrived. There was a 4.0% chance each try of getting the first clue, 3.0% for the second clue and 2.0% each try for the third clue. That means that the first team to find one will have taken an average of 25 tries, but the third team needs 50 tries. Jaime/Cara took 2nd and Tammy/Victor 3rd.

The next clue sent teams to find a Surfboard Farm at Kaohu Farms Peahi slightly inland from the north coast of Maui near the northern end of the Hana Highway, infamous for its 20 miles of continuous curves further south. Margie/Luke maintained a healthy lead. Jaime/Cara's taxi driver did not know where to go and took them to the wrong surfboard farm. The driver's dispatcher responded to their call "tell your people that I am not their personal concierge" and refused to help. Jaime got smart and called the police, who say Kaupakalua is at Mile marker 16 on the Hana Highway. Then the driver needed to refill his gas tank. When Jaime now said this is how we lose the race, she was right this time. By the time they got to the ROADBLOCK "Who's ready to relive it?" selecting and arranging surfboards in order of the episodes represented from a 300+ pile of surfboards, they were a substantial margin behind. There was a frame with 11 slots, one for each leg of the race. A surfboard picture with a representation of any part of that episode goes into the slot for it. There is a judge who instantly says right or wrong. The chosen ones were Luke, Victor and Jaime since physical strength moving the surfboards was important. In the middle of this, Luke and Victor strip off their shorts; regrettably, Jaime did not follow their lead.

The logos for the surfboards by leg were:
1 Locarno St. Church of San Antonio
2 Ruhpolding Gondola
3 Romanian Gymnastics
4 Krasnoyarsk Yenisei River Dam
5 Novosibirsk Lada automobile
6 Jaipur pit stop nose flutes
7 Phuket Esso the tiger at the zoo
8 Bangkok Long-Tailed Boats
9 Guilin Cormorant
10 Beijing Reflexology
11 Beijing Delicacies—scorpions

Luke had attacked this problem-solving exercise in a positive manner. He filled a majority of the slots before Victor arrived in second place. Luke got the first 9 without difficulty, in the order leg 1, 4, 8, 7, 6, 5, 3, 4, 9, then 2. Getting 10 and 11, both Beijing, confounded and frustrated him. Victor steadily progressed and placed 10, 11, 4, 2, 6, 9, 7?, 3?, 1?, 8, 5. Jaime finally got going and was completing them at a rate quicker than Victor. Finally Luke moved one from slot 11 where it was wrong to slot 10 where he had already tried over a dozen others without success. This time it was right, so only #11 remained. Victor needed only #5 and Jaime only 2 surfboards. Victor found it first and Tammy/Victor left in first place. Now Jaime was coming on strong and she is on the last one. Luke helped with her final surfboard placing, the church at #1. She reciprocated by helping Luke in a way that should never be allowed if it wasn't already clear that neither team could win after Margie urged Victor to work with Jaime. Jaime showed Luke each surfboard in order so he could compare and see what was missing. Jaime/Cara left in second place, Margie/Luke minutes later.

All teams took their taxis to an undiscovered location with statues near the ROADBLOCK location. There they found the clue to the King Kamehameha Golf Club maybe 15 miles away. A short sprint took them to the finish line where all the eliminated teams cheer the teams as they finish. Tammy/Victor arrive first and get the "3 continents, 9 countries, 40,000 miles and 22 days" speech from Phil. Jaime/Cara arrived second and Margie/Luke third. During the taxi ride, Luke required assurance from his mother that he had done well even though they did not win Amazing Race 14. He was tantalizingly close to doing so having run an excellent race. However, Tammy/Victor and Jaime/Cara also did well and they experienced less of a frustration factor on the critical ROADBLOCK. I think these are the right 3 teams to be there and I think the best team, judged by victories in prior legs, won.

I think we witnessed the curse of the international tax driver's union. That union took Christie/Jodi out in Jaipur and now they have ended Jaime/Cara's dreams of being the first female/female team to win the Amazing Race U.S. and win the $1,000,000. Their performance was exemplary except on the pig-carry, where they lost less than 5 minutes because of the short distance, and the drive to the ROADBLOCK, where they lost an undetermined amount but probably 15 minutes or more. Why did Jaime end up finishing behind Victor? There is no explanation except the taxi driver. Karma bites back. It's truly amazing how many karma-related situations seem to occur in Amazing Races. This is not the result of editing, although editors do tend to over-dramatize them.

AMAZING RACE ASIA 1

The new Amazing Race Asia is produced by Australia's Active TV and its leader Michael McKay. The host is Allan Wu, not well-known in the U.S. before this series but developing into a fine host. Teams:

Ernie/Jeena, husband/wife, businessman and homemaker, 42/35
Aubrey/Jacqueline, actress and model, age 26 and 23
Sahil/Prashant, models, age 26 and 26
Melody/Sharon, best friends, entertainment and headhunter, age 28 and 31
Howard/Sahran, best friends, tour operator manager and interior designer, age 39 and 31
Andy/Laura, engaged couple, entrepreneurs, age 28 and 37
Mardy/Marsio, brothers, civil contractor and photographer, age 36 and 34
Andrew/Syeon, dating 3 years, Managing Director and Business Development Manager, age 26 and 28
Sandy/Francesca, dating 1 year, personal trainer and model, age 29 and 27
Zabrina and Joe Jer, co-workers, TV producers, age 26 and 29

Ep.1 "I Don't Think I Can Do This"

Teams started at Merdeka (Freedom) Square in Kuala Lumpur, capital of Malaysia. The task "Shop Till You Drop" was both team members ascending to the top of tall Berjaya Times building, descending 8 stories of the open middle area of its shopping mall within a designated time using a doubled rope coiled around the body and attached to some higher point. Sandy/Francesca were unable to get a taxi.

Next was DETOUR Paint or Pot. In Paint teams had to do a traditional silk batik painting based on the design shown. In Pot a team member at a pottery wheel makes a clay pot of minimum quality while the other controls its spin. Sandy/Francesca's taxi is stolen by Andy/Laura. The only team to try Pot was Ernie/Jeena; Ernie cracked this joke: "Harry Potter, Jeena Potter" to explain his wife's success at the wheel.

The clue received there is to Shah Alam Stadium for 4 consecutive good laps in go karts. Mardy/Marsio and Aubrey/Jacqueline used the pay-taxi-to-follow method. Every time I see that method, I detest it and cringe although it is now common practice in both Amazing Races and Amazing Race Asias. "There ought to be a law" banning that practice. I would settle for an Amazing Race rule.

Teams were then sent to Kuala Lumpur Tower by winding, difficult-to-follow trail in Buka Nanas Forest Reserve to the tower base. Andrew/Syeon had the advantage of being locals and knowing Kuala Lumpur area roads. Andrew and Syeon reached the pit stop first, but had to redo it since they hadn't followed the trail properly.

Most of the tasks this episode were highly physical. You would expect the least physically fit team of Mardy and Marsio would not do well, but they actually finished first. The finishing order was:

Mardy/Marsio
Ernie/Jeena
Zabrina/Joe Jer
Aubrey/Jacqueline
Andrew/Syeon (2nd time after going back)
Melody/Sharon
Andy/Laura
Sahil/Prashant
Howard/Sahran
Sandy/Francesca, non-eliminated

Sandy/Francesca balanced bad luck with their taxi drivers with good luck of non-elimination, but they lost all their money. Amazing Races place racers in driving situations that are new and uncomfortable. It was no surprise there was a fender-bender, this time with Ernie driving.

ARA1, Ep.2 "They're Speedy, They're Fast and They're First"

The release times from the pit stop were:
Mardy/Marsio   211am
Ernie/Jeena   221am
Zabina/Joe Jer   227am

Aubrey/Jacqueline 237am
Andrew/Syeon   242am
Sharon/Melody   257am
Andy/Laura   257am
Howard/Sahran   343am
Sahil/Prashant   400am
Sandy/Francesca 438am

Sandy/Francesca received no official money for this leg and needed gifts from every other team. They supplemented by begging at the airport. The clue was going to Jakarta Indonesia. With the first flight many hours off, the teams all Bunch at the airport waiting for the AirAsia flight. The clue sent teams on arrival to Ragunan Zoo. The chaotic taxi race there is termed by Melody "Ragunan Zoo Race".

The ROADBLOCK "Who likes animals?" was next. This required the selected individual to enter an enclosure filled with large non-poisonous Indonesian snakes and retrieve the clue from a tree in the middle in 2 minutes. It was not for the timid or those afraid of snakes. However, surely the snakes had been totally fed earlier.

The clue packet received at the zoo gave teams some choices. One was FAST FORWARD "Find SONY Walkman" and the other the regular tasks, the next of which was the Mainangkabu Plate Dance. The Walkman task was going to SMA60 School by taxi to find 50 students in the yard and determine which one has the one Walkman (Note product placement) with the message "You have the correct one." Ernie/Jeena got a poor taxi driver who got them to the neighborhood but could not find the school. They elected to abandon the taxi and walk, a big mistake. Sahil/Prashant were able to get ahead of them at the school and started their task well ahead of Ernie/Jeena. The laws of probability usually determine outcomes, so Sahil/Prashant found the correct Walkman after about 25 tries and exchanged it for directions to Monas National Monument, the pit stop, before Ernie/Jeena ever located the school. Ernie/Jeena then had to do the plate dance task that everyone except Sahil/Prashant was required to do. The plate dance was easy enough that all teams finished quickly.

After the Plate Dance task, the next clue led to DETOUR Push or Sell. Both options involved 10 carts of bakso (meatball soup). In

154

Push teams navigated a marked course while singing a traditional Indonesian song and not spilling too much soy sauce until 10 carts were at the end point. Teams realized the only way to complete this in reasonable time was to proceed carefully and steadily. Sell required teams to sell 15 bowls of bakso or eat 15 bowls of bakso. Ernie/Jeena caught up to Sandy/Francesca doing Push desperate to make up time as they didn't have the luxury of slow and steady; they spilled soy sauce and had to go again. Sahil/Prashant won first place because they won the FAST FORWARD. Mardy/Marsio were next because as Indonesians they knew the Jakarta area well. This was an object lesson on the perils of losing a FAST FORWARD competition. It was also another example of how taxi drivers frequently determine episode outcomes (see chapter on Taxis).

The finish order was:
Sahil/Prashant
Mardy/Marsio
Howard/Sahran
Zabrina/Joe Jer
Melody/Sharon
Aubrey/Jacqueline
Andy/Laura
Andrew/Syeon
Sandy/Francesca
Ernie/Jeena, eliminated

ARA1, Ep.3 "Give Me the Strength, Give Me the Strength"

The pit stop release time was:
Sahil/Prashant   159am
Mardy/Marsio   227am
Howard/Sahran   238am
Zabrina/Joe Jer   240am
Sharon/Melody   240am
Aubrey/Jacqueline 241am
Andy/Laura   242am
Andrew/Syeon   246am
Sandy/Francesca   307am

Sahil/Prashant started 28 minutes ahead of the next team, not a very good return for their FAST FORWARD effort in the prior episode. Mardy/Marsio were next and then the following 6 teams were within 9 minutes of each other. Sandy/Francesca started last. It all made no difference because there was a major Bunching again at the Jakarta airport for the Air Asia flight to Denpasar Bali. Teams are directed to the famous Kuta Beach for a ROADLBOCK "Who digs the seaside?" This one turned out to be the mother of all ROADBLOCKS (tying AR7, Ep.3 for that honor). It was a classic needle-in-a-haystack task where digging volume is rewarded, but being lucky in choosing the right spots to dig was the key. Teams look for something 18 inches down (it turns out to be a miniature wooden surfboard), but they dug only with a small spade. All teams struggled. After about one hour Andy/Laura used the strategy that Rob took in the Mendoza 4 pounds of meat eating challenge. They expressed willingness to take a 4 hour penalty. Mardy/Marsio did the same. Umbrellas were brought for remaining teams at 2 to 3 hours to provide shade for diggers and drinks were allowed. I could not identify the individuals, but Sahil/Prashant finished the ROADBLOCK first and Howard/Sahran second. There was only an hour left in the digging time limit when Aubrey/Jacqueline took the penalty. Andrew/Syeon quit after Syeon's hands get bloody. Why was she doing this ROADBLOCK in the first place? What a poor choice by their team! Shovels were finally allowed in the waning minutes. Sandy, who has moved mountains of sand, made good use of his shovel and found the surfboard. Sharon/Melody got lucky and they found it just before the time limit expired. Zabrina/Joe Jer became the 5th team out of 9 to take the penalty.

Next task was at the Ubud Monkey Forest with 200 clues, only 10 of which had actual instructions for the next clue. This was the second needle in a haystack task in a row. Is Michael McKay nuts? Coming out of the Monkey Forest the order before application of penalties to teams was Sahil/Prashant first (only team to finish before 6pm closing). Aubrey/Jacqueline finished the Monkey Forest last.

Next was DETOUR Wet or Dry. Dry was an Elephant Walk and Wet was White Water Rafting. These tasks had no impact on relative positions of teams in the race although the 3 km Dry appeared faster than 6 km Wet. Sandy/Francesca, Mardy/Marsio, Howard/Sahran and Zabrina/Joe Jer chose Dry while Sahil/Prashant, Aubrey/Jacqueline, Sharon/Melody, Andy/Laura and

Andrew Syeon did Wet. Getting taxis from a hotel near both DETOURs proved to be very difficult. Andrew/Syeon stole a cab from Sahil/Prashant but this will only move Sahil/Prashant down one place in the finish order while for Andrew/Syeon it meant solidifying 8th place and staying in the race. Teams are directed to Uluwatu Caves then to the pit stop at Tanah Lot Temple. Zabrina/JoeJer made up a huge amount of time reaching the pit stop first. After their penalty was applied it guarantees them 5th place. Howard/Sahran arrived seconds behind and they check in as the top finisher. Next were Sandy/Francesca in second place. Mardy/Marsio, Andy/Laura and Andrew/Syeon arrived in the next 3 spots guaranteeing 6th, 7th and 8th place when their penalties are applied. Sharon/Melody were next and finished in 3rd place. Sahil/Prashant arrived and took 4th place. Aubrey/Jacqueline, last to arrive of those taking the penalty and in last place, were eliminated. This team fits the "dumb blonde" stereotype. On arrival, one of them exclaimed "oh, yay." Not able to grasp the finer points of ARA fniishes, they failed to realize that their finish meant elimination.

The separation of teams caused by the DETOUR of elephant ride or white water rafting was not much, but the last few teams left at the Ubud Forest task faced sharply diminishing returns. Consider that with 9 teams and 10 clues, the probability of finding a valid clue on each try started at 5.0%. By the last team, that probability had dropped to 1.04% (two out of 192) meaning that the expected time for a valid clue is much longer.

ARA1, Ep.4 "Just Shut Up and Do It"

Teams leave Denpasar to fly 8000 km via Singapore to Sydney and find Dawes Point. Times for pit stop release were:
Howard/Sahran   1231am
Sandy/Francesca 1255am
Sharon/Melody   155am
Sahil/Prashant   206am
Zabrina/JoeJer   430am
Mardy/Marsio   511am
Andy/Laura   553am
Andrew/Syeon   555am

Options for teams to do flight reservations are frequently restricted in Amazing Race episodes and Amazing Race Asia episodes, but not in episode 4. Teams could phone in a reservation, book on the Internet, or just get the reservations with tickets at the airport. It did not matter which method they use. All managed to find the same best flight combination back to Singapore then nonstop to Sydney.

Most teams easily found Dawes Point, but one taxi driver had great difficulty. Teams received DETOUR Elevation or Crustacean. Elevation involved the famous walk on top of Sydney Harbor Bridge (also used in AR2 Ep.9). Crustacean was cleaning 14kg of prawns. Teams that had the focus and concentration for the bridge climb finished in the top 4 four positions this DETOUR. One thing you could count on throughout ARA1 was Mardy/Marsio choosing a food detour if it was offered.

Next was a trip to Mrs. McQuarie's Chair, which is a famous rock formation in Sydney. The clue received there sends teams to SONY Central HQ Store to get a HANDYCAM (product placement). There were many famous Australian songs like Waltzing Matilda and some lesser known (outside of Australia) songs. In the latter category is "Click Go the Shears," a sheepherder's ballad. Teams needed to find a local who could sing "Click Go the Shears" while being taped for playback. Videos with the song incorrect were rejected. Teams redoing it with new talent were Mardy/Marsio, Sharon/Melody and Sandy/Francesca.

Completion got teams the clue to Manly Wharf Ocean World, reached by a ferry, to walk with an animal. Well those animals turned out to be 50 sharks and full diving gear was required for this to walk on the bottom of a 4 million liter tank to retrieve an object. Isn't the ROADBLOCK title "Who's ready to dive with a nurse?" one of the most creative? That schedule mostly dictated the order of teams leaving Ocean World. Howard/Sahran and Andy/Laura took the first ferry, a slow one, but landed behind other teams whose fast ferry started later but finished ahead. Sandy/Francesca misdirected their taxi driver to the Sydney Harbor Bridge, but that delay caused them to get the first fast ferry and take the lead. Once at Ocean World the walk was short and teams held their positions except for Howard/Sahran. Howard couldn't do this ROADBLOCK due to extreme nervousness and had to take a 4 hour penalty. This

ROADBLOCK was a visual feast for viewers.

One issue for a team was Laura injuring her left leg, requiring medical attention, but staying in the race. The clue received on completion sent teams back on the ferries to the downtown side of the harbor to find Tall Ship Bounty, the pit stop. Sandy/Francesca got a slow ferry and finished 3rd behind Andrew/Syeon and Sharon/Melody. Mardy/Marsio were 4th. Sahil/Prashant went from last arriving at Ocean World to 5th by lucking out with the fast ferry. Zabrina/Joe Jer and Andy/Laura were 6th and 7th. Howard/Sahran were next to last before the penalty, but non-elimination saved them, with all money confiscated.

ARA1, Ep.5 "It's Blowing Like Your Mum's Pants on a Windy Day"

Teams are released from the pit stop at these times:
Andrew/Syeon   1230am
Sharon/Melody   1232am
Sandy/Francesca 1241am
Mardy/Marsio   105am
Sahil/Prashant   131am
Zabrina/JoeJer   136am
Andy/Laura   138am
Howard/Sahran   536am

Howard/Sahran were left money by all teams except Andy/Laura (why did they give to Sandy/Francesca but not Howard/Sahran?). They begged in Sydney. The flight was 2150km to Auckland New Zealand, one more Bunching as Howard/Sahran catch up. They went to the north shore suburb Devonport to find a child on a swing near the ferry terminal going from/to downtown Auckland terminal. On arrival Andy/Laura stole their second taxi of this race, this time from Mardy/Marsio. Sahil/Prashant observed and commented that other teams can't stand Andy's whining. Despite maneuvering for an edge, all 8 teams get the same ferry to Devonport.

In Devonport, it was a figurative zoo. Teams paid no attention to "near the ferry terminal" and were all over this 11,000 population town. They investigated all schools and playgrounds. Andrew/Syeon stepped off the ferry, turned left along the waterfront and

159

immediately found the girl and the next clue. Zabrina/Joe Jer and Andy/Laura barely joined them on the first ferry back. Mardy/Marsio barely avoided a transportation penalty and finished the task. Melody/Sharon also made that ferry, leaving Sandy/Francesca, Sahil/Prashant and Howard/Sahran behind. 3 times Sahil/Prashant accepted private car rides, warned by Sharon/ Melody it was illegal under ARA1 rules, but as the test case it remained to be seen how Michael McKay deals with it (how much time and when to apply it). All trailing teams got the same ferry back.

Teams returned to Auckland by ferry for DETOUR Rugby or Rigging. In Rugby it was taxi to Victoria Park to make 3 goals inside the posts and above the bar from 22 yards out. This would be relatively easy for any who can kick a rugby ball up with some velocity. Rigging was go to WestHaven Marina and copy knots and lines to rig a moored sailboat.

Next was Auckland Sky Tower and a 44 meter Vertigo Climb to 270 meters above ground. While up there the next clue is ROADBLOCK "Who's ready to make the leap of faith?" One team member leaped from the Sky Tower down 192 meters while the other on the ground shoots a photo on a SONY Cybershot (product placement). Andy/ Laura arrived first, were first to the top, first to the bottom and on to the next task. The order of team arrival predicted their order of task completion. That order of task completion was:
Andy
Andrew
Zabrina
Howard
Prashant
Francesca
Marsio
Melody

That clue sends them to the Auckland Museum pit stop. Andy/Laura got first place, followed by Andrew/Syeon and Zabrina/Joe Jer. Howard/Sahran were 4th. Next to arrive was Sahil/Prashant, but they received a 1 hour penalty before they could check in. In the interim, Mardy/Marsio, Sandy/Francesca and Melody/Sharon finished. That eliminated Sahil/Prashant, very upset at the rule interpretation that led to their penalty.

ARA1, Ep.6 "What Have You Been Eating?"

Teams release from the Auckland Museum pit stop at these times:
Andy/Laura   430am
Andrew/Syeon around 445am
Zabrina/Joe Jer   459am
Howard/Sahran   513am
Sandy/Francesca   622am
Mardy/Marsio   633am
Sharon/Melody   640am

All teams take the same 800am flight from Auckland on the North Island of New Zealand to Dunedin, on the east coast of and bottom of the South Island of New Zealand. Teams arrived and picked up a marked 4 wheel drive car to self-drive 5 hours to Queenstown and were specifically warned to obey local speed limits. Along the way that limit was 100km/hr. Zabrina/Joe Jer are clocked at 110, but got off with a warning. Andy/Laura were clocked at 146 km/hr, which resulted in a NZ$600 fine for Andy and confiscation of his driver's license. I wonder where they got that much money to pay the fine. The scenery along the drive was spectacular in the Queenstown area. Teams must do some of the extreme sports that Queenstown is noted for. First they gassed up at the Caltex station (product placement) for the clue to the Gondola Ride up Bob's Peak. On top was a DETOUR of Ledge or Luge. Ledge used a Bungee Swing 400 meters above the surrounding countryside, on a long tether but with plenty of safety equipment (the reputation of Queenstown is so visitor-friendly that it can't afford to lose any tourists there). Luge was the option for those too scared to do Ledge. Luge teammates did a relay race 8 times, alternating team members, up a chairlift and down a 430 meter summer luge course. The first 4 teams all chose Ledge and finished in the order they arrived, Mardy/Marsio, Andy/Laura, Sandy/Francesca and Andrew/Syeon. Sahran says "I can't do this (referring to the bungee swing)" so Howard/Sahran did Luge, as did Zabrina/Joe Jer and Sharon/Melody.

The clue sent teams to Arrowtown to find the clue box. This was extremely tricky and it took quite a while for some teams. However, it made no difference as there was now a hours of operation Bunching all teams at Off Road Adventures involving quad bikes. Teams reaching the hours of operation delay agreed among themselves that they would all honor that order of arrival the following morning. Several teams were concerned that Andy/Laura, with their history of sharp dealing, would try to cut the line. Off Road Adventures had team members maneuver separately through very difficult terrain. Andrew, Sahran and Sharon all get stuck in mud and are assisted by course personnel to get out. Completion of that task sent teams to the world-famous Nevis Valley Bungee Jump ROADLBOCK "Who can drop 134 m in 9.5 seconds?" Since there was no opportunity to change positions unless someone chickened out, the order of arrival was the order of departure. That order (also the order of team arrival at Chard Farm Winery) was:

Sandy
Laura
JoeJer
Andrew
Mardy
Howard
Sharon

Sharon was frightened, but she did the bungee jump. Chard Farm Winery was the pit stop. Andy/Laura received their penalty, 2 minutes for each km/hr above the speed limit, for a total of 92 minutes applied to their upcoming pit stop release. If assessed this episode (and why shouldn't it?), then I think Andy/Laura would have been narrowly eliminated. Michael McKay used some logic to assess it at the beginning of the next leg, where it washed out with Bunching at the airport. Sharon/Melody were eliminated.

ARA1, Ep.7 "Don't Stand There Doing Nothing!"

Teams are released from the pit stop at these times:
Sandy/Francesca 254am
Zabrina/Joe Jer   315am
Andrew/Syeon   405am
Mardy/Marsio   422am
Howard/Sahran 425am
Andy/Laura   605am????

What happened here? If you estimate that jumping times at Nevis

Valley were 10 minutes apart, you conclude that Andy/Laura would have finished around 305pm. Add 12 hours and the 92 minute penalty and you get to 435am. Why was there 90 minutes extra in their release time? What has Michael McKay not told us?

The clue said get to a specific Caltex station (product placement) in Singapore. The flights were Queenstown to Auckland connecting there to Auckland to Singapore. First departure was at 11am and arrival was around 830pm. The stop in Singapore is the most criticized set of tasks in the history of all Amazing Races and Amazing Race Asias. Sandy coined this slogan: "all the way to Singapore just to wash a car." Sandy didn't consider the important product placement taking place for FORD with its Focus make being washed for Caltex! He just told it like it is. Teams then got a pointless trip to Suntec City's Fountain of Wealth for the next clue, on to Bangkok. Teams Bunched again at Singapore airport and flew to Bangkok. On arrival teams grabbed taxis but several drivers had a huge communications gap and are changed out by those teams. The destination was Wat Niwet Thamaprawat in the Ayutthaya historical complex, 85 km north of Bangkok. However, its hours of operation were 0630 to 1900, so all teams Bunched at the entrance. Order of arrival was critical because the limited entry transportation system involved cable cars across the Chao Phraya River that could take only one team at a time. At that temple Zabrina/JoeJer were the first to find the next clue, a coin with an unidentified temple on it; Howard/Sahran were last.

Teams took taxis to Bangkok after they figured out by various means (mostly their taxi drivers) that a Thai 2 baht coin portrays the Pukao Tong (Golden Mount) in the Wat Sawet temple complex. A ROADBLOCK "Who rings a bell?" was waiting there. The selected individual climbed 316 steps and searched 560 golden blessing bells with 100 capsules hidden among them but only 6 of which have correct clues. All teams but Howard/Sahran had made it to the golden bell. Andy found the first correct clue, surprising as his was last of the first 5 teams to arrive. This was a classic needle-in-a-haystack task with the probability of finding a valid clue each try diminishing as valid ones are found.

Next was a DETOUR Bacon or Egg. Bacon meant directing a taxi driver to Ha Long Latadong for a clue and then to locate and the Pig

Monument with the necessity of figuring out where it is first. Egg was to find an egg stall and transport on a dolly 20 wholesale trays 3/4 mile through a busy market. Broken eggs had to be replaced. The confusing nature of Bangkok streets plus communications issues with taxi drivers made navigation to the Pig Monument very difficult. Some tried "Oink, Oink" to convey the destination, but it has a different meaning in the Thai language. Finding the egg stall was also unusually difficult. Andy/Laura used the home team advantage (they live in Thailand) and partial knowledge of the language to good effect to find the egg stall first. Many teams were finding that Asian politeness of never wanting to say "No" or "I don't know" to a foreigner complicates accurate communications. Howard/Sahran and Andrew/Syeon finally made it to the Pig Monument, but Andy/Laura got to the delivery point for their eggs first for the clue to the pit stop at Wat Pho, the temple of the Reclining Buddha. Andy/Laura also gave directions from near their egg destination to help Sandy/Francesca to locate the origination egg stall.

Team finish order was:

Andy/Laura
Andrew/Syeon
Howard/Sahran
Sandy/Francesca
Mardy/Marsio
Zabrina/Joe Jer, still in the race with a non-elimination leg but receiving no money leaving the pit stop

ARA1, Ep.8 "My Legs Are Shaking Like Jelly"
Teams are released from the pit stop at:
Andy/Laura   100am
Andrew/Syeon   105am
Howard/Sahran   111am
Sandy/Francesca 135am
Mardy/Marsio   155am
Zabrina/Joe Jer   327am

The clue sent teams from Bangkok's Southern Bus Terminal to Krabi, 800 km south. Fans of Amazing Race 1 will remember Krabi as the destination of the taxi rides that resulted in Rob/Brennan and

Frank/Margarita earning a significant advantage, Joe/Bill dallying reaching there after a FAST FORWARD and Nancy/Emily eliminated there after a 24 hour penalty earned in the Bangkok area. Zabrina/Joe Jer were left enough money by other teams to reach the bus terminal and buy tickets to Krabi, but they needed to supplement it by begging. The express bus with Zabrina/Joe Jer, Andy/Laura and Sandy/Francesca left at 7am, arriving at 6pm. The other 3 teams left on a local bus to Prachuap (only 1/3 of the way to Krabi) hours earlier, but gaining an advantage leads to suboptimal results. They hadn't checked connecting schedules properly; on arrival at Prachuap the bus to Krabi is 10 hours and put them way behind. They received conflicting advice from locals and bus drivers on how to proceed. They developed the strategy of making many short segments heading south, first to Chumpon and then Menang Mai (where the driver arranged a special private bus to meet and transport them direct to Krabi instead of continuing through Phuket to reach Krabi). They arrived at 730pm instead of at 830pm. Teams were then directed to a local beach, using taxis. Mardy/Marsio had wiped out their funds on new lighter backpacks before the bus trips, so 100 baht from Andrew/Syeon allowed them to continue.

None of the 6 teams arrived by the 600pm closing time for the Hat Phi Phi National Marine Park on the beach at Hat Nopharrat Thara Bay. Mardy/Marsio begged and attempted to sell clothing, successful enough to stay in the race. The following morning they get the clue to marked long-tailed boats as the means of transport. The cluebox offer of a FAST FORWARD was declined by all teams at that time. All teams went to Ko Poda Island and a DETOUR of Smash or Grab. Smash was use a small hammer to open up any of 75 coconuts to find 1 containing desired red dye. Grab was to swim to one of 100 buoys with clues, but only 10 had real clues. Both DETOUR options were luck-based tasks.

Mardy/Marsio were a little behind the other teams and could see that none were going for the FAST FORWARD. They changed focus and direction instantly and went to Pranang Bay to navigate a two-person kayak among the caves there. Mardy had never kayaked, so they adopted a conservative approach of one balancing and one paddling, slower than a normal approach but safer. Their strategy worked fine; they found the FAST FORWARD, whose clue sent them to the pit stop at Ko Phak Bia. Andrew/Syeon was initially the only team to do Grab, but their immediate success motivated most of the other teams to switch. Andy/Laura completed Grab and Sandy opened the red dye coconut. Zabrina/Joe Jer next completed it, leaving Howard/Sahran in last place and Howard suffering from massive blisters on his hand.

Next was the Rock Climb at Railey East 123 Wall, a task with a professional anchoring the safety line and providing safety advice. The clue was 20 yards up the wall. It looked easily reachable to me. Even Sahran, complaining "Oh my god" and "I can't do it," surprised himself by climbing relatively quickly despite his fear of heights. Teams left in the same order they arrived and the same thing happened at Koh Hong Lagoon where teams were only picking up a clue to the pit stop.

Andrew/Syeon's boat captain picked the wrong island so they went from 2nd to 5th place. Howard/Sahran finished in last place and eliminated. They complained they were not ready to leave this race, but most observers disagree even though they were the 2 most colorful ARA1 characters.

ARA1, Ep.9 "This is Totally, Totally Out of This World!"

The release from the Krabi pit stop was at:
Mardy/Marsio   437am
Andy/Laura   441am
Sandy/Francesca 443am
Andrew/Syeon   444am
Zabrina/Joe Jer   459am

So we see that Mardy/Marsio took enough time doing the FAST FORWARD that they were only 4 minutes ahead of the next team to arrive. An alternate explanation is that Michael McKay's design of this leg did not properly compensate the FAST FORWARD, but I don't believe that. Teams flew to Kolkata, India 2700km away. During that period Sandy predicted that "We should eat before we get to India because we are probably not going to be eating in India." Since this is an Amazing Race and we haven't seen eating challenges yet, Sandy's logic does not hold up for me. Other teams accuse Andy/Laura of hiding secret maps in their luggage, but nothing happened as a result.

The first task in Kolkata was to find Theresa of Avila's church to light a candle or not. All teams except Mardy/Marsio went to Mother Teresa's church (a well-known tourist attraction vs. the less popular Theresa of Avila church) and found nothing. The chaos of Kolkata's city road traffic was clear. The next clue sent teams to Tollygunge railroad station, to shoeshine men waiting to instruct them for ROADBLOCK "Who wants to shine?" 7 shoeshines need to be completed at the minimum price of 5 rupees, with teams keeping their earnings (around 75 U.S. cents). Their task was to sell shoeshines and to shine those shoes. Everyone had a good time watching or doing this. The task was easy; everyone knew there won't be any huge lead for anyone.

Next task was the antithesis of Sandy's prediction. Each team member had to eat a traditional Bengali meal at the Aaheli restaurant in the Parak Lee Inn Hotel. Everything has to be eaten, including lentils, dal, sheep's eyes, trays of vegetables and meat dishes, huge mounds of rice and dessert. Mardy/Marsio were so hungry they asked for more rice. They got it but after a few more courses they were feeling unwell. It was a large amount of food to eat, but not as bad as other eating challenges like meat in Mendoza in AR7 Ep.3. There was a lot of barfing off camera and loud farts on camera, but all finished and Mardy/Marsio did not improve their relative position, arriving last and departing last.

Results of the eating challenge are negated as teams received the clue for Kanishka's Sari Boutique. Its hours of operation are 9am to 7pm. This was another Bunching point and all teams enter at the same time to find a sari within all the bolts of material throughout this shop. It was a classic luck-based random task. Andrew/Syeon finished first. Andy/Laura came out second and negotiated a higher price with Sandy/Francesca's taxi driver, whom they stole. Andy/Laura knew how to make friends and influence people. They have a knack for treating the other teams that gets them wished a speedy visit to Sequesterville.

The next task was a DETOUR Count or Carry. Carry used a headpiece as the base for stabilizing jugs of milk on top to carry a distance to a large urn with a minimum fill line representing 80 gallons. Count required counting of about 1000 betel nuts in a basket; if the accurate count was missed they had to redo it until right. For several teams, that was multiple times. Andy/Laura did Carry and breezed through.

Teams go to B.P.Gangooli St. Kolay Market on top of the Bank building across from Schiava Train Station. Allan Wu met them with a direction CONTINUE with a new clue rather than the "You are team number ___." expected. This was a classic To Be Continued (TBC) leg.

ARA1, Ep.10 "War Has Begun!"

Some people label this episode as 9, part 2 but my counting system says it is episode 10, the back end of a To Be Continued leg. Teams behind Andy/Laura finished the COUNT task one-by-one, Andrew/Syeon, then Mardy/Marsio, then Zabrina/Joe Jer and Sandy/Francesca all arriving at the Bank Building roof to meet Allan Wu. Teams are directed to Sealdah station for a major Bunching followed by a 19 hour train ride to New Delhi. Once they arrive there will be a taxi to Red Fort, where a YIELD awaits. Mardy/Marsio and Andrew/Syeon discuss yielding Andy/Laura, but Sandy/Francesca arrive first and YIELD Andy/Laura.

Next is a DETOUR of Donkey or Deliver. Donkey started with located donkeys at Cycle Market, Chandni Chowk in Old Delhi, then delivering a load of onions to the onion vendor at Lahori Gate Crossing. Deliver was locating Sunny International in the Gadodia Market in Old Delhi and delivering bags of chili powder to a spice shop with Sunny International identified only by a picture from a SONY Cybershot Camera (product placement). Both were fraught with many perils, including the twists and turns of the routes involved, asking locals for help, onions bouncing out of the basket, and the bulk and weight of the chili powder bags. Not shown problems for Sandy/Francesca included Andy/Laura making up the entire YIELD time and catching up to Sandy/Francesca. Crossing Sandy is not a good idea; when Andy tried to take the lead Sandy cut him off. All 3 teams doing Donkey had big navigational problems. Their attempts to ask locals frequently resulted in misinformation. Sandy/Francesca completed the DETOUR first.

168

Next was ROADBLOCK "Who's ready to help out at the farm?" at Tibetan Monastery market. The task was make dungcakes for fuel out of carried buckets of cowdung and water, then place them to stick on a large wall. This task was hot, difficult and messy. After difficulty finding the correct route inside the Monastery, Sandy excelled at this. Andrew and Mardy seem to be OK. Laura struggled but was well ahead of Zabrina/Joe Jer. The actual finish order was Andrew/Syeon, Sandy/Francesca, Andy/Laura, Mardy/Marsio, Zabrina/Joe Jer, the last 3 close.

In the most climactic scene in all of ARA1, competition for taxis among the last 3 teams proved to be crucial. Andy/Laura had trouble getting one, Mardy/Marsio found one and left, and Zabrina/Joe Jer got one just before Andy/Laura. Andy/Laura were fifth to arrive despite their magnificent comeback from the YIELD. It wasn't a non-elimination leg so they are eliminated. Taxi bingo had its perils as several teams change positions by 2 spots. The final finish order at pit stop Jain Mandir Dada Bari temple, with very hot tiles to walk barefoot across, was:

Sandy/Francesca
Andrew/Syeon
Mardy/Marsio
Zabrina/Joe Jer
Andy/Laura, who are eliminated

ARA1, Ep.11 "This Is going to be Embarrassing!"

Teams are released from the pit stop at:
Sandy/Francesca 147am
Andrew/Syeon   153am
Mardy/Marsio   155am
Zabrina/Joe Jer   215am

Syeon had a foot injury and reportedly cannot run. Teams flew 2,000 km to Dubai to take a taxi to Burj Dubai water taxi station to hire an Abra water taxi. Andrew/Syeon claimed a money-only alliance with Zabrina/Joe Jer and an everything-but-money alliance with Mardy/Marsio. There's an unused YIELD opportunity at Burj

169

Dubai station. Mardy/Marsio are delayed by engine problems their driver is able to repair as Andrew/Syeon pass.

The next task was ROADBLOCK "Who wants to Play Around?" at a 9 hole par 3 golf course at Dubai Creek Golf & Yacht Club. The selected team member got one ball, one putter and one club. If the ball is lost they must go back to the beginning of the first hole to get another one. Zabrina and Francesca both played solid rounds and complete it quickly. Despite her foot problem, Syeon managed to complete the course. Mardy and Marsio are delayed by a breakdown of their water taxi. Marsio is the choice for this ROADBLOCK, but he was a poor choice, as Mardy admitted they made a mistake by choosing the wrong team member (Mardy plays golf and Marsio doesn't). Marsio lost a ball on the 6th hole and went back for another. He finished 3 holes behind Syeon, or about 30 minutes behind. Mardy/Marsio then suffered additional transportation problems when they discovered their taxi had left and they needed to locate another one to keep going.

The next clue sent teams on a useless trip to find their next clue at The Leopard of Dubai. First they needed to figure out what that is and where. It is a boat moored at Dubai International Marine Club. The clue found there directed teams to Ski Dubai at the Emirates Mall. The DETOUR is Hack or Hike. In Hack the clue was in the middle of a 150 pound block of ice. Using a small hammer and chisel for each team member, they had to chip enough ice to get the clue. Hike was for each team member to be outfitted with 25kg backpacks plus the rope needed for safety, then go up to the top of the ski lift by ground, retrieve the clue and walk down. Sandy/ Francesca and Andrew/Syeon chose Hack, both completing it rapidly. Zabrina/Joe Jer and Mardy/Marsio chose Hike and had trouble getting up the slope.

The next clue sent teams to Gold Souk mall to find the Modern Jewelry store matching a photo only. There were 500 gold stores in the Gold Souk area, so it's a classic needle-in-a-haystack random task. Andrew/ Syeon got lucky and found it quickly. Sandy/ Francesca were more systematic and eventually found it. Zabrina/ Joe Jer phoned ahead, but this didn't help them. Mardy/Marsio found it relatively quickly.

The final clue sent teams to a marked 4 wheel drive vehicle to ask its driver to go to Margham Desert Camp, the pit stop. Teams finish:
Sandy/Francesca
Andrew/Syeon
Zabrina/Joe Jer
Mardy/Marsio, who are non-eliminated and would not receive money on pit stop release

ARA1, Ep.12 "Oh, My Goodness, I Have to Eat a Brain!"

Here are the times for the release from this pit stop:
Sandy/Francesca 745am
Andrew/Syeon   751am
Zabrina/Joe Jer   806am
Mardy/Marsio   820am

The first clue sent teams by SUV to Desert Area 53. There is DETOUR Ride or Seek. Ride is to have both team members on the back of the same camel and navigate it through a course to retrieve 5 poles. If you got a cooperative camel, this task could be completed quickly; if not, it was a nightmare. Either way, it's really good TV to use balky animals in Amazing Races. Sweep was use a metal detector to sweep a large area of sand to find a miniature metal camel. Sandy/Francesca got an uncooperative camel, switched to Seek, found out its difficulty and came back to be assigned a new camel, which is a good one. Andrew/Syeon got a good camel, but later they got stuck in the sand. Zabrina/Joe Jer had a moderately balky camel. Mardy/Marsio, who did the task quickly, got stuck in the sand leaving and also had a good camel.

Next clue sent teams to the Eye of the Emirates, a ferris wheel on a scale close to that of the Eye of London. This was a quintessential luck-based task, but a bit of skill applies to prevent you from ever repeating the same number. There were 42 cabins and 5 clues in them. Keeping track of which numbers you have selected is important since the first team will have a 12% probability of success for the first pick and it increases as numbers are theoretically eliminated. The fourth team will have only 2 clues and a 4.8% probability for its first pick. It took the first team an average of 8 tries to hit one of the cabins with a clue and the fourth team an average of 21 tries. The physical manifestation of a selection was that you step out of your current cabin and wait until the wheel comes around to that other cabin. If there are other teams there it complicated the process, decreased the probability of a hit (due to the wheel turns that are not for you), and increased the number of tries it will take. Andrew/Syeon got incredibly lucky and hit cabin #19 on their first try. They are done and on their way with the next clue. Zabrina/Joe Jer took many rotations but finally #26 hits for them. Mardy/Marsio arrived long after Sandy/Francesca and had the disadvantage of not knowing which numbers have not worked. Sandy/Francesca barely beat them.

Next in ROADBLOCK "Who's got the brains on this team?" Syeon was selected for this misdirection task, eat brains at a local restaurant. She had a difficult time. Zabrina was an eating machine and made up time to finish just after Syeon. Francesca guessed it might involve brains so she had Sandy take it. He demolished the plate of brains quickly. Mardy arrived and indicated that they, despite a reputation as great eaters, don't eat organ meats. He ate slowly and fell farther behind.

Next was an unnecessary trip to find Sheikh Saeed al-Maktoum's house. Teams don't have much trouble there except for Sandy/Francesca trying to find taxis to/from it. Teams received a clue to Wild Wadi Water Park to ride the Jumeirah Sceirah giant water slide, the largest and fastest outside of North America. This was a cool-looking task but from a competitive standpoint nothing changes in the relative positions of the racers. All teams stayed in the same order. How boring!

The pit stop was at the Mirna A' Salam Beach near the Burj al Arab Hotel. The final finishing order was:

Andrew/Syeon
Zabrina/Joe Jer
Sandy/Francesca
Mardy/Marsio, who are eliminated and do not make the Final 3

I think the Final 3 teams have an interesting mix of brawn (Sandy) and brains (both of the other 2 teams). The finale will be interesting.

ARA1, Ep. 13, Finale "24 Days, 15 Cities, 39,000 Kilometers, and it Comes Down to This"

A question for the finale is whether the producers paid exorbitant sums for them to stay at the Burj al Arab Hotel, a self-proclaimed 7 star hotel which is one of the most luxurious and expensive in the world. I doubt it. Times for release from the pit stop were:
Andrew/Syeon   323am
Zabrina/Joe Jer   340am
Sandy/Francesca 426am

Teams had to solve a puzzle to find their next destination. It is the Menara Kuala Lumpur, the first pit stop of this race. All teams went to Dubai International Airport for 6100km flights to Kuala Lumpur. The first two teams connected in Singapore, Sandy/Francesca in Bangkok. This was supposed to result in an unstated advantage of some minutes for Andrew/Syeon and Zabrina/Joe Jer, but in actuality they arrived at the same time. All teams went to the base of Menara Towers for a clue to Kuching, Sarawak East Malaysia by air. Now, this was almost as absurd as sending teams to Singapore for a car wash. Why didn't Michael McKay send them directly to Kuching in the first place? Teams Bunch at Kuala Lumpur airport, but it's the last we see of it in ARA1.

Teams first find a marked car in the airport car park, then find the Cat Statue in Kuching for their next clue. Andrew/Syeon believed their Lonely Planet book on Kuching can direct them anywhere they need to go. We'll see how that worked out for them, but now it worked OK and they found it first. Zabrina/Joe Jer hired a taxi for the day, a very smart move, and ended up finding the correct statue (there are 5 different ones). Sandy/Francesca attempted it without help. They got there third.

Next was another useless task where they are sent to the Old Court-house on Gambia Road to find the next clue. That sent them to the DETOUR Brawn or Brain. Brawn was carry 30kg of fruit from a boat to a wet market. Brain was to assemble a bench using provided tools, parts and a SONY Cybershot Camera (hopefully the last product placement of ARA1). All teams chose Brain. Andrew/ Syeon started and finished in first position. Sandy/Francesca did a

173

great job and caught up a bit from arriving last. Zabrina/Joe Jer did OK but finished 15 minutes later.

Next was drive 35 km to Sarawak Cultural Village. Navigating from Kuching was the difficult part causing Andrew/Syeon to lose ARA1. Their Lonely Planet didn't help them enough. They ended up arriving third at least 15 minutes behind at the Sarawak Cultural Village. It was now a 2-team race. Sandy/Francesca hired a taxi to follow. Zabrina/Joe Jer arrived the same time.

At Sarawak Cultural Village the first task was find the clue. Longhouses needed to be checked. Teams next went to the Blowpipe range and shot darts at colored pineapples until each team member had 3 hits. They had to alternate colors hit and shots by team members. Sandy/ Francesca had a slight lead in finishing this. However, they lost it by turning the wrong way, not taking a direct route back to the parking lot. Zabrina/Joe Jer chose a direct route and got slightly in front.

Teams drove behind leading taxis 32 km to Permai Rainforest Resort for ROADBLOCK "Who can swing like Tarzan?" One team member was selected for a Treetop High Rope Walk and Balance Beam Challenge. It was Francesca vs. Zabrina. However, with the use of take-a-number and only room for one person to do that challenge at a time, Zabrina's earlier arrival was critical. They both did well and finished it with Zabrina 2 minutes ahead of Francesca. Then teams went to the adjacent Damai Beach for a motorboat to Bako National Park, where you run or walk across a small strip of sand to a mangrove boardwalk. At the end of that short boardwalk was the traditional array of all the eliminated teams, Allan Wu and the Finish Mat. There was no place to pass another team except on the sand. With boat captains going at a regulated speed there wasn't going to be any position change. Zabrina/Joe Jer won by their route to the parking lot back at Sarawak Cultural Village. Sandy/Francesca finished 2 minutes later, Andrew/Syeon 15 minutes after that. Zabrina/JoeJer won $100,000 US for traveling 39,000 miles, 14 cities, 9 countries. I commend Michael McKay for his casting of Andy/Laura, Mardy/Marsio and Sandy/Francesca.

AMAZING RACE ASIA 2

10 teams assemble with host Allan Wu on the grounds of the Asian Civilisations Museum in Singapore. It's ARA2! The teams are:
Marc/Rovilson, TV hosts and best buddies, age 31 and 30
Pamela/Vanessa, sisters, artist manager and professional dancer, age 29 and 24
Adrian/Collin, gym buddies, Business Development + Sales, age 25 and 29; Adrian with a hearing disability communicates in sign language with Collin
Ann/Diane, mothers who are known for their dancing, Business Owner and Marketing Manager, age 40 and 33
Paula/Natasha, best friends, Actress/Model+Public Relations, age 24 and 24
Sawaka/Daichi, sister/brother, Singer and Interpreter, age 28/26
Sophie/Aurelia, ex-housemates, Writer and model, age 27 and 27
Henry/Terri, husband/wife, Retired U.S.Navy and Housewife, age 48 and 44
Edwin/Monica, dating 10 years, Event Organizer and Actress/Model, age 26 and 28
Brett/Kinar, dating, model/actress and physiotherapist, age 26/28

Note that ARA2 didn't provide pit stop release times or titles.

ARA2, Ep.1

Each team received a postcard of a different Singapore icon. They have to find the 1 of 10 taxis within 300 yards with that postcard on its window. Finding their taxi, they received their next clue and proceed to Mt. Faber (site of the AR3 Ep.8 elimination of John Vito/Jill) to locate the Merlion statue. 2 teams lag behind, Edwin/Monica (due to fatigue carrying her heavy bag plus his own) and Brett/Kinar. Pamela/Vanessa reached the Merlion statue first and received a clue plus a Nokia N95 cell phone. They must use the phone as a GPS system to take them the correct distance in the right direction. Henry/Terri, Brett/Kinar and Edwin/Monica trailed and have difficulty finding a taxi. Adrian stated "It's just like you are 007 in the movies" on Nokia N95 as a GPS system.

Directions on the N95 led to Suntec City Tower 3 for DETOUR Dare or Stair. Dare is to go up 45 flights by elevator, hook to a Tyrolean traverse line strung to the top of Tower 4, have your partner pull it across, go down those 45 flights of stairs in the Tower 4 elevator, then cross at ground level to Tower 3 and take the elevator up 45 flights of steps there. Stair involved going up and down 45 flights of stairs and then going up 45 flights in the adjacent tower. All teams Dare. Rovilson quipped "I should have gotten a girl partner."

Next was a flight to Manila. Rovilson requested the airline ticket agent "send them to Paris," pointing to Adrian/Collin. Is this a repeat of the route of Colin/Christie in AR5 to the field with the ox? Henry/Terri and Edwin/Monica weren't in time for the last flight and arrive next morning. The stage was set for their race to avoid elimination.

The first 8 teams made the first possible flight and go to Asian Promenade at CCP Complex in Manila. Finding the cluebox location outside in the park was difficult. The next clue sent teams to Plaza Miranda night market to a Balut egg seller where teams consumed a total of 8 balut eggs. Balut is a Philippines delicacy and reputed aphrodisiac, mostly developed duck embryos with feathers and beaks. Each team had a different reaction to balut eggs. Pamela/Vanessa and Marc/Rovilson (no surprise, the Filipino teams) finished on top. Aurelia on Sophie eating balut eggs "I've never seen anyone who can talk and swallow and chew at the same time." There is no "i" in "teamwork", Aurelia.

The final clue led to the pit stop at Fort Santiago. Teams walked uphill the last part of the trip. Finish order was:
1. Pamela/Vanessa
2. Marc/Rovilson
3. Ann/Diane
4. Brett/Kinar
5. Sophie/Aurelia
6. Paula/Natasha
7. Adrian/Collin
8. Sawaka/Daichi
9. Henry/Terri
10. Edwin/Monica were non-eliminated, with a 30 minute Marked for Elimination penalty if they fail to finish first next episode.

ARA2, Ep.2

Teams took taxis to Green Star Bus Centre. Their destination was the Municipal in Pila Laguna, a 3 hour bus ride with buses every 15 minutes. Teams are spread over 6 buses. Paula/Natasha impressed Adrian/Collin begging money from bus passengers. A ROADBLOCK "Who has an animal instinct?" was guide a carabao and plow around a muddy field in a figure 8 pattern, as in "My Ox is Broken" task from Amazing Race 5. Many couldn't control their carabao; all eventually finish.

Next teams took one of several buses back from Pila to Manila and located a Caltex Starmart. There they loaded 4 boxes of donations into the back of a jeepney and delivered them to a local children's orphanage in Ermita Shrine. A comedy of errors occurred next. Pamela/Vanessa could have been on the lead bus with Marc/Rovilson but they misread the clue and search Pila. Adrian lost a contact lens in the field, affecting his vision. There was valuable interaction with the children from some teams while others kept going immediately.

The next clue led to DETOUR of "Heel or Wheel?" Heel matched up 250 pairs of shoes and Wheel was to assemble a bicycle using only the parts and tools provided. This DETOUR highlighted a classic confront-ation between a luck-based option (Heel) and a skill-based option (Wheel). If a team had mechanical aptitude then Wheel was the best choice; if a team did not, then they should choose Heel and devise a system of classification. Marc/Rovilson and Pamela/Vanessa did Wheel while Adrian/Collin, Paula/Natasha and Brett/Kinar did Heel. Natasha quipped about this task: "Paula probably has more shoes in her closet than what we saw. It's not a challenge because we have been there." Marc/Rovilson finished first after having to redo the handlebar angle. Ann/Diane and Sophie/Aurelia arrived and Ann/Diane blitzed through Wheel and finished second.

The final clue was to Paco Park and Cemetery for the pit stop. Marc/Rovilson arrived with national pride and won $5,000 each, followed by Paula/Natasha, who won a find-a-taxi contest with Ann/Diane. The last two teams were Edwin/Monica and Henry/Terri, with Terri following this mandate from Henry: "I'm the expert on the bike. All she has to do is shut up, not mess with me and it is going to be my time." That philosophy worked to finish next-to-last.

Order of finish was:
1. Marc/Rovilson
2. Paula/Natasha
3. Ann/Diane
4. Vanessa/Pamela
5. Adrian/Collin
6. Brett/Kinar
7. Sophie/Aurelia
8. Daichi/Sawaka
9. Henry/Terri
10. Edwin/Monica, who were eliminated due to their last-place finish

ARA2, Ep.3

Here we have the second most ridiculous task in the entirety of the Amazing Race and Amazing Race Asia. The ultimate destination is Auckland, New Zealand. However, first teams must first fly to Hong Kong to count Hong Kong currency and coins at a Standard Chartered Bank. Now that company is a gem for their sponsorship of ARA2, but this was taking the product placement concept a bit too far. Does fly thousands of miles out of your way to publicize Standard Chartered Bank in Hong Kong sound to you like something worth televising? Michael McKay lost the respect of many in the Amazing Race community for the Hong Kong part of this episode. It was not quite as bad as the infamous ARA1 Singapore carwash only episode, but was close. Sending teams to a major metropolitan area for a very minor task and then on to somewhere else is not my idea of good episode design.

Teams flew 1,000 km and go to Central Pier, Marc/Rovilson after a 242am release from the pit stop. Teams took the MTR train line from the airport, except for Brett/Kinar who took a taxi. Teams had difficulty finding the Central Pier clue box. The clue sent them to Standard Chartered Bank at Causeway Bay for counting large stacks of Hong Kong bills and coins. Paula/Natasha had to recount 10 times. Sawaka/Daichi just did it and finished this task first by using their eyes plus good arithmetic skills. The next clue sent teams to Auckland New Zealand to find marked cars in the airport parking lot. Arrival back at Hong Kong airport revealed that the schedules from Hong Kong to Auckland caused all teams to be Bunched again. There was so much slack in the schedule that the worst counting performance would be as good as the best counting performance in moving forward. Michael McKay was cursed by some racers and by viewers.

Arriving in Auckland, teams got cars and self-drive to Hotwick Historical Village, a 5 acre colonial New Zealand restoration. Marc/Rovilson, Adrian/Collin and Ann/Diane found a local guide; other teams had trouble. Teams took pictures after arriving at Hotwick with a SONY Cybershot camera (more appropriate product placement) of 3 specific items wherever they could be found in the village. They delivered the pictures to the Hotwick Court House. Since there were more than 30 houses in the Village, this was a standard luck-based task of moderate difficulty. Teams responded by trading information so it is easier to find items that another team has already located. Marc/Rovilson impressed me once more by getting this task completed without any help from other teams. Brett/Kinar took the longest to reach the Village.

In ROADBLOCK "Who wants to take the plunge?" teams drove to Auckland Harbor Bridge and one from each team must bungee jump off the underside of it. Nobody had problem with this, but Vanessa noted about Collin "It's funny to hear a guy scream."

The next clue was the DETOUR Wall or Waka. In Wall teams drive to Birkenhead Leisure Center and both teammates scale a wall to get the flag on its top to receive the next clue. In Waka teams drive to North Shore Rowing Club for a waka (Maori boat) for both to row gathering 3 flags to earn their clue. Marc/Rovilson again excelled going right up the wall. Paula/Natasha could not finish the wall and switched to Waka. Adrian/Collin handled the wall with ease and speed. In Waka several teams flipped their boat, adding a swimming task to the main one including Henry/Terri, Pamela/Vanessa and Sawaka/Daichi. Henry: "I think that's what the N in Navy stands for. Non-swimmer." Diane: "We were relieved some teams spent time in the water. That meant we could catch up." Sophie castigated Aurelia for not being able to climb the wall.

Teams next drove to Ascension Vineyards in Makatana, with King Seed Psychiatrist Center on its grounds and behind that was

Spookers Haunted House. Fake ghouls and demons there were trying to frighten people. It impacted some, but definitely not Adrian. His deafness came in handy at the Haunted House. Each team on finishing the Haunted House received the clue to find the pit stop behind the Haunted House. Marc/Rovilsson finished #1, Adrian/ Collin #2, Ann/Diane #3, Paula/ Natasha #4, Terri/Henry #5, Daichi/Sawaka #6 and Pamela/Vanessa #7. Sophie and Aurelia had done poorly due to driving hours out of their way to the wrong place, but finished in 8th place 7 hours behind and found out there is still one team left back at the wall. Brett and Kinar can't climb it and the site of the waka is closed so they are eliminated.

ARA2, Ep.4

Aurelia/Sophie were unlikely to stay in the race. Unless there is significant Bunching they will not survive. This episode started with a drive to the Rotorua area, then a stop at a Caltex station (another product placement) in Tirau for the second half of the clue. After filling gas tanks, teams drove to Okere Falls Scenic Reserve, center of white water sledging. Popular in New Zealand, sledgers put on helmet, elbow pads and knee pads plus a life preserver before going down the strong currents of the river. Again Henry's disdain for swimming emerged. Natasha asked "Has anyone ever died doing this?" Next was a clue to Lake Tikitapu where one team member pilots a 450hp Agrojet boat around an obstacle course, the other providing navigational guidance. Teams were now close to Hell's Gate, a natural geothermal area.

Hell's Gate had a ROADBLOCK "Who's the real stick in the mud" as selected individuals must bathe in 40 degree Centigrade (104 Fahrenheit) mud in a pool and locate a clue hidden inside a stick there. Pamela's team did not have enough strength to pull out the stick. Rovilson quipped: "If they ever made Driving Miss Daisy, part 2, the boat version, Marc would definitely be the main actor."

The next clue was to Te Puia for DETOUR Flax or Stick. Flax is using flax plant leaves weave a Maori headband. In Stick teams must toss 4 sticks back and forth (2 from each person) to the beat of a drum. You can't drop them or you must start over. This is a traditional Maori game to improve hand/eye coordination needed in battle. Adrian/Collin Stick to the type of task they expect to be good at. Diane messed up and hit Ann in the eye with a stick. Henry had difficulty at the headband task so they switch to Stick. That was worse so they go back to Flax. Henry was having a difficult time, exclaiming "we cannot work together. Even in our house we can't work together." Terri, who had been on the sidelines all day, snatched the headband and finished it rapidly.

The pit stop greeter was a Maori warrior with his fierce war cry. Marc/Rovilson checked in first, followed by Adrian/Collin 2nd, Paula/Natasha 3rd, Ann/Diane 4th, Daichi/Sawaka 5th, Pamela/ Vanessa 6th, Terri/Henry 7th. Sophie/Aurelia reached Okere Falls to discover its hours of operation are finished. Allan Wu went there to eliminate them.

ARA2, Ep.5

The clue directed teams to Tokyo Japan, giving Sawaka/Daichi a hometown edge. It is 8,800km to Tokyo. A 4am start allowed major Bunching, all on the same flight. On arrival in their homeland, Sawaka/Daichi didn't want other teams to follow them. They moved rapidly to minimize that risk, but other teams found their way on their own. The next clue sent teams to Shiba Park at the Zojoji temple in Tokyo. Teams then transferred from rail to taxis which let out all around Shiba Park. Parts of the park were unlit; it's difficult for teams to find the cluebox. In what is essentially a random search, once again Marc/Rovilson got lucky and found it first. Sentiment against Ann/Diane was rising from all other teams. Daichi stated "the Malaysian moms are rude and it seems that everyone hates them". Terri said "Diane is the sneaky evil one. Outside she is sweety sweety but deep inside she's the devil."

Teams next took a rickshaw to the SONY building in Ginza. At SONY Plaza they received SONY handycams (product placement) and instructions to find an individual who can sing the folk song Sakura about cherry blossoms and record that performance, then bring it in for verification. Marc and Rovilson attempted it first, but their singer flubbed some of the lyrics and they had to do it again. Sakawa/Daichi had a hard time finding a singer who did it well but they got the next clue. Pamela/Vanessa had this problem: they

181

recorded a singer one of them had inadvertently hit the RECORD button when receiving the camera and so they turned it off when they thought they were turning it on. Henry also messed up not hitting the RECORD button.

The next task was at Mark Shopping Center to select a young girl matching a photo provided from several in anime costume.

Next was DETOUR You Catch It or You Cart It. In Catch It find the restaurant and scoop 40 goldfish; the "catch" is that you use a traditional rice paper paddle to Catch with before it dissolves. Cart It is find a dry cleaner and get a Japanese kimono to deliver to a local address receiving a token identifying task completion. This was doubly difficult as finding the store and the local address are both challenging if you can't read Japanese. That problem didn't affect Sawaka/Daichi who selected Catch It because Daichi did this as a young boy, but he has lost the touch; they switched to Cart It. Once more Marc/Rovilson had apparently incredible luck by chancing on a newspaper delivery person who leads them to a dry cleaner. However, it wasn't correct so they still had to find the right one. Sawaka/Daichi finished this DETOUR first.

The next task was a difficult ROADBLOCK (unless you are Japanese) "Who is cold and calculating?" The selected individual enters the Ice Bar Tokyo and gets small cubes of ice with English letters displayed they must combine into blocks to spell a Japanese city (which is Fukuoka, the name of the next destination for ARA2). Sawaka blitzed through this. Vanessa was frustrated but finally solves it. Henry was in the same room trying to solve it using an identical set of blocks. He duplicated Vanessa's solution which she neglected to rearrange in her joy at leaving. Henry: "Otherwise I would still be in there."

All teams now went to Shinigawa Train Station for the bullet train to Fukuoka Congress Centre. They had a long wait for the first train at 5am. The train zipped 1,100km in about 3 hours. Given the previous extensive tasks, they expected that the pit stop will be close on arrival. They were almost correct. There's a mad dash to taxis. Allan Wu was on the mat without any greeter. He told teams to Keep Racing.

The next clue was to Hakata Port Ferry terminal in Fukuoka for a 24 hour ferry to Busan, South Korea, a distance of 320 km. The first tasks in Korea were take a taxi to Jongro, find a taekwondo school and break 3 boards. Leaving the ferry terminal, Marc/Rovilson deliberately held all teams up so they can ask directions to Jongro since no taxi driver knows where it is. As Rovilson puts it "we got the first cab and kind of held everyone up while asking for directions" for a while.

Marc/Rovilson and Adrian/Collin arrived first and all four broke their boards with ease. Later karate black belt Daichi was unable to break his boards. Paula/Natasha and Pamela/Vanessa broke the boards with ease. Teams went on to the Jagalchi Market to find the Golden Pig Statue and decide to YIELD another team or not. Then they chose the DETOUR Slither or Deliver. Slither was find the fish market and "fish" out two tokens while an octopus is in the tank. Deliver involved delivering 3 trays of food, one to each of 3 locat-ions but some of the addresses may not have a name. Unless you are squeamish it is clear that Slither was the way to go; it can be completed in a few minutes while Deliver might take a half-hour. Marc/Rovilson expected Adrian/Collin to YIELD them and were glad it didn't happen. When Sawaka/Daichi arrived, they could YIELD Ann/Diane but elected not to. "We would have YIELDed the moms if we knew they were behind us." They could elect Slither, chosen by every other team, but chose Deliver. After reaching their frustration level, they returned and switched to Slither, but lost time going back to Jagalchi market. Henry/Terri arrived and unsuccessfully tried to YIELD Marc/Rovilson, a lost opportunity.

The task was to find Nurimaru APEC House; then the challenge was to find a way in since there are no gates or roads leading to it. Teams improvised and climbed the outside wall. Ann/Diane and Sawaka/Daichi were trying to solve that issue when the former team attempts to hood-wink the latter with "next clue to the airport" to encourage moving in the wrong direction. That didn't happen, but on completion of this task Sawaka/Daichi were in last place.

Teams travelled to Yogousan Park and found the keeper. He handed them a key to try to open any of a set of locks. It took only a few tries for teams to open a lock, so this task may not have accomplished its intended objective. It pales compared to the AR6 Lock ROADBLOCK. The pit stop was Beomeosa Temple. Once again Marc/Rovilson were first. Marc states "We have gone beyond dumb luck. I call it retarded luck." Ann/Diane stayed in front of Sawaka/Daichi, who were eliminated.

ARA2, Ep.7

Release times from the pit stop are:
Marc/Rovilson leave at 1030am
Adrian/Collin
Henry/Terri
Vanessa/Pamela
Paula/Natasha   1047am
Ann/Diane

All day the teams meandered from Busan to Seoul, first by self-drive to Seoil soybean farm in Anseong in Gyeonggi province in southern South Korea. This trip was 80 km. Teams found their next clue at this farm. All teams were slowed down by Korean street signs and some by having the driver on the left side of the car. Marc/Rovilson arrived in first place. In this ROADBLOCK "Who's Bean the Most Patient?" each team must search 1,500 soybean jars for their next clue; one jar holds a bonus of US$50 from (product placement ahead) Standard Chartered Bank. It's obvious that there must be at least 6 clues scattered about. With these "needle-in-a-haystack" luck-based tasks, early arrivals finished fastest with more clues around for them to find than later ones.

Natasha was driving on the highway; at a tollbooth she gently crashed her van into a barrier. This left her tire torn to shreds, so they enticed a policeman to change their tire. All other teams passed them. Pamela/Vanessa arrived at Seoil farm as Marc/Rovilson left with the next clue. It said drive to Woncheon Resort, an amusement park in Suwon, where they looked for a flagged boat and paddle to a buoy to find their next clue. Getting there Marc/Rovilson drove on the shoulder for speed. Adrian/Collin had navigation problems and take a longer route, but eventually got there. Pamela/Vanessa finished and headed out to Suwon. Adrian/

Collin found the clue with the $50 bonus and also left for Suwon. Ann/Diane obtained assistance from a local to be led to the farm. Once arriving, Diane made a mistake and searched inside one of the jars, getting the soybean paste all over her arms. A farm employee set her straight. Henry/Terri were hopelessly lost. There were a lot of negative interpersonal interactions happening in their car. Ann/Diane found a clue, then so did Paula/Natasha. Henry/ Terri finally got close and convinced a local to lead them to the farm.

Adrian/Collin found Woncheon Resort and closed in on the buoy as Marc/Rovilson arrived. Adrian/Collin reached the buoy first, took their clue and headed back to the dock. Marc/Rovilson found the buoy and clue soon. Marc calls Adrian/Collin "The terminators, that's what we call them. No emotion. They just keep coming at us. They are very businesslike. They are a tough team." Terri searched for the clue, Henry had a suggestion, but Terri was very negative. Henry said, "She's gotta do it her f*cking way and that's why we f*cked up." Terri heard him, responding by her version of a Death Stare. He convinced her to get back in the race. Terri found the last clue. He "has to find out where they are so he can tell Terri where to go." It's unclear if this was literal or figurative.

Adrian/Collin made it to Korean Folk Village and opened their clue, a DETOUR with options Too Ho or Too Heavy. In Too Ho, teams toss 3 bamboo sticks into a cylinder from 4.5 meters away. Teams with good aim finish quickly in this traditional Korean game. In Too Heavy, teams deliver 30 logs to a house using a traditional Korean carrying device known as a jigae, which Adrian/Collin chose. Marc/Rovilson arrived and chose Too Ho. Vanessa/Pamela have reached the buoy, get their clue and head back to the dock. The Dancing Moms have reached the amusement park. Ann/Diane found their marked boat and started to paddle. Ann/Diane finished their task and get ready to go to their vans. Pamela/Vanessa reached the dock and left the amusement park 3rd. At Woncheon Resort, the moms finished their task and went to their vans. As they're preparing to leave, Paula/Natasha were arriving.

Adrian/Collin delivered their second batch of logs. Marc/Rovilson finally figured out how to throw the sticks into the small cylinder. They threw 2 of the necessary 3 sticks in the round container. Adrian/Collin stacked the logs for the monitor. Marc threw the final stick into the cylinder; his team is the first to get their clue. Adrian/ Collin got their clue, but they're farther away from their van. Both teams are instructed to drive from Youngin to Seoul and Olympic Peace Park, featured prominently in the 1988 Summer Olympic Games. Vanessa made a mistake on a turn and took them many km out of the way. They had no knowledge of local roads and were fortunate to get back on the best route. With all the navigation/ driving problems, Ann concluded getting from one place to another, particularly by self-driving, was the hardest part, not doing a task. This is not always true but in my Amazing Race experience it is most of the time in non-English speaking countries.

Vanessa's wrong turn took them far out of the way until a toll collector allowed them to do a for-real U-Turn. Paula and Natasha practiced their stick-shift driving, as they are rather pathetic at it. When road signs were not in recognizable characters, it was that much more difficult. Paula/Natasha arrived at the Korean Folk Village and chose Too Ho. But after taking a wrong turn, they reached the Too Heavy task instead. Paula looked over the jigae and correctly surmised how to do it and Natasha said she'll carry the logs on her back. What's really heavy was the traffic around the Seoul area. Adrian/Collin hired a Seoul taxi driver to lead them to Olympic Park. Marc/Rovilson enlisted a local FERN who's a slow driver to take them to the Pit Stop. Ann/Diane finally reached the Folk Village and chose the Too Ho task. Paula/Natasha delivered 30 logs and earned the next clue. Ann/Diane reached Too Ho and threw bamboo sticks at the cylinder but after lack of success they decided to switch tasks.

Marc/Rovilson finished first again, barely ahead of Adrian/Collin. Ann/Diane finished at the Folk Village. Terri/Henry reached the amusement park. It's dark but they eventually reached the next clue at the buoy. At Olympic Park, Pamela/Vanessa finished team #3, Paula/Natasha team #4 and Ann/Diane #5. Henry/Terri finally arrived on the mat in last place, to be spared by a take-all-your-money non-elimination leg.

ARA2, Ep.8

The pit stop release was known for the first and last teams but can be estimated very well for teams 3, 4 and 5:

Marc/Rovilson   748am
Adrian/Collin   807am
Vanessa/Pamela 947am
Paula/Natasha   1004am
Ann/Diane   1026am
Henry/Terri   1207pm, money gone and receiving no start funds

Teams flew from Seoul to Frankfurt, over 8000 km. There are 4 different flight combinations depending on when teams reached Seoul-Inchon Airport. An alliance was formed by Marc/Rovilson, Paula/Natasha and Pamela/Vanessa to YIELD the moms when possible. Arrivals only vary by 1.5 hours from Marc/Rovilson to Adrian/Collin, Ann/Diane and Pamela/Vanessa, with Paula/Natasha in between after booking standby on 3 different flights. Ann attempted to obtain an earlier flight, stating that her aunt was "very sick". That may have been true but that aunt was almost certainly not anywhere near Frankfurt. Her ruse failed. Henry/Terri connected Hong Kong due to arriving Seoul after all non-stop flights were full. They arrived the next morning about 12 hours after Marc/Rovilson. Frankfurt Old Opera House had the next clue, go to Prague, Czech Republic by train and find the famous Charles Bridge over the Vltava River to find a holy or holey statue. Teams had to locate the main train station, the site of major Bunching. During the wait, Marc and Rovilson go slumming in bars in the adjacent area to beg for the money Rovilson earned doing a pole dance. All teams except for Henry/Terri made the 1138pm departure, 412 km to arrive Prague the next morning. Since few international trains leave late night, it looks like their gap, which had compressed while the other teams were waiting for the train, will widen again.

The clue was in a holy or holey statue on the bridge. Ability to find it varied. The next clue was to a puppet shop in the Karlova Street #3 building. This didn't open until 11am, so Hours of Operation and more Bunching occured, making it that much easier for any lagging team to catch up. The ROADLBOCK "Who will rescue a damsel in distress. (And not take all knight!)" was next and sent them to Kinsky Palace in Old Town Square. The selected individual donned knight's armor to go to the Hotel Prince to find a damsel in distress; the non-selected individual had to carry their team backpacks/ possessions. By using a rope with a hook teams first sent a key up to the damsel and received a clue in return. That clue is to Beroun Town Square 30km by train.

Marc/Rovilson, Adrian/Collin and Ann/Diane all got the earliest train (1226pm). Paula/Natasha arrived but waited for a train leaving 40 minutes later. Pamela/Vanessa finally found the holey clue and took the next train to Beroun. Henry/Terri arrived but the holey clue had them stumped. Teams in Beroun had to search for a local with a Nokia N95 mobile phone (product placement) and their picture on it.

The clue directed them to drive to the town of Nizbor for a DETOUR, Blow or Bow. In Blow each team member produced a crystal glass with a clear and thick star-shaped marking for their next clue. In Bow teams used a traditional cross-bow for each shot at a red/yellow target 25 feet away. All teams except Paula/Natasha chose Bow. Marc/Rovilson finished first. Paula/Natasha made 3 incorrect glasses before getting one right each. The clue was drive yourself to Karlstejn Castle, the pit stop. The video showed Henry/Terri now on the train to Beroun.

The order of finish is:
1. Marc/Rovilson—6th straight first-place finish
2. Adrian/Collin—6th straight second-place finish
3. Ann/Diane
4. Pamela/Vanessa
5. Paula/Natasha
6. Henry/Terri – last, 2nd straight non-elimination leg, alive with 30 minute MARKED FOR ELIMINATION penalty, hard to overcome.

Henry remarked to win a team must really possess great fitness and good communications skills. Thinking his team has neither one Henry is quoted saying "If we were to win this, it would be a fluke."

ARA2, Ep.9

Release times from the pit stop were:
Marc/Rovilson	217am
Adrian/Collin	224am
Ann/Diane	240am
Pamela/Vanessa	310am

Paula/Natasha   417am
Henry/Terri   1035am

Marc/Rovilson were released from the pit stop and go to Prague's Petrin Hill. They counted the number of steps to the Observatory. The timing allowed all teams except Pamela/Vanessa and Henry/Terri to catch up. Marc/Rovilson and Paula/Natasha plan to team up if there is an Intersection. There was an Hours of Operation delay until access to the hill opens at 9am. That allowed Pamela/Vanessa to catch up. It also is great for Henry/Terri who have yet to be released. While Marc, Rovilson, Paula and Natasha got to know each other better, Adrian/Collin and Ann/Diane hit the Internet and discovered there are 299 steps at Petrin Hill. It was smart of them to do that research during down time. Marc/Rovilson, Pamela/Vanessa, Adrian/Collin and Ann/Diane all got the correct number although the first 2 actually had to count it. Paula/Natasha were off in space and counted 311, which meant going back to the bottom of the hill and recounting to get 300 (also wrong), so they went back for a 3rd pass and get the right number. Teams took the funicular down and reached Strelecky Island on the Vltava River.

Once there, teams rowed a rowboat 140 degrees east southeast using a compass. Teams found the spot with the next clue, sending them to Prague Castle. Rovilson claimed "I'll do the rowing because my first name is Ro. Rovilson" and was super. The planning Marc/Rovilson did on who to partner up with is wasted with Paula/Natasha making rowing mistakes and slowing. Marc/Rovilson accepted the invitation of Adrian/Collin to partner up for the Intersection found in Prague Castle: "It was just the wise choice, to pair up with the next team that came along." The first task was get to the Ice Hockey Arena in Prague, position themselves from 3 different angles to shoot and score goals against a live goalie. 12 goals, 3 from each participant, must be scored for the clue. I heard no claim that it was an All-Star goalie, so kudos to Michael McKay for honesty. Ann/Diane waited at the Intersection point when Pamela/Vanessa arrived, they decided to team up. That meant when Paula/Natasha arrived it will be many hours for Henry/Terri to join them and those 2 teams will be fight it out for 5th place. With two back-to-back NELs there is not going to be another one. When Paula/Natasha arrived at the Intersection point, Henry/Terri were just released from the pit stop and so have 30km transportation plus

189

2 tasks to complete to reach the intersection point.

The next task was the DETOUR Snap or Roll. In Snap the intersected teams took a photo of each of 3 historic monuments to Josef
Manes statue verification. Roll was to deliver two 50-liter beer kegs
to the Admiral Boatel. Marc/Rovilson/Adrian/Collin did Roll easily.
They were released from the Intersection on delivery of the beer
and went back into competitive mode. Finding taxis proved difficult.

That clue sent them to a ROADBLOCK "Who wants to make a
splash?" at the swimming pool; they changed into swimming gear
and the selected individual (Rovilson, Collin, Vanessa, Ann, Henry
and Natasha are those) climbed to the top of the 10 meter diving
platform and dove off it to get the clue. Rovilson completed it first
and Collin/Adrian next.

Ann/Diane and Pamela/Vanessa did OK on the hockey goal task,
but chose Snap and had serious problems with each of the first two
monuments. They stopped and switched to Roll, completed fast.

Henry/Terri reached the Intersection point and joined with Paula/
Natasha to go to the hockey arena. Vanessa elected to dive but got
a serious cut on her lip. Outside, Vanessa blanks out. Pamela:
"Whether it's bungee jump or the scariest thing we did, it was not so
terrifying as that moment so far in the race." Marc/Rovilson were
first at pit stop Vrtbovska Gardens for a 7th consecutive first place
finish. Adrian/Collin finished soon after, then Ann/Diane and
Pamela/Vanessa. Pamela/Vanessa were 3rd after finding the
correct entrance/ parking area. Ann/Diane were 4th. The race is last
2 teams to avoid elimination.

The final 2 teams scored goals easily and picked Snap. Natasha
had done sightseeing in Prague previously, so finding the 3
monuments went smoothly for them. Then they were released from
the Intersection and both head for the large indoor swimming pool.
Henry was quicker to the top, so Paula/Natasha were forced to wait.
One of the strangest incidents in any Amazing Race is about to
occur. On successful completion Henry received the clue to the pit
stop, but when he and Terri get outside the taxi driver in front was
engaged in an extensive conversation so they went down the road
to find another one. In the interim, Paula/Natasha came out and

Natasha charmed the first driver into taking them. They barely beat Henry/Terri to the pit stop for 5th place and are still in ARA2. Henry/ Terri lose one time too many and are eliminated. Henry says "We've been crushing everybody. It's just little things and bad luck." I disagree. It's consistent inability to complete tasks in a timely fashion. They only crushed themselves.

ARA2, Ep.10

Release times from the pit stop were:
Marc/Rovilson
Adrian/Collin
Ann/Diane
Pamela/Vanessa
Paula/Natasha

On release teams went to Keleti Train Station in Budapest, Hungary for the next clue after a 7 hour, 443km trip. Marc/Rovilson book a nonstop train leaving at 730am. Adrian/Collin researched it, finding a combination to Budapest via Vienna taking one hour longer but arriving 1.5 hours ahead. They booked this 5am train and pray that no other team finds it. Ann/Diane and Pamela/Vanessa do not. Paula/Natasha had only 30 minutes to make the 730am train and make it. Rovilson in a joking manner said they are so far ahead now they are in Season 3 already: "Collin and Adrian have been using a fourth dimension that we haven't been using; and that is the Internet." It isn't rocket science to check train schedules carefully. Shame on the 3 teams that did not!

Adrian/Collin arrived in Budapest; the clue directed them to Batthyany Square. The next clue said to find a marked car and drive it to Magyar Farms 20km in the exurbs. When the other 4 teams arrived, Paula's limited manual transmission skills emerged; Vanessa was in even worse shape, taking precious time to practice. The DETOUR at the farm was Pitch or Pull. In Pitch teams fully loaded a donkey cart with hay and delivered it to the farmer for the clue. In Pull teams picked a goat to milk and extracted 200ml to get their clue. Adrian/Collin did well on this hard labor task and finish immediately. Paula/Natasha did Pitch; Ann/Diane did Pull. Pamela/Vanessa and Marc/Rovilson are lost. Ann/Diane cannot get any milk at all, so they have to switch to Pitch. Paula/Natasha finished and saw Marc/Rovilson just arriving and Pamela/Vanessa arrived soon after. Pamela/Vanessa started Pitch but immediately switched to Pull; after some no-milk periods they finished. Marc/Rovilson did Pitch.

That clue at the farm directed teams to ROADBLOCK "Who wants to really Zoom up in a view?" at Fun Extreme Canopy and its Flying Fox trails of ziplines up high in the trees. The task is complete each of 3 stations and add the 3 numbers to get a total, correct if 1000. Adrian/Collin arrived first; Adrian got 1039. They tried again, got it right and received the next clue. Paula/Natasha arrived and failed with 988. Ann/Diane navigated better than Marc/Rovilson, earning the 3rd opportunity. Diane didn't understand the special requirements of this ROADBLOCK and was practicing manual transmission driving when needed at the start.

Marc/Rovilson moved up and got it right. Next Ann failed and Natasha succeeds on her second try. Pamela arrived but had to redo, so Ann/Diane and Pamela/Vanessa fought for 4th place. Can adding numbers in your head be that difficult? That is roughly a fifth grade skill, taking into account that by memory does make it a little harder. Is that generation so inept at arithmetic they can't do it without a calculator?

Teams went from the Fun Extreme Canopy to the site shown on the Hungarian 1000 forint note, which is at Visegrad Castle. Teams had to team up with a local to find out where that is. Ann intelligently went into a bank to ask them. Adrian/Collin found the Hercules Fountain at Visegrad Castle easily and so does Marc/Rovilson. They are directed to the pit stop at Salamon Tower, with a special parking area and special marked entrance difficult to find in order to check in. In their desire to get to the pit stop, Adrian/Collin used a regular parking area and regular entrance. Allan Wu immediately sent them back to do it right. The second try was right for their first 1st place victory after 7 in a row for Marc/Rovilson. Marc/Rovilson finished second and Pamela/Vanessa tried to do what Adrian/Collin tried with similar zero results. After they went back and found the marked parking area and marked entrance, they were still in 3rd place. Ann/Diane checked in 4th. Paula/Natasha were last, but are saved by a non-elimination leg with the penalty of 30 minutes should they fail to place first in the following leg.

The Marked For Elimination penalty is a great motivator, but the issue is whether the Ep.11 task sequence will be kind to them. The only example I know of first place for a team after one was AR11 in Kuwait where David/Mary were able (with major help from Erwin/Godwin and Hours of Operation delays) to get the FAST FORWARD and a first-place finish.

ARA2, Ep.11

The first clue sent teams to the Little Princess Statue, but it is up to the teams to find it (on the promenade along the Danube River) in Budapest. Adrian/Collin and Marc/Rovilson got help and to that statue simultaneously. The FAST FORWARD Count Fence Posts competition is available if a team wants to go for it. If you have been watching the competition between Marc/Rovilson and Adrian/Collin you know both were going to go for it. The task is to walk across Elizabeth Bridge between Buda and Pest, counting the number of posts on one side of the bridge. Their count is to be entered on a safe at the other side and the correct number will open the safe and reveal directions to the pit stop. Collin and Adrian left markings on the rails in Chinese so no other team can take advantage of them. Rovilson used a belt to measure the number of belt units, each a specific number of posts. Adrian/Collin went for it and put in the wrong number. Marc/Rovilson also got it wrong the first time. Marc/Rovilson counts faster than Adrian/Collin on the second pass. They submitted 2376, not correct. Adrian/Collin submitted 2377 and the safe door opened to give them their clue to the pit stop at Gellert Hill Citadel. Marc/Rovilson may now catch up to the 2 other teams who are doing regular tasks, but Paula/Natasha haven't even been released from the pit stop. Pamela/Vanessa decided to go for the FAST FORWARD, poor judgment based on 2 prior teams doing so. They quickly found the FAST FORWARD taken and went back to the other tasks. Ann/Diane started those tasks ahead of Marc/Rovilson but are behind them by the Buda Castle Labyrinth, with a ROADBLOCK "Who's ready for Raiders of the Lost Clue?" for the selected individual to go down into the labyrinth and search for treasure chests, open any found and evaluate for clues. Pamela says "I don't think I look like Lara Croft, but I feel like it here, especially in my Tomb Raider shorts."

Marc/Rovilson opened many chests; none contained a clue. Paula/ Natasha were fortunate to find a FERN who escorted them right to the Labyrinth. Marc/Rovilson finally found a clue, by taxi to the South Entrance of Margaret's Island near the Pest side of the Danube River. They rode a pedicab and found the home of St. Margaret to win a souvenir and return to the pedicab vendor for their next clue.

The next clue took teams to Heroes' Square, historically significant for Hungarians and site of a major uprising June 16, 1989 marking the end of the Soviet domination of Hungary after 43 years with massive commemorative statues of 14 famous men in Hungarian history. Marc/Rovilson responded to a request from Paula/Natasha to help them stay in the race to avoid last. "Paula and Natasha are going to have a hard time making up the time, but the YIELD may help them." So they YIELDed Ann/Diane, holding them there for about 30 minutes. Next for Marc/Rovilson was a DETOUR, Say It or Play It. Say It required correct pronunciation of all 14 men whose statues are there, using a new tutor for each. You need a minimum of 14 locals to train you. Pronouncing Hungarian is tricky due to many character combinations representing difficult sounds. Play It has teams solve each of 6 sides of a Rubik's Cube, easy compared to solving all sides simultaneously; it should be easy for all teams that elect it. Marc/Rovilson elected Play It. Pamela/Vanessa chose Say It because Vanessa does not know what a Rubik's Cube is. Pamela/Vanessa did well to get the next clue. As Ann/Diane's YIELD expires, they tried Say but switch to Play It.

Marc/Rovilson finished 2nd at the Citadel. Pamela/Vanessa finished 3rd. The only issue remaining is whether Paula/Natasha can slip in ahead of Ann/Diane, but Ann/Diane finished and headed for the pit stop. Paula/Natasha chose Say It and finished in record time. Their luck ran out on reaching the pit stop after Ann/Diane; they were eliminated from ARA2.

ARA2, Ep.12

We are at the penultimate episode of ARA2 and 4 teams go for 3 spots in the finale. Who will not make the Final 3? I think Marc/ Rovilson and Adrian/Collin are reasonably safe due to their superior performance so the third spot is likely to go to either Pamela/Vanessa or Ann/Diane. Pit stop release is 810pm for Adrian/Collin.

The pit stop clue was fly to CapeTown South Africa. Rovilson cannot visually locate either Collin or Adrian, quipping "they are probably setting up a website and chatting with someone in CapeTown already." Ann/Diane, taking a major gamble that all of the other teams can't get the best flights, left early, connected in London to arrive if on time in CapeTown at 750am the next morning. Marc/Rovilson and Pamela/Vanessa got confirmed space on a connection through Frankfurt, arriving CapeTown at 5am. Adrian/Collin had made a strategic error on arrival at Budapest airport trying too hard to optimize and that put them on the waiting list for the Budapest to Frankfurt flight. They succeeded in getting confirmed space in Frankfurt for the same flight to CapeTown that the other 2 teams have.

The 3 teams got taxis to Signal Hill 10 minutes away. The taxi driver for Pamela/Vanessa did not know the way, so they were quickly behind. They found the hill opens at 830am, which theoretically gave Ann/Diane 40 minutes to make it there, but they did not arrive for the opening. Marc/Rovilson got the clue first and discovered they need to get a marked car and drive to the top of Signal Hill to search for their next cluebox. It is now apparent this is a push button/start vehicle and the mechanism for starting it is perhaps not common in Asian countries. Marc/Rovilson started it quickly, it took Pamela/Vanessa a bit longer and Adrian/Collin had to get help from a local. It is foggy and misty on Signal Hill, but teams found a clue to Killarney Motor Racing Circuit.

Marc/Rovilson got a huge break when they pull over to study a map and a FERN who had given them directions on the way up tapped their window to help them with more precise directions to where they now knew to go. Pamela/Vanessa reached the circuit first and selected Vanessa for ROADBLOCK "Who has a need for speed?" The selected individual did 4 laps of the circuit in a racecar in 7 minutes or got a 5 minute penalty; in either case they had to come in for a brief maintenance check, then heads out for the final 4 laps. At about this time Ann/Diane arrived on Signal Hill, got their car and found that they too do not know how to start it. Marc/Rovilson and Adrian/Collin arrived at Killarney at the same time; Marc and Collin suited up and get on the track. Vanessa and Collin incurred 5 minute penalties and Marc got none. However, Vanessa was still ahead starting the last 4 laps. Then Pamela remarked "Someone just realizes she has a heavy foot now." Rovilson added "Now she's showing off." Vanessa finished 1st and drove to Khayelitsha Township, where a Standard Chartered Bank (a big ARA sponsor) has a support vehicle with painting supplies. Then they have to find their way to Inyatyambo Community Project and paint a marked section of a day care center to satisfy the master painter there. Collin again couldn't get his car started as his team and Marc's head for the painting task. Ann/Diane finally got to Killarney but chose Ann for that ROADBLOCK. She does not drive manual shift; Diane does but it is too late. Pamela/Vanessa were lost; Marc/Rovilson were first to arrive at Inyatyambo. Adrian/Collin arrived next, then Pamela/Vanessa. Ann got the 5 minute penalty and then finished the final 4 laps. Marc/Rovilson finished and delivered a $5000 Standard Chartered Bank check to the daycare center. Once completed teams must self-drive to Aquila Game Park Reserve 2 hours north of CapeTown. Adrian/Collin and Pamela/Vanessa finished. What a fabulous move by Standard Chartered Bank and of Active TV led by Michael McKay to put such an uplifting tasks (painting and giving a company's donation) into this episode! Ann/Diane eventually arrived, did their painting, gave their check, and moved on toward Aquila Game Preserve. Vanessa commented on her team's lack of navigation skills: "We're just getting lost this whole trip".

Marc/Rovilson reached Aquila and found the center of the cheetah compound to get their clue. A ranger drove them to the elephant habitat. They received DETOUR options of In One End or Out the Other. In One End is feed elephants 100 kg (that's 220 pounds) of food and wait for them to finish eating it. Out the Other teams must clean out an elephant stall of dung, using the provided tools and taking the dung to a marked area. Marc/Rovilson selected Out the Other because they sense a good fit with their personalities. They found they are limited to one small garden spade, which takes longer than expected. Adrian/Collin arrived and chose Out the Other. Collin claimed to have never seen so much dung in one place. Marc quipped "Oh, you haven't seen us after Nacho Night." They finished and got the clue to go to the Aquila Private Game Reserve, the pit stop. Pamela/Vanessa chose Out the Other also and Pamela predicted that it might involve small tools (extremely perceptive observation). Vanessa responded they will just use their hands. That's how they guaranteed themselves a Final 3 spot.

Marc/Rovilson finished first. Adrian/Collin finished second and Pamela/Vanessa finished third. Ann/Diane also chose Out One End: "We were thinking it was going to smell, but I can tell you, a baby's poop is much smellier" and finished in fourth place, eliminated from the race. They probably realized that their conservative decision to take the safe, longer flying route to CapeTown caused their demise. Arriving 3 hours after the other teams was too much of a handicap to overcome.

ARA2, Ep.13, the Finale

This is it, the final episode of this 50,000+ km race. Teams drove back from Aquila to CapeTown District 6, an area where residents were forcibly removed from their homes under apartheid, to find the District 6 Museum. Teams received a SONY Vaio Notebook (product placement) and unlocked it using a password from one of the original street names in District 6. Marc/Rovilson guessed and quickly succeeded in unlocking their computer. It tells them to go the wall and read one paragraph about the history of the district.

Next is a trip to Victoria and Albert Waterfront where they chose between the DETOUR options Search or Assemble. Search is to go to the Scratch Patch where tens of thousands of gems await and find the 3 marked gems with a red dot. This is a 3-needles-in-a-haystack task. Assemble is to make a radio out of a collection of parts and actually receive something on it. Marc/Rovilson chose Search but the difficulty of a needle-in-haystack search motivates switch to Assemble. Pamela/Vanessa picked Assemble. Adrian/Collin picked Search. Marc/Rovilson were fast putting the radio together and receiving on it in record time.

The next task is to go to the FC Carlstadt soccer field and score three penalty kicks from the penalty line. Marc/Rovilson did not appear to be soccer wizards. Adrian/Collin were soon on their way and then Pamela/Vanessa also with this keen insight from Vanessa "Anything can happen on the road while I'm driving." All team finished and followed the next clue, to Atlantis Dunes to ride an all-Terrain Vehicle aka Quad Bike.

Another luck-based task awaits them. Teams had to find the one container which has the clue; the other 17 have hourglasses which are flipped and the resulting time lost before selecting the next one. It should take an average of 9 tries to complete that so teams are likely to take the average time of an hourglass times 9, which could be minutes or hours. Marc/ Rovilson found a clue and tried hoodwinking Adrian/Collin. They fear that team so much they want them to pass right by the only container with a clue. They stay right there for a long time and do not leave until they think Adrian/Collin are focusing elsewhere. Marc/ Rovilson claimed brilliant acting skills for their part in this play. After Marc/Rovilson left, Adrian/Collin went to that container, opened it and found the next clue. So much for brillliant acting!

It sent them to Cape Point Lighthouse to tell the lighthouse keeper where they think they will travel next. At Cape Point Lighthouse, Marc/Rovilson elected to travel down and Adrian/Collin went up a funicular. Marc/Rovilson reached a dead end and had to turn back. Pamela/Vanessa found the correct container and were on their way.

Adrian/Collin guessed Malaysia and Singapore to get their next clue. Until you are correct you keep guessing but it doesn't take long. The clue sent them to the Raffles Statue near the Asian Civilizations Museum. Marc/Rovilson guessed Singapore; Pamela/Vanessa guessed Singapore. Why bother with this charade? It's a useless task! No purpose was served. Just tell teams where their next desination is!

All 3 teams are on the same 9,700 km flight and are raring to go after landing at Singapore Airport. At the Raffles Statue, Marc/ Rovilson barely beat Adrian/Collin there. The clue directs Final 3 teams to Tanjong Beach on Sentosa Island. Marc/Rovilson asked their taxi to stay and they get off right away. Adrian/Collin neglected to do this and were delayed finding another. Pamela/ Vanessa finally arrived at the Statue. Pamela said "we are going to win as Vanessa is not driving." Pamela/Vanessa also took the precaution of asking their taxi to wait.

ROADBLOCK "Who can flag their worldly knowledge?" awaited, a challenge to stick national flags for each country visited this season into the sand in correct order visited. Rovilson was selected, the result of their pattern of rotating every ROADBLOCK. Marc claimed ability to do a better job: "It's very frustrating to watch this, especially when you know the flags and see your teammate picking the wrong one." That may be so, but there are ROADBLOCK Balance Rules to make sure one member of the team does not have an unfair share. That too might have dictated the choice of Rovilson. Vanessa was selected and she is having trouble too. She said that "I actually forgot the Philippine flag, which is so silly because the boys have it on their bags." Adrian/Collin now arrived and selected Adrian. He apparently was a flags wiz as a result of his mother buying him a flag book when young and he has forgotten little. He just put each correct flag into its rightful place almost instantly and they are done. Rovilson commented: "He was in the middle and chucked the flags into the holes and he was done."

Adrian/Collin received the final clue, which is to the pit stop Chinese Gardens. Allan Wu proclaimed them ARA2 winners after 10 countries, 15 cities and 51,534km. They finished in first place and won the US$100,000 prize. Vanessa finished and Pamela/Vanessa were off to the pit stop and finished second. Rovilson finished and Marc/Rovilson reached the pit stop, checking in third. Rovilson's final comment on this was "I was hoping for an eating challenge. I was hoping to eat the flags." I think that is a good exit line for Marc/Rovilson, not beloved by fans outside of the Philippines. Adrian/Collin earned this with consistently steady performance and taking advantage of the many Bunch points to stay in it until they could find a task where they clearly excelled over Marc/Rovilson. It happened at the best place, just before the Finish. Pamela/Vanessa, a delight to watch, showed their joy at most tasks.

I want to revisit the lack of release time information. Titles are superfluous but not quantitative performance information. Shame on Michael McKay for dropping them!

AMAZING RACE ASIA 3

The teams competing for the prize for this season are:

Pailin and Natalie, former beauty queens, age 25 and 26
Neena and Amit, cousins, actress/model and real estate consultant,
age 24 and 27
Mai and Oliver, best friends, actress/model and model/student, age
24 and 26
Vince and Sam, friends, comedian + university lecturer, age 32/32
Faeza(Fuzzie) and AD, friends for 15 years, writer + teacher, age
34 and 34
Geoff and Tisha, dating couple, model and Business Development
Manager, age 26 and 32
Niroo and Kapil, father and son, actor + HR executive, age 53/25
Bernie and Henry, sister and brother, actress/TV host and chef, age
39 and 43
William and Issac, brothers, sports TV host and sports agent, age
26 and 29
Ida and Tania, friends, actress/director/producer and real estate
investor, age 44 and 36
This cast has many well-known Asian celebrities.

ARA3, EP1

Teams assembled at the Rama I Monument in Bangkok to start this
race for a $100,000 US prize. Allan told them there are 11 legs and
7 elimination points. What he does not say is that, allowing for a
finale, there will be 3 Non-Elimination Legs (NELs) or To Be
ContinuedLegs (TBCs). The first task at Khao San Road is titled
"Never Race on an Empty Stomach" with both team members
eating a local delicacy, which means fried bugs, maggots, frogs and
scorpions. Yummy! Michael McKay wanted to give teams a shock
they would never forget to start this race with a nasty eating
challenge and set the tone of grueling legs. Fuzzie tries to set her
tone for the race: "When you're lazy you're a lot better at finding
ways of getting things done quicker, because you're finding the
quickest way." Natalie's approach is "Who says beauty queens
can't eat bugs?" This is the Michael McKay way!

The next task is travel to another province to a Caltex station (product placement) to clean a vehicle. It turns out that this was a 22 passenger bus. This sends another shockwave through the teams. Michael McKay promised it would be the toughest race ever and it is clear that he is not joking about that. Ida stated that she never has to clean her own room; her mother does it for her (she is an actress and away a lot). The difficulty is underscored when it starts to rain long before the cleaning is completed. William on the first 2 tasks: "I didn't expect a walk in the park, but a bowl of insects and a 2-story bus?" Teams completed bus cleaning, signing up for 1 of 3 buses to Wat Phai Rong Wua. The first bus has Bernie/Henry, Neena/Amit and Pailin/Natalie. The second has Mai/Oliver, Geoff/Tisha and Ida/Tania. The third bus has the other 4 teams. Clues are placed randomly on hundreds of statues and it's quite dark. On arrival, a bus has 20 minutes before it departs for Chiang Mai bus terminal. The close arrival of the second bus after the first gives teams lucky at finding a clue the opportunity to leave 20 minutes later. If teams haven't finished the task, they must wait for the final bus. This has the net effect of making it hard to get anything other than the third bus, which waits until the last team is done before it leaves. Mai/Oliver and Geoff/Tisha get the first bus. Only Bernie/Henry made the second bus. That means 7 teams are on the third bus going to Chiang Mai bus terminal. All buses take about 8 hours, not counting the original bus trip to Wat Phai Rong Wua.

Chiang Mai DETOUR was Rice or Race. In Rice teams pound rice to make 2 rice balls using traditional methods based on sweat equity. In Race at X-Centre teams drove an off-road buggy on a 8km dirt track. Completion brought teams a clue to the pit stop Ratchaphruek Garden World.

Going to the pit stop, Mai/Oliver and Geoff/Tisha shared a cab. Since they will finish at the same time, they determined in advance by a game of chance which team will get the higher placement. It is Mai/Oliver that won and those two teams finish first and second, appropriate for making the first bus. Mai/Oliver received a cash prize of $5000 US. Tisha says are entitled to it. Vince/Sam neglected to pay their taxi driver and have to go back to do that before they can check in. Order of finish is:
1. Mai/Oliver
2. Geoff/Tisha
3. Bernie/Henry

4. Pailin/Natalie
5. Ida/Tania
6. William/Issac
7. Vince/Sam
8. Fuzzie/AD
9. Niroo/Kapil
10. Neena/Amit-eliminated, surprising because first legs traditionally NEL, but ARA3 wants to break new ground; I welcome innovation.

ARA3, Ep.2

Mai and Oliver released from the Chiang Mai pit stop at 1035pm. The clue sent them to Flight of the Gibbon Adventure Park where they will take a jungle heights course of zip lines and parallel drops to fly in the treetops 50 meters above the jungle. They had bitter arguments during the pit stop, presumably over racing strategy and tactics, particularly about Oliver's concerns of Mai's too-relaxed attitude toward racing. Mai and Oliver know the opening hour won't be until after daylight, so they relaxed and chilled without proceeding to the park. Geoff/Tisha and Bernie/Henry did not dally and went straight to the park entrance. There finding the park opens at 930am and also uses a "pick-a-number" system they draw #1 and #2. With ziplines one thing that is certain is that time is spent to make sure a team is clear before the next team can go. This will result in lagging teams delayed awaiting their turn. Mai and Oliver were well-rested but #9 as the last arrival.

Next was a banana plantation where the ROADBLOCK "Who's Steady on a Fire?" awaits. Geoff/Tisha arrived first and Geoff was the selected individual who must search a fenced area for a backpack with the next clue while subject to hidden sniper fire that will use 329 km/hr paint-balls. Anyone hit by a paintball had to go back and do it again. Although starting the prior task last, Mai/Oliver were second at the ROADBLOCK. Progress was slow. Tania finished first, crawling the entire way. Fuzzie's good eyesight and avoidance skills took second.

The clue directed teams to Ho Chi Minh City (formerly Saigon), Vietnam where they find their next clue at the Saigon Opera House. Flights were mostly full, so this severely limits flight possibilities for teams. There were two basic routes, one connecting in Siem Reap, the other connecting in Bangkok. Ida/Tania were the only team successful at getting a mid-afternoon flight. 5 teams booked the Siem Reap connection and reached Ho Chi Minh City that night. The other teams, William/Issac, Pailin/Natalie and Oliver/Mai, reached Bangkok that night but must wait for the first connecting flight in the morning. That put them a half-day behind the first 6 teams so 1 of these 3 teams will be last. Natalie threw a prima donna fit, uncomfortable with Pailin's decision to save money by sleeping in the Bangkok airport even though this was what the other 2 teams are doing. Pailin behaved with great restraint, as she was stuck with a partner uninterested in giving her all: "I just don't think anyone would die by sleeping at the airport. I mean I slept at the same airport." What race did Natalie think she was on? Has she never seen an Amazing Race before she went on this one? Did Natalie think this race was for prima donnas who wanted to be coddled? And where are Dustin and Kandice of AR10/AR11 fame when you need a team of beauty queens? The task in Ho Chi Minh City was go to Saigon Pho Café for gamers and play the Nokia racing game System Rush to receive the next clue. Next was to go to Binh Tanh Market and a specific flower store. Fuzzie/AD arrived at Saigon Pho an hour after the other 4 teams on their flight, but made up some time by winning the game rapidly. Vince/Sam reached the Binh Tanh Market and saw a sign identifying 7am as its opening hour. However, Fuzzie/AD are sharper and, at the actual flower shop, found it opens at 6am. Some teams arrived at its opening and others about an hour later (but not the 3 who haven't yet left Bangkok).

The next task was a bus to the Cai Be bus terminal, 2 hours from Ho Chi Minh City. In Cai Be they found a DETOUR Sampan or Some Walk. Sampan is choosing a boat, loading it with fruit and delivering it to a trader upriver. Paddling upstream against the current is difficult. Some Walk is to catch 20 live chickens, put them in a cage and deliver them on foot to a specific individual in a Vietnamese market. Navigating the market was confusing and difficult for anyone not speaking Vietnamese (which none of the racers do). Ida/Tania and Geoff/Tisha attempted to row but give up and switched. Catching chickens proves to be tricky and the walk to the market is draining, but the big problem is finding the right market stall. Bernie/Henry succeeded first. There is an altercation for Ida/Tania and Geoff/Tisha. Ida/Tania had put a basket of chickens down and Geoff took them. Ida insisted they be returned, as she selected young small chickens deliberately to ease the burden of the walk. Geoff did not win friends and influence people generally with his sharp personality or by blowing his high-pitched taxi whistle in the market. Kapil said "We are very happy with the way we are working as a team because we are not complicating things by strategizing." Natalie said "I only do things if it makes sense, or if there is a reason to do things." Allan Wu should tell her there are 50,000 reasons!

There was a brief interlude to check on teams just arriving at Saigon airport. Natalie was bummed up both by having to sleep poorly at Bangkok airport and by the lack of cleanliness on the race. Natalie: "We are treated as subhuman." Pailin responds "I knew what I had signed up for." Teams finishing the market took the bus back to Ho Chi Minh City and went to the Hanh Nu Jeanne D'arc Van Lang Church for a clue. Next they randomly picked a representative of various Ho Chi Minh City area charities. Each team received $500US to fulfill the needs expressed on that charity's needs list. Some need electronics, some furniture, some art supplies, some groceries and some musical instruments. Teams spend the $500 all on the needed things. One charity wants only money, making the task trivial for Pailin/Natalie who chose them. Completion gets a clue to Saigon Post Office, where they receive a clue to the pit stop at the Museum of Vietnamese History.

Bernie/Henry finished first at the charities task. The final 3 teams arrived at the chicken DETOUR and caught them in the dark. Wiliam/Issac noticeably lack energy and fall behind. It stayed that way all the way to the pit stop. William/Issac were eliminated.

ARA3. Ep.3

The clue was to Hue, an unstated 1000 km by bus. The trip was 25 hours; teams except Kapil/Naroo learn that at the bus company ticket office. Bernie/Henry and Kapil/Niroo got the 1st bus. Vince/Sam, Geoff/Tisha and Fuzzie/AD got the 2nd bus. Pailin/Natalie and Mai/Oliver made the 4th bus, so Ida/Tania must be on the 3rd bus. Buses leapfrogged as 2 of them have flat tires and bus #1 is passed. The bus line probably had specific instructions from

Michael McKay, as bus #1 easily regained its lead without any response from the driver of bus #2. Natalie continues griping, causing Geoff to ridicule her: "This is so not top model." Natalie was at her limit and considering withdrawal: "I did underestimate the part of the race. Being dirty is worse than anything in the world." The clue in Hue was to a specific service station not open until 930am; most of the teams were Bunched there. The task was grubby, change a tire and engine oil on a marked jeep. Fuzzie: "We changed the oil and, trust me, we are never doing it again".

Teams finished and got a driver for that jeep to Quai Dinh tomb. However, the catch was that the team must provide the navigation instructions. There was a ROADBLOCK "Who's In Line for King's Ransom?", to find the tomb of Ming Mang, get 7 coins representing the 7 emperors of the Nguyen Dynasty, return to the Quai Dinh tomb, then place those coins into correct order based on the reign of each emperor. Vince hoped "It'll be like Indiana Jones." Some selected individuals were careful to jot down information available about each coin and others just blew through it. Teams that aren't correct have to return to the tomb to find the needed information, on the jeep over and back. Henry, a careful note-taker, finished first. He gives his coins to Sam and tells him to share it with Ida. Natalie, doing poorly all race, suffered a breakdown due to heat exhaustion.

Next was DETOUR Sticks or Stalks. Teams in Sticks made 10 incense sticks using incense paste and materials. In Stalks, teams thrashed rice stalks to collect 2 baskets full of rice grains.   Bernie/ Henry chose sticks and, after learning how not to do it from trial-and-error, eventually finished 10 sticks. Most teams chose Stalks.

Teams must head to Quoc Hoc Park and find a cycle rickshaw or cyclo that one must push with the other as passenger. In AR3, Ep.11 cyclo was the means of transportation to a ferry and from it to a local café. Teams arriving in Quoc Hoc are looking for a traditional cluebox, but this task doesn't have that. Teams found the clue on the seat of the cyclo. Brakes exist, but since they are under the peddler's seat only a few teams figure that out. Without brakes they were at the mercy of the maneuvering of local traffic. In this time frame Natalie, totally unsuccessful at getting the coins in the right order, finally gave up and took the 4 hour non-completion penalty. It doesn't matter much as they're so behind the chances of catching up before the penalty application are about 0. The cyclo was team transportation to Hue Citadel, the pit stop. Some teams have difficulty with the cyclos. Henry swerved a little bit left when he made contact with a car there, fell, the cyclo tipped and Bernie spilled on the road. Despite that and their many problems with jeep breakdowns all day long, Bernie and Henry finished in first place.

Order of finish is:
Bernie/Henry
Sam/Vince
Ida/Tania
Fuzzie/AD
Tisha/Geoff
Oliver/Mai
Kapil/Niroo
Pailin/Natalie, last and eliminated; Pailin: "I felt a bit let down because she told me she didn't want to race anymore, which is heartbreak for me. I really want to do it and it takes 2."

ARA3, Ep.4

All teams traveled back to Ho Chi Minh City, by plane to get a connecting flight to Taipei Taiwan 3,000km away. Vince/Sam had an advantage there because they speak Mandarin. On arrival they found marked cars at the airport and self-drove to Xi Men Ding for their next clue. Navigation referencing street signs in Chinese characters was difficult. The destination was a clue box, which gives further directions for the DETOUR Shoot It or Shape It. In Shoot It, teams go to the Miniatures Museum and must find a small item they will recognize when they see it, take a picture of it, print it at a special station and then the next clue will be on the back side. In Shape It, teams go to Rao He street market, search for a specific stall and do a Chinese tangram set that has 7 pieces to create 4 specific shapes. The pieces can be used in 2 horizontal ways by rotating it 180 degrees. Two teams had serious trouble reaching the DETOUR locations. Fuzzie/AD were in the area late and the Miniatures Museum was closed; they have no real choice but to do the puzzle. Kapil/Niroo were clueless about how to deal with the ignition key being stuck. Mai/Oliver found the clue first, a miniature Amazing Race logo. They cheated on an alliance with Sam/Vince. Vince was the next to find it on his own and his expressed joy brings every other team there to where he is. All took their photos and were on their way. Kapil/Naroo arrived while the others left.

The next clue, written in Braille, was to the Institute for the Blind. A blindfolded team member relays information about each character to the other, who has a Braille chart and decodes the message. One clue contains a $20,000 check to Institute for the Blind; Sam/Vince got that. Mai/Oliver were the first team to reach the Institute and first to solve the puzzle: "Go to Sheng Keng", which forces teams to a small town in southern Taipei County I find to be correctly spelled "Shen Keng".

In Shen Keng was a ROADBLOCK to eat a bowl of stinky tofu, consisting of duck blood, fermented tofu and vegetables. Information about stinky tofu varies, but most people except for Taiwan natives say that it is pretty noxious stuff. Serious puking by any individual can and does impact on the others eating stinky tofu. Ear muffs should be standard equipment for Amazing Race eating challenges. Ida said "I love tofu but this is the most horrible tofu I've ever had. Sorry Taiwan."

Finishing, teams got the final clue to City Hall Square in Taipei. Ida/Tania arranged a police escort and finished first. Finish order was:
Ida/Tania
Sam/Vince
Mai/Oliver
Ida/Tania
Bernie/Henry
AD/Fuzzie
Geoff/Tisha
Kapil/Naroo

Kapil/Naroo got to the restaurant last. Kapil knew he can't eat stinky tofu and immediately took the 4 hour penalty. It was moot as they were last with or without the penalty. Kapil/Niroo were eliminated.

ARA3, Ep.5

Releases from the pit stop were at:
Ida/Tania   200pm

Sam/Vince   217pm
Mai/Oliver   253pm
Bernie/Henry 255pm
AD/Fuzzie   256pm
Geoff/Tisha   354pm

The first clue sent teams from one point in Taipei to the New Sogo Department Store's SONY Style Store. Teams found a task to use their own Blu-Ray disc player to try out any of 1000 Blu-Ray discs. I believe that only 6 of them had the message "You are correct." earning the team the next clue. The others had the message "Sorry, try again." This was a test of organization skills but mostly a luck-based task. Early arrivals had a mathematically higher chance.

Vince/Sam were the lucky team to get the first CORRECT. That gave them the next clue plus first shot at a FAST FORWARD. This one creates serious debate: to do or not to do. A team attempting the FAST FORWARD must find the tattoo parlor. Each team member is required to get a small "FF" tattoo on their body. Vince/Sam decided to go for it to obtain the advantage of the FAST FORWARD. It's quick and they are on their way to the Taiwan Astronomical Museum, the pit stop.

Geoff/Tisha were the last team to arrive at the Blu-Ray task and they found Ida/Tania and Mai/Oliver still there. Geoff taught Tisha his system for determining whether a disc has already been seen (in which case it is definitely of the "Sorry, try again" variety); this was to examine it for fingerprints and avoid it there are any. Ida/Tania and Geoff/Tisha finished, leaving Mai/Oliver there with a diminished probability of finding one of the remaining discs. They were still there as the store closes at 8pm and were given the clue despite not having finished there. They took a taxi but, when it breaks down, they decided to spend the night in it, hoping for non-elimination to stay in the race.

Next was drive to the Coal Mine Museum at Pingshi and do ROADBLOCK "Can you dig it?" The selected individual must find a small silver AXN token in a large cart full of small coal pieces. A shovel assists them as well as a second empty cart to shovel the coal into. You know that they will place the target close to the bottom, so it was hard work to remove many cubic yards of coal. I am going to take a rough guess of 6 feet long, 4 feet side, and 5 feet high to the top of the coal pile. That would mean 120 cubic feet as the approximate volume of its contents. That's a lot of coal to move. Although this appeared to be a luck-based task, it really isn't. Only sweat equity finds the silver token in a reasonable length of time, near the bottom.

Next was driving to a DETOUR back in Taipei of Pick or Pail. In Pick teams operated an arcade game machine claw crane to retrieve 3 soft toys in a specific mall. In Pail teams filled a wooden bucket and carried it up many steps at the Grand Tong Temple to deliver it to a monk who measured the remaining volume of water. Finishing either DETOUR option teams went to Tawian Astronomical Museum for the pit stop.

The finish order for this episode is:
Vince/Sam—due to the FAST FORWARD
Bernie/Henry
Fuzzie/AD
Geoff/Tisha
Ida/Tania
Mai/Oliver, who are eliminated

ARA3, Ep.6

Release times from the pit stop were:
Vince/Sam   611am
Bernie/Henry   1007am
Fuzzie/AD   1008am
Geoff/Tisha   1109am
Ida/Tania around 130pm

What was important is not the release time of teams but their flight schedules from Taipei 800km to Hong Kong. Vince/Sam were "ready to rock and roll" with their hometown advantage. There are 3 flights each hour throughout the day, so that should not delay them more than half an hour above the minimum time. Here were the flight departures:

Vince/Sam   1035am

Bernie/Henry   1230pm
Fuzzie/AD   115pm
Geoff/Tisha   115pm
Ida/Tania around 330pm

The clue has teams arriving Hong Kong go to King's Park Sports Ground, home of the Standard Chartered Rugby Football team, to see which teams are intimidated to run/jog/walk through the team as it was practicing. Team task times had to be quite similar as it looked like no more than 5 minutes to complete. Geoff observed "all the other teams are grouping and we're definitely not a team they want to group with" and the cool kids don't need a group anyway.

The earned clue led them from Kowloon to Hong Kong Island to Central, corner of Hollywood Road and Peel St. Next is ROADBLOCK "Get Fishy or Get Lucky". Get Fishy was to clean and gut 15 large fish at a nearby Gong Kei seafood market. Get Lucky was a classic luck-based DETOUR at Mee Lun St. to open by biting as many of 300 fortune cookies needed to find the next clue. The jar opening was narrow and teams work at a small circular table so no teams apparently turned the bowl upside down and started from what is now the top due to space constraints (or maybe unstated restrictions in the clue). That's what I would have done, as I expect that the winning cookie would be low in the initial pile and therefore relatively high in the inverted pile. Henry is a chef and Bernie knows how to clean fish, so their choice was obvious; they were the one team doing Get Fishy. Vince/Sam found the correct cookie with only 10 left; its fortune read "You're very lucky. You eat well and now you will get your next race clue." Geoff/Tisha arrived after Fuzzie/AD but were lucky and they finished before Bernie/Henry could complete scaling/gutting and before Fuzzie/AD finished.

The next clue directed teams to take a taxi to Central Pier and the Star Ferry to Tsim Tsat Tsui and take a taxi from there to the Ladies Market at Tung Choi St. in Kowloon. Fuzzie commented "If you are a taxi driver in Kowloon, you don't know what is happening Hong Kong side." This ROADBLOCK "Who's got any eye for the ladies?" required good eye-sight to choose a ladies bag from a rack and find a woman in the Market with the exact same bag. This was another random task involving a small amount of skill. Sam does OK and finished before any other team gets there. They continued to the pit stop at Blake Pier in Stanley Bay.

All 3 teams were able to make the same Star Ferry, roughly 15 minutes apart, to get to the Ladies Market. Bernie/Henry sent Bernie through the Ladies Market task and she finishes before Tisha and AD. Bernie kept the bag, which she was not required to return due probably to the time consumed in that big market. They finished 2nd, Geoff/Tisha got third and Fuzzie/AD were 4th. Nobody had seen Ida/Tania all day. They stroll through their tasks and eventually finish. Ida said of Tania's shopping proclivities "If we had Tania in the streets of cloth and bag, we would never see her again." Their belief in a non-elimination leg was honored by it being a NEL; they lost all their money but in ARA3.

ARA3, Ep.7

Release times from the pit stop were:
Sam/Vince   547am
Bernie/Henry 653am
Geoff/Tisha   712am
Fuzzie/AD   724am
Ida/Tania   957am

This episode opened with Bunching, as teams went to Mong Kok to deliver 4 goldfish. The catch is the aquarium they deliver to didn't open until 11am. Ida/Tania got a late start due to a last-place finish and supplement HK$300 three other teams left them by begging.

The clue at the aquarium says travel to Macau on the ferry, then to the fountain in Senado Square to find the next clue. Vince/Sam were locals and knew that traveling to the ferry on foot is quicker than in a cab at that time of day and are 15 minutes ahead. Geoff/Tisha made what seems like a small improvement by getting 2 other passengers to trade tickets for the 1130am ferry for the 1135am ferry tickets Geoff/Tisha hold. The next instruction is look for a clue at Macau Tower. A YIELD was coming up and it could change the destinies of teams affected.

Next is ROADBLOCK "Who wants to climb the ladder of success?" to climb the mast of Macau Tower, 338 meters high. You get to the

61st floor in an elevator, but have to climb from the 61st to 77th floors inside, then outside. Strategy associated with use of YIELDs comes up as Vince and Sam had differing views of whether to go for this one. Vince was adamant to not use it at this time (if used, eliminating the possibility of any later yields). Geoff/Tisha come next and YIELD Bernie/Henry, who have to hold for maybe 30 minutes but don't really lose their #3 position with Bernie climbing against Fuzzie. On discovery of being YIELDed, Henry's ackowledgement to Geoff is "Scum!" Weather conditions deteriorated and Fuzzie had a difficult time both up and down the Tower. By the time Ida/Tania arrived, they discovered Geoff/Tisha left HK$70 for them, but those weather conditions are so nasty that all tower climbing is suspended minutes later. Ida/Tania were given their next clue without really earning it. I expected Michael McKay to assess an equalization penalty based on the slowest time for any other team climbing up and down, but that was not done.

Next was Dragon Boat Pier of Sai Van Lake for a dragon boat paddle around the buoys of a course. Vince/Sam were barely ahead of Geoff/Tisha here. Teams went to the pier for the DETOUR Dance or Chance. In Dance teams learn/demonstrate a perfect lion dance routine. Geoff/Tisha were the only Dance team and finished quickly and ahead. In Chance, teams changed to formal attire, played blackjack and must beat the dealer 9 times. That means playing an average 19 hands given equal skill, and since it isn't, a few more. Vince/Sam chose Chance. Bernie/Henry finished at Macau Tower and headed for the DETOUR. AD says "this is the first time I have worn a dress since I was 8."

The next clue was for a task in front of the pit stop, which was at A-Ma Cultural Village in the Coloane section of Macau. It relies on knowledge of the Chinese Zodiac or ability to use clues to assist them in putting the 12 animals of the Chinese Zodiac in correct order as displayed on 12 lanterns. Geoff/Tisha made some wrong tries before Vince/Sam arrived, but then got it right. That opened the huge door to the cultural center. Vince/Sam finished soon thereafter. Bernie/Henry finished Chance and had taxi troubles, so Fuzzie/AD beat them to A-Ma. AD knew the Chinese Zodiac enabling no delay in getting in. Bernie/Henry finally arrived. Ida/Tania arrived later and found it is another non-elimination leg. They expected to lose their money but Allan Wu has a surprise for them.

They are MARKED FOR ELIMINATION, a 30 minute penalty if they fail to finish first in the next leg. Replacing lost funds is typically easy in most Amazing Races, but most teams have been eliminated by being MARKED FOR ELIMINATION. Finish order was:

Geoff/Tisha -who got a huge return from their ferry ticket swap and
    maybe a smaller one for yielding Bernie/Henry
Vince/Sam
Fuzzie/AD
Bernie/Henry
Ida/Tania - last but non-eliminated, MARKED FOR ELIMINATION

ARA3, Ep.8

The first clue sends teams to the ruins of St. Paul's Church. There they got a clue returning to Macau Tower. Since its opening hour is 8am (I believe just for ARA3; it's normally later), the first 4 teams Bunch at its base. Awaiting them was a ROADLBOCK "Who wants a bird's eye view?" for the selected team member to jump off the Tower in a controlled fall of 233 meters. Tisha went first and she won a special prize, a helicopter ride from Macau to Hong Kong courtesy of Caltex. Tisha states "It was like having a FAST FORWARD. It zoomed us ahead." This has to be considered a partial FAST FORWARD, excepting a few tasks in Hong Kong and in Cochin. This departure around 0813 on the helicopter saves them more than 1 hour over other teams who take the ferry and a taxi. The helicopter takes Geoff/Tisha directly to next task at MASKargo Warehouse back in Hong Kong. Teams searched for a package with their name on it, opened it and read it. This is a classic random task. The clue they received directs them to a temple near Cochin India. Tania at the ROADBLOCK says "I've been saving my bungee jump for the right moment in life." Vince/Sam departed Macau on the 900am ferry, Bernie/Henry and Fuzzie/AD on the 930am ferry. Ida/Tania get a 1030am ferry.

The critical factor now becomes which flight combination teams booked and made. Geoff/Tisha finished at MASkargo and rush to the airport. There they see their options and the best is clearly nonstop to Singapore, connecting with a late afternoon nonstop flight to Cochin. They try for tickets for that combination and are on their way to Singapore and Cochin, 7000 km away on the most direct and quickest route. Vince/Sam were next to reach the airport but they were too late for that flight combination (note the value of Geoff/Tisha doing Dance, placing first and getting the unexpected bonus of the helicopter ride). They book the next flight to Singapore connecting to flight to Mumbai and there connecting to a flight to Cochin that arrives around 3am. Fuzzie/AD were able to book a Hong Kong to Mumbai flight, connecting there to the same flight to Cochin as Vince/Sam. Bernie/Henry arrived, bump into Vince/Sam and end up on the same flight combination. Ida/Tania by unknown means got the same flight combination as Fuzzie/AD.

So the issue now is will flights be on-time. Geoff/Tisha experienced no problems and arrived on schedule. The Singapore flight that Vince/Sam and Bernie/Henry are on arrives in Mumbai late and the transfer from international to domestic terminals goes badly. Both teams miss the last flight to Cochin. Fuzzie/AD and Ida/Tania arrived earlier in Mumbai and made that flight to Cochin. That leaves the two stranded teams to sleep in Mumbai airport and not arrive at Cochin until 7am the next morning. Unless there are absurd hours of operation in Cochin one of those teams will be eliminated due to reaching the pit stop last.

Geoff/Tisha were well-rested on arrival at Neelam Kumangara Devi temple. Fuzzie/AD and Ida/Tania arrived well before its opening hours of 6am so there is a mini-Bunch there. Teams were blessed and the clue sends them to Kumbalam for elephant washing. Each team washed one elephant with a dry coconut shell to the satisfaction of its mahout (driver). Taxi drivers had problems finding the site except Ida/Tania's taxi driver, who gets them first place. Fuzzie: "You've got to be kidding me. I am not touching an elephant." However, she has no choice.

Teams are now directed back to Cochin where they have a DETOUR Fish or Fill. In Fish they need to carry six 20kg fish for about 1/3 mile to a seafood restaurant. In Fill they fill an intricate geometric design on the floor using matching colored rice powder for each segment. Vince/Sam and Bernie/Henry arrive and try to make up some lost ground. As the first 3 teams finish in the order Geoff/Tisha, Ida/Tania and Fuzzie/AD, Ida/Tania has to wait the 30 minute penalty so Fuzzie/AD are actually checked in in second place. Vince/Sam with a 2 minute lead pick Fish and Bernie/Henry pick Fill. Henry was averse to physical tasks through this race, but this was not a ROADBLOCK so both team members had to contribute; he wanted to be artistic so they went with Fill. It proved to be their undoing, as Vince/Sam were more effective than they were. The pit stop was at Bolgatty Palace on an island in Cochin's harbor. Vince/Sam took 4th. Bernie/Henry were eliminated.

ARA3, Ep.9

The clue sends teams to Pune, 120km south and east of Mumbai. Teams determine that they need to fly 1,000km to Mumbai and get a taxi from Mumbai airport to Pune's local cricket stadium to find the next clue. It's the usual Bunching at Cochin airport. All teams take the same flight to Mumbai. Ida/Tania use a cab by the road while the other 3 teams use a taxi service, but that delays them while the drivers get the cars out of the Mumbai airport car park. On reaching Pune some taxis find their drivers have no local knowledge; one accepts that and the other two switch to a local Pune taxi. Ida/Tania were first to the Nehru cricket stadium. They have to bat against a local cricket team up to 36 swings and hit the cricket ball against a specific wide fence. Teams that fail to do so receive a 10 minute penalty. They are unable to hit to the fence and get the penalty. Geoff/Tisha were the next to arrive but they end up with the 10 minute penalty. Geoff makes a sage comment "We played a dismal game of cricket, because I don't play cricket." Vince/Sam arrives and Vince powers one into the fence. Fuzzie/AD arrived and Fuzzie got lucky and hit the fence.

The next clue uses a Nokia N6120 Navigator to give their auto rickshaw driver directions to the next clue. It takes them to a palace fort park where 50 men walk on different carefully planned routes and under phetas (hats under which for 4 of them is the statement "Correct"). This is your typical luck-based ROADBLOCK "Who has better pheta?" Ida has trouble remembering the men already checked, but she keeps at it and finally succeeds. Vince is second to find one. Fuzzie/AD were next to finish, then finally Geoff/Tisha. The probability of success per try dropped from 8% for the first team to 2% for the last.

The next clue was to SONY World for a SONY Handycam (product place-ment) for videotaping a funny joke told by any local a team selects. Judges determine if a joke was funny enough; if not, you find another local. Ida/Tania got a local whose joke is judged not funny enough. They film another person whose joke they don't think is funny enough, but the judges think it is. Vince/Sam found a person whose joke is good enough to earn their clue on the first try. Fuzzie/AD had 2 unsuitable attempts, but on their 3rd they got a joke the judges found appropriate. Fuzzie says "We found this lady and instantly, I knew she could tell a joke. She had a face." Geoff/Tisha needed another attempt.

Next was a DETOUR Push or Crush. In Push teams must travel to a pottery shop, load 75 pieces of pottery on a cart and deliver them by pushing the cart on foot 1 km, breaking no more than 5. In Crush they must take sugar cane stalks and feed them into a press making 40 glasses of sugar cane juice. That juice is then sold for a total of at least 200 rupees to get the clue, given its price of 5 rupees a glass. Vince/Sam made a batch that turned out to be short of 40 glasses volume. Sam says "I think sales and public relations are a field I can enter. Charm can sell anything." Geoff/Tisha and Fuzzie/AD finished their sales simultaneously. Which team will be quicker to the finish?

The next task was the U-Turn preceding the next clue. Any team U-Turned will have to do the other DETOUR option, probably taking about 30 minutes including transportation. Vince/Sam arrived first and chose not to YIELD any other team. They got a clue to the pit stop at the Gokhale Institute. Ida/Tania were next and they wanted to YIELD Geoff/Tisha but have lost the picture of themselves that is an integral part of the YIELD process. Without it, they cannot exercise the YIELD. By getting to the U-Turn point quicker, Geoff/Tisha YIELD Fuzzie/AD to solidify their hold on 3rd place. Geoff/Tisha reached the pit stop next. Fuzzie/AD were delayed by about 30 minutes doing the other DETOUR and they get to the pit stop that much later. They would normally be eliminated but it is their lucky day. This was the last Non-Elimination Leg (NEL), so they got the 30 minute Marked for Elimination penalty.

ARA3, Ep.10

Teams were released to find Bhaja Caves. 815am opening hour meant teams had hours to wait, so they get a room for that period. Teams finished Bhaja Caves quickly as it's a "Go to" clue, take a train back to the center of Cochin. Ida commented on train travel "there's that madness of India that you can only find in India." Teams must carefully view the Mahatma Gandhi statue in front of the train station and then find the Standard Chartered Bank (product placement) building.

Fuzzie/AD inadvertently had their taxi driver bypass the statue and go directly to the bank. The PIN number needed is the year of Mahatma Gandhi's birth. Ida/Tania arrived first at the bank and they did not write it down. They had 10 minutes before their turn expires. They asked locals, who know it is 1869. That worked as the PIN # and the resulting printout reveals the next clue, to go to Muscat Oman and find a clue inside a marked car. Fuzzie/AD asked locals and got the same results. Vince/Sam arrived and entered the correct information from the statue. Geoff/Tisha arrived and put in 3 wrong numbers, then had to take a 10 minute penalty for not getting it right in 3 tries.

As usual, all this frenetic effort produces nothing in differentiation between the teams. They are Bunched at Pune Airport for 1,700km flying to Muscat. On arrival they drove to the Al Alam Palace. Ida/Tania were first to complete it. They self-drove 140km to Nizwah fort. All teams arrived there to discover Hours of Operation opening at 7am. They must find the cluebox, which is hidden in one of many spaces at the top of different steps up. That gave some teams trouble, particularly Fuzzie/AD who are left behind when the others have left. The next clue directs teams to Mutrah Souq. Ida/Tania were first once again and find DETOUR Carpet or Count It. Carpet involved finding an exact match between 2 carpets among a showroom full of carpets. This was a typical luck-based task. Count It is count a basket full of dried limes. This is harder than it looks. Geoff/Tisha switched to Carpet, but this task was so daunting they switched back to Count It. Teams can realistically switch only when the DETOUR options are nearby.

Vince/Sam got the first correct count, 1601 for their basket. Vince/Sam had an alliance with Geoff/Tisha but forgot to honor it with the exchange of the correct number. Vince explained this away by saying that the baskets probably have different number counts (true), so their information would be of no value to Geoff/Tisha. After their next try was incorrect, Geoff/Tisha returned to Carpet. After some negative experiences doing it a second time, Geoff/Tisha switched one more time back to Count It. Fuzzie/AD elected to choose 1599 for their first try and got that same number on their second time, but went with 1598, which was correct. Then Geoff/Tisha finally got it right.

The next clue led to Wadi Tanuf 2.5 hours away in the desert. Teams are lost in the desert and happy to meet up with other teams. Fuzzie observes "There are things on the map not on the road signs and things on the road signs not on the map." After being directed to the correct road, teams face ROADBLOCK "Who's ready for a cliffhanger?" of unusual difficulty. It is 2 parallel horizontal zip lines across a canyon, to a secured post, and then back around to the original spots. The selected individual must pull himself over and back using just his own strength. Those with high strength to weight ratios will do better at this horizontal rappel. There were two sets of lines parallel to each other. Sam is first, but he became stuck with no strength left about half way on the return journey. Ida went and made it all the way, then a short distance to the pit stop. Geoff arrived and blitzed it, finishing second. Fuzzie went last and got part way, but her arm strength gave out. Sam was smart enough to take the 4 hour penalty first. That guaranteed Vince/Sam third place and Fuzzie/AD fourth place and elimination.

ARA3, Ep.11, Finale

Teams leave the pit stop for the final leg at these times:
Ida/Tania   542am
Geoff/Tisha 554am
Vince/Sam 1004am

It's obvious that Sam/Vince have to catch up or risk being left behind. They were determined to do just that. The first clue led to the Office of the Governorate of Muscat. The Hours of Operation of not opening until 8am there removed about 2 hours from the deficit that Vince/Sam face. This was only another clue directing them to

218

Said's Camel Farm in the desert. Teams transfer 10 camels from their stall to a holding pen. Any task involving animals has an Amazing Race and Amazing Race Asia history of proving great entertainment. I would only rate this as good entertainment, observing the differing strategies to this task. Tania/Ida each took one camel each loop. Geoff took 2 and Tisha 1 camel each loop. When they arrive hours later, Sam and Vince took 1 camel between them for the fist 4 loops and then took 1 each. If you work this out, Geoff/Tisha took 4 loops, Ida/Tania 5 and Sam/Vince 7. It is clear that Sam/Vince did not catch up here.

Teams next drove to a marked sand field at Hubra Sands for ROADBLOCK "Who has the keys to your final destination?" using a metal detector to find any of 70 buried keys. Only 7 would open the cluebox. This was a luck-based task; getting there first is an advantage of 10.0% probability for each key found to be correct vs. Vince/Sam a 7.35% probability. Teams had a serious hazard driving in/out of this site of getting stuck in the sand. Ida/Tania and Geoff/Tisha were stuck long enough that Vince/Sam caught up to less than one hour behind at that point. Next stop was Muscat International Airport to fly 6,100km to Phuket Thailand. Teams booked the next available flight and Ida/Tania got an incompetent travel agent there. Geoff/Tisha booked a Dubai connection for Bangkok plus a connection there to arrive Phuket 850am. Due to the booking delays, Ida/Tania can't make that Dubai connection, so they fly Dubai to Singapore to Phuket, arriving at 935am. Vince/Sam arrived later at Muscat airport but got the same flights as Geoff/Tisha. How did that occur? I don't know. Flights arrived Phuket on time and Ida/Tania started with a 45 minute deficit.

Taxis hired at Phuket airport got teams to Thai Trade Food Ice Factory. There teams had to find a small plastic cube in a barrel of shaved ice. As at the Coal Mine Museum in Taiwan, you know that the cube will be near the bottom to ensure maximum effort in moving shaved ice. It is sent to the ground where it will quickly melt but it's still necessary to move many cubic feet of ice out of the barrel. Next was a taxi to the Sam Kong Temple, where Vince/Sam got into the lead as Geoff/Tisha's driver led them off-target, the only change in position this episode.

Next it was from Lam Hin Pier in a traditional long-tailed fishing vessel to a point between islands where a marked fisherman with clues can be found. It's a DETOUR of Plunge or Pull. Plunge is to snorkel to find a giant clam shell, open it and take the plastic pearl inside to exchange for the next clue. Pull is to kayak to an oyster farm and pull up oyster lines from underwater until you find a shell with an ARA3 logo, which is exchanged for the clue. Vince/Sam Plunge, but then switched to Pull. Geoff/Tisha Pull. Ida/Tania were very relaxed when they arrived there and chose Plunge, as they knew that they were destined for 3rd place.

That clue sent teams to the final task, go to Rang Yai Beach and find a marked sand pit and dig with your hands to unearth a treasure chest which contains $100,000US, then carry it to the Finish Line for the key from Allan Wu. Vince/Sam were there first after "7 countries, 11 cities and 21,600 km." Geoff/Tisha arrived later. Ida/Tania arrived maybe 45 minutes after Vince/Sam. Normally Michael McKay is good for a more cerebral task but this is his self-described most difficult Amazing Race Asia ever, so he is going with a luck-based task that gives an edge to individuals with good digging skills. The luck factor applies to the choice of where to dig but volume of dirt moved was critical. The first team done and receiving the contents of the treasure chest was Vince/Sam. Geoff/Tisha were second and Ida/Tania last. They have traveled 21,600 km to 11 cities in 18 days. I rate this as one of the finest closing legs in the history of Amazing Race Asia and Amazing Race U.S.

Hong Kong and Macau were normal legs, but all other legs had some elements of major difficulty. I think Michael McKay succeeded on his quest for an exceptionally difficult Amazing Race.

ANIMALS in AMAZING RACES 10 to 14, ARA1, ARA2, ARA3

Animals play key roles in many Amazing Race episodes; they can get star treatment from the cameras or can influence the results.

In AR10 in Mongolia, teams in Gorkhi Terelj National Park started riding horses to a clue featuring a DETOUR. Kimberly got knocked off her horse being careless with an approaching tree branch. Dustin and Kandice and either Erwin or Godwin lost their hats and had to find them before they could get back on their horses and exit. Teams could choose Take It Down, which was to pack up a yurt and attach it to a camel, or Fill It Up, which was fill water jugs for transportation by a hynik. This large beast of burden got out of control with Peter, who promptly switched to the other DETOUR.

Possibly the most decisive statement by an animal was made by the donkey in AR12 guided by Ari/Staella to deliver 15 blocks of peat in a basket at Cleggan Farm in northwest Ireland. That donkey refused to move for a 7 hour period, causing Ari/Staella to be outed instead of Nathan/Jennifer, who only lost 4 hours to theirs.

AR12 teams went to Bingo Burkina Faso for a ROADBLOCK to milk a camel to a certain mark and drink the milk. Most camels were docile but Julia/Marianna and Lorena/Jason got difficult ones. The time lost milking their camel eliminated Julia/Marianna.

The following Burkina Faso episode, a ROADLBOCK at Tampouy Goat Market involved the transport by bicycle of a live goat.

In AR14 Jaipur camels received the ROADBLOCK's bounty for "Who's ready to drink?" Selected team members delivered buckets of water and baskets of hay to feed the camels and have a good supply of drinking water. These camels were well behaved.

In Phuket for AR14, an elephant and tiger got star treatment. The tiger was restrained with chains to pose for cameras. The elephant performed a routine of lightly stepping on each teammate's back and showing great control on its haunches hovering over humans.

What do you find on Said's Camel Farm in Oman? This is not a trick question so the answer is camels. The ARA3 Final 3 teams went there to transfer 10 well-behaved camels from 1 pen to another.

For ARA1 Jakarta, teams visited Ragunan Zoo. Their mission was to snatch a clue from the cage of several large Indonesian snakes.

In the next episode in the Ubud Monkey Forest of Bali, the challenge is to find a valid clue among 200 clues scattered about. Unfortunately the resident monkeys were having a blast eating the clues. If they ate any of the maybe 10 valid clues, they could sharply reduce the probability for the lagging teams to find a valid clue. Those clues were for the DETOUR WET or DRY. In DRY teams got to ride an elephant over a 3km course. Who would not want to do that? Actually, several teams chose WET instead because it was white water rafting, also quite neat.

Later in ARA1, teams got to Manly Wharf Ocean World, a huge 4 million liter tank with all kinds of fish, sea vegetation and inhabitants of the seas. The only ones that were a potential threat to humans were the sharks. This ROADBLOCK required one team member to walk on the floor of the aquarium as sharks and fish cruised above them. Howard was so frightened of it that he took a 4 hour penalty.

In India, ARA1 teams on the DETOUR Donkey found the onion vendor and delivered a load guiding a donkey from Cycle market in Chandni Chowk to Lahori Gate Crossing. These donkeys were OK.

ARA1 teams at Desert Area 53 picked a camel to respond to commands and allow stakes to be picked up by humans riding on its back. These camels were well behaved, with 1 team in trouble.

In ARA2 near Manila, Michael McKay tried a duplicate of "My Ox is Broken" AR5 ROADBLOCK causing Colin grief using a carabao.

AR13 Almaty had 30,000 chickens for Golden Egg ROADBLOCK packed into a large henhouse, making human movement dicey.

I generally found the use of animals to be appropriate and reasonably "natural". The exception was AR14 at Phuket Zoo where the tiger and elephant were performers being exploited.

SADDEST ELIMINATIONS

The best approach to this subject is a comparative analysis of who might qualify, race-by-race, and a nomination of my top 3 saddest elimination teams across all the Amazing Races. This is a judgment call on relative emotional values since all of these teams were eliminated in middle episodes of their race. You will not see any third or second place teams here, so do not be disappointed that I define my qualifications for "saddest" to not include them. What is sad to one person may not be sad to another since this judgment is highly subjective. Even so, my standards for "saddest" are reason-able. Teams eliminated due to factors beyond their control deserve major consideration; those eliminated but could had choices should not be considered saddest material. This is particularly true of random tasks where pure luck typically causes the outcomes. My standards will exclude teams who "did it to themselves" and honor those who suffered bad luck. With the top 3 teams in each race excluded and the fact that we do not see enough about early elim-inated teams to really care for them, the teams most carefully considered here will be between the bottom 3 and top 3.

AR1—My first nominee is Kevin/Drew. They made it to the end of episode 11 in Beijing, China and were dead even with Joe/Bill coming out of a restaurant and needing a taxi ride to Temple of Heaven Park's South Gate. Joe/Bill's taxi driver was superior in maneuvering through the very heavy traffic. Kevin/Drew elected to get out at the West Gate and jog through the park. They weren't faster than Joe/Bill in the taxi and lost by several minutes. Nancy/Emily in Ep.9 had a lousy break caused both by their fatigue and by the confining instructions they received in Bangkok. First they competed with Joe/Bill for the FAST FORWARD at the Temple of the Dawn, a counting exercise. Joe/Bill won, which forced Nancy/Emily back to the regular tasks. They had a choice of finding a marked car in a specific area of several blocks of Bangkok or of taking the public bus to the long-distance bus station. They were tired and it had been a tough day, so they decided to use a taxi instead. That got them to the bus station fast and they make it to Krabi, the pit stop. They even arrived before Joe/Bill, who had lolly-gagged in Bangkok as they had a tendency to do. However, the 24 hour penalty (the stiffest in amazing Race history and designed to eliminate anyone who received it) caused Nancy/Emily to be eliminated. Which one is the sadder? For me it is Nancy/Emily.

AR2– Gary/Dave climbed Sydney Harbor Bridge in Ep.9. They fell a little behind and they are the only team to not make the first charter flight to Cooper Pedy. Their arrival 30 minutes behind can't be overcome due to the structure of the remaining tasks. The Ep.8 scene of Oswald/Danny enjoying life in and shopping near a world-class Hong Kong hotel was too amusing! They get frappucinos and cologne while awaiting their travel agent finishing ticketing to Sydney and providing a limo to the airport. How big a commission must have motivated that! They made the final 4 and then were up against Alex/Chris, Wil/Tara and Blake/Paige in Ep.11 in New Zealand, who were much more intense in their approach to life. After Bunching leveled the playing field, teams descend on ropes at the famous Lost World Caves and climb out. Alex/Chris got a small lead over Oswald/Danny and kept it all 100 miles into Auckland's WarBirds Airport. Oswald/Danny were eliminated there for fourth place. By my criteria actually Oswald/Danny in AR2 don't qualify for "saddest" as the critical Lost World Caves task could have been done better. Gary/Dave were the AR2 saddest.

AR3-John Vito/Jill were sweethearts on this race. They did well and I expected them to reach the Final 3, but they had difficulty with navigation. In a foreign country, inability to read a map correctly places you at the mercy of helpful locals who may or may not know how to properly direct you. In Singapore Ep.10 they had to find an apartment on the fringes of downtown and navigate from there to Sun Tec City Fountain of Wealth. They got lost and had difficulty getting back on track. Their elimination in 5th place was truly a blow to their many fans (me included). Derek/Drew stayed in for one more leg. Ep.10 went to HoChiMinh City, Vietnam and required them on arrival back there from an expedition to the countryside to find a specific storage area for cyclos, a semi-covered cycle rickshaw or pedicab that you pedal yourself. They went across the river to the pit stop to see if Flo, who was romantically involved with the unmarried twin brother, would help them. But when Ken/Gerard (presumably a less competitive team) came, she directed them to precisely where the cyclos are, resulting in the elimination of Derek/Drew in that episode. I used to think losing John Vito/Jill was sad, but the reason for their elimination was poor navigation, which was in their control. They failed to develop sufficient map-reading and associated skills before the race started. So the nod goes to Derek/Drew, no better or worse than Ken/Gerard in finding the cyclos until Ken/Gerard got special help withheld from Derek/Drew.

AR4- Jon/Al were at Seoul-Incheon Airport with the 3 remaining teams. Jon/Al booked Korean Airlines, but its departure was severely impacted by a fog delay. They tried to switch to the flight the other 3 teams were on, but reportedly their WRP credit card was not processed properly and they missed it. They got to Brisbane Australia well after Chip/Reichen, Jon/Kelly and David/Jeff and almost catch up, but are eliminated. Tian/Jaree only made it to Ep.8 in Alleppey, India. They started the critical DETOUR Trunks by picking an elephant and getting on top. However, they have forgotten 2 fabric bales which must be delivered. In the time it took to fix that, Reichen/Chip arrived and started Baskets, catching 10 live chickens and forcing them into a basket on a bicycle that they have to navigate to deliver them at a farm. Both DETOURS end with a clue to the pit stop. The time disadvantage that Tian/Jaree created for themselves couldn't be overcome. They finished just after Reichen/Chip and were eliminated. My pick for AR4 "saddest" is Jon/Al.

AR5—the fourth place team was Linda/Karen. They ran a classy race all the way to Ep.12 off El Nido Island, Philippines. They moved from equal to Colin/Christie at the start to 40 minutes ahead in a theoretical skill task, find the Philippines flag. Colin/Christie made a different and wrong guess. They maintained that 40 minutes in a boat ride to the Lagen Wall, a sheer cliff on which a ROADBLOCK required use of an ascender to pull the selected individual up that wall. Karen went halfway up before Colin/Christie arrived but once Colin, an extreme sports fanatic, arrived he shot up the wall in record time. Linda/Karen did nothing wrong except compete against the greatest single task achievement in Amazing Race history. They were at the wrong place at the wrong time. Karen had to do unusually well in ascending to finish by Colin/Christie's arrival. Linda/Karen are AR5's saddest elimination.

AR6– In Ep.3 near Stockholm Sweden Lena and Kristy arrived at a large open field covered with 270 hay bales at Haggvik Farm, with only 20 of those containing a clue. The ROADBLOCK "who's got hay fever?" was selected by Lena. At the start the odds were 7.4% that any unroll of a hay bale would result in a clue. Lena started unrolling and watched as each of 8 other teams went past her. The odds on her finding a hay bale were then down to 4.4% but even then unrolling to find one of the 12 clues in the remaining bales should not have taken more than 23 tries on average to find it. Lena was up to approximately 100 over an 8 hour period. There is a rumor that there were several clues in the bales she had unrolled, but I cannot verify that. This was a tragic outcome for Lena/Kristy, who were eliminated in that field. I am very fond of Bolo/Lori. They made it to Ep.9 ROADBLOCK "Who has strong legs and a keen eye?" at Sir Lanka Lion Rock. Teams purchased tickets at the bottom, then the selected individual climbed about halfway up to reach the entry point for the second half of the climb. Lori got there without her ticket and had to go back down. Freddy had a similar problem although was not quite as high when he somehow figured this out, but his turnaround time at bottom was minimal. Lori when she turned back was last and she could not alter that. Lori/Bolo were eliminated at the pit stop. Hayden and Aaron made it to the Final 4. In Ep.12 the "Which of you is more methodical?" ROADBLOCK Hayden joins the other 3 females on this task. There are 3,000 locks; you must find the one that your keys fit. When 3 hours or so elapsed it was a few minutes before closing time. Hayden and Rebecca were still there. Hayden/Aaron stopped and took the 4 hour ROADBLOCK non-completion penalty. Almost immediately after, Rebecca's key turned a lock. Hayden/Aaron had no effective options. They will be in last place when they reach the pit stop and eliminated. I used to think that Lena/Kristy was extremely sad, but I don't any more. The revelation that Lena had poor eyesight or unrolling skills takes them out of my "saddest" category. Lori/Bolo also did themselves in. The only truly "saddest" AR6 team is Hayden/Aaron, losing a luck-based task.

AR7—In Ep.7 in Botswana the ROABLOCK "Who's ready for a real roadblock?" 2 teams reached the pit stop at the Khwai River Lodge without completing the precise requirements for finishing. Uchenna/Joyce and Meredith/Gretchen had to go back on the course they had been navigating to correct a minor discrepancy for Uchenna/Joyce and missing a clue and several intermediate points for Meredith/Gretchen. Brian/Greg got onto the course late by missing a turn in the first half of this episode. They needed a huge break to stay in the race. They went through the course decently, but not enough to catch Lynn/Alex, who had been delayed by 2 vehicle replacements. Brian/Greg did well, but didn't pick up enough time to stay in the race. They were eliminated. Bad performance in the episode's first half disqualifies Greg/Brian for "saddest". In my judgment there is no AR7 team that qualifies.

AR8– The only AR8 team to consider is the Gaghan family. They ran a good race up until the ROADBLOCK at the Doka Coffee Estate, Costa Rica was "Search 800 pounds of coffee beans to find one red coffee bean." This is the classic random task, with the finishing order potentially quite different than the starting order. Tammy Gaghan was 2nd to the beans, but last by 30 minutes leaving. It was gut-wrenching to watch her search for the red bean. The issue is whether it qualifies for "saddest." Despite the judgment call made for AR6 with Lena/ Kristy, there no is culpability on this random task. Somebody has to be last; it was unfortunate that last leaving Doka also meant last at the pit stop at the beach. Design of this leg gave the Gaghans no opportunity to catch up. Caused by a random task, the elimination wasn't the result of Gaghan family performance and the Gaghans are the saddest of AR8.

AR9—In Ep.8, Fran and Barry took a taxi to Freemantle Prison and then after a task from there to Freemantle Sailing Club The pre-arranged taxi driver supposed to meet them at the ferry did not, so their planning ahead move came back to bite them. They lost time on both trips and dropped into last place, resulting in their elimination. Another team to think about is Lori/Dave in Ep.5, starting 21 minutes behind Lake/Michelle and over an hour behind Joseph/Monica and Fran/Barry. They stayed behind all day, as this leg was designed with no opportunity to make up time. So, which team is the "saddest"? By my criteria, Lori/Dave are not saddest material due to poor performance on leg 4 (Lori's inability to put the statue together). Fran/Barry were eliminated in spite of their efforts to optimize taxi support. That is not only ironic but it makes Fran/Barry my candidate for AR9 "Saddest".

AR10— In Ep.6 Peter/Sarah in Kuwait do the DETOUR "Automatic", drive yourself to the Camel Racing Club, choose a robotic jockey, attach it to a camel, and use a voice-activated remote control that causes the jockey to lightly whip the camel drive it to the end of a 140-yard track. This was irrelevant because Peter and Sarah never located the club despite hours of effort. They finally ended up by chance at the used FAST FORWARD site and the Manual DETOUR before receiving a clue to the Al Sadiq Water Towers pit stop. However, in their case it was after all others teams checked in, so they were eliminated there. In Ep.8 David/Mary join Lyn/Karlyn in the Intersection. In the joint "Long Sleep" DETOUR they deliver 8 mattresses to a specific address in Antananarivo. Then teams were released from the Intersection and there was a ROADBLOCK "Who can cut through the red tape?" to obtain 4 matching stamps from market vendors. David/Mary were behind all teams starting the ROADBLOCK, finished that ROADBLOCK next to last but their Marked for Elimination penalty officially made them last. Mary had helped Lyn on the ROADBLOCK. In Ep.9 in Kiev, Ukraine Erwin/Godwin finished the Find the Music DETOUR and attempted to get to the pit stop. With all teams converging in a very close time range, Erwin/Godwin self-driving made a wrong turn to an unfamiliar street. It was marked closed and they were pulled over by local police and ordered to present papers. That was enough time lost to solidify them in last place and elimination. Dustin/Kandice in Ep.10 ahead of the other teams self-driving through Morocco to find DETOUR Grind It at a business sign near Idelssan 4 miles from where they received the DETOUR clue. They missed the sign and drove on by, turning back after a few miles but not soon enough. When they arrived each of the 3 workstations was full, forcing them to wait until Tyler/James were finished. By then Rob/Kimberly and Lyn/Karlyn were close to done. Dustin/Kandice had no chance to catch up on them during the drive to a Berber camp in route to Marrakech. They survive this non-elimination leg but are Marked for Elimination; they have to get first place in the next episode or they will be get a 30 minute penalty. David/Mary had been given a FAST FORWARD opportunity to recover, but not Dustin/Kandice. In Barcelona they pick the DETOUR Lug It and become costumed as giants to navigate on foot and with limited sight to a plaza 1 mile away. They do not do well, losing not only to Tyler/James directly but also to Rob/Kimberly and Lyn/Karlyn who did the Lob It DETOUR. When they reach the pit stop they are last before the application of the 30 minute penalty and are eliminated. So we have 4 teams who could qualify for the "saddest". Which one really is? Peter/Sarah were eliminated by their own actions. David/Mary aided their direct competition causing their own elimination. Dustin/Kandice made a serious navigation mistake which ended in their eventual elimination. None of these teams qualify according to my criteria. However, Erwin/Godwin do qualify. They were defeated by events beyond their control in Kiev.

AR11-There are several teams to consider here. I start with Rob/Amber in Ep.4 at the bottom of South America. In Punta Arenas they run into the Sign It DETOUR. They are next-to-last reaching the boat dock for Isla Redonda. At the world's most southern post office (except for Antarctica), the "Who's Good at Sorting Things Out?" ROADBLOCK pits Rob against Mirna. It is a classic luck-based task; Mirna was lucky and Rob was not. Rob and Amber were eliminated before they can leave the post office as Charla/Mirna had already finished. There are two conflicting elements here, the poor performance at the DETOUR and the bad luck at the ROADBLOCK. We'll see which prevails in my thinking. Ian/Teri did OK in the Mozambique episode, but in Ep.6 they and other teams were caught in an unexpected shortage of available flight seats from Mozambique to DarEsSalaam. They got there along with Joe/Bill, reaching Zanzibar Island about 24 hours after Mirna/Charla. Ian/Teri and Joe/Bill went head-to-head on a puzzle solving DETOUR "Solve It". Joe/Bill earned a slight lead and never relinquished it. Ian/Teri were eliminated. In Ep.7 Joe/Bill arrived with Eric/Danielle to compete in a variety of tasks resulting in the non-elimination of Joe/Bill and a 30 minute Marked for Elimination penalty. In Ep.8 in Warsaw and Krakow, Poland Joe/Bill qualify for the later bus of the 2 going to Auschwitz/Birkenau concentration camp. They are forced into an Intersection with Eric/Danielle and choose the "Eat It Up" DETOUR, arrive at a sausage factory and eat 2 links per person. Eric knows that Joe/Bill have to get ahead of someone to avoid elimination via the 30 minute penalty; he deliberately eats slowly so they really have no chance once all 4 are released from the Intersection. The ensuing ROADBLOCK had no impact on the order of teams. Joe/Bill never had a chance and they were eliminated when Eric/Danielle arrived at the castle just after they did. Ep.9 had teams flying from Krakow to Kuala Lumpur via at least one connecting point. Conservative approaches by other teams contrasted with Uchenna/Joyce deciding to risk going through Frankfurt international airport, infamous for its flight delays. They arrived from Krakow and had over one hour to get to and on the connecting flight. Some paperwork expected from Munich (figure that one out, because I can't) did not arrive and so the valid reservations Uchenna/Joyce had were not honored; they missed the one Malaysian Airlines flight that could keep them in the race. Their fault was to attempt a riskier flight combination than necessary. Then a chain of random events brought them down and eliminated them as on arrival in Kuala Lumpur they were guaranteed last place. Ep.12 starts in the Macau/Hong Kong area and flies to Guam. The 4 teams know that one will not make the Final 3 this episode. Oswald/Danny chose Engine Care, a DETOUR requiring washing a B-52 Bomber engine pod, as did Dustin/Kandice and Eric/Danielle. They were roughly even when they finished. The ROADBLOCK "Who's Ready to Search Far and Wide" was next and Charla, Dustin, Oswald and Danielle were chosen as the selected individuals. This involved a naval search and rescue training exercise with a hand-held GPS they navigate through the jungle to find one of 4 Search and Rescue Training Officers; once there that officer would reprogram the GPS to get the selected individuals to a helicopter pickup point. Oswald/Danny fell behind in this critical task and car navigation, were unable to make up lost time and were the last AR11 team eliminated. For Rob/Amber their culpability in falling behind is not overcome by the random nature of the letter sorting DETOUR. For Joe/Bill they had a minor amount of culpability in finishing poorly to end leg 7. For Uchenna/Joyce they had free choice of any route. Oswald let Danny down in the Ep.12 ROADBLOCK. I award the AR11 "saddest" award to Joe/Bill.

AR12-- In Ep.6 Azaria/Hendekea had problems in Vilnius airport on the way to Dubrovnik. They were mistakenly given business class seats but did not catch it quickly enough. They arrived in Dubrovnik a half hour behind Nicolas/Donald. There were tasks and a find-the-cluebox exercise. By the time Azaria/Hendekea started rowing in the Long and Short DETOUR, Nicolas/Donald were still in sight. Azaria started rowing hard but not getting far. It appears he had failed to release an underwater line, so all his effort for about a half hour was wasted. He had the physical prowess to catch up with the other team, but failed to do so due to his own negligence. Azaria/Hendekea finished last and were eliminated. In Ep.8 in Mumbai India Kynt/Vyxsin had to do a SpeedBump as a result of non-elimination in the prior episode. They were competitive through several tasks. They got to their SpeedBump task, which required taking a taxi to a yoga master, doing a quick yoga exercise routine and getting back to a U-Turn decision point. Amazingly, despite the approximately 30 minutes that the SpeedBump had taken, Kynt/

Vyxsin were not last. They knew nothing about other teams. They made a judgment call and decided to U-Turn Nicolas/Donald, who were already past the U-Turn point. The team behind them was Nathan/Jennifer who used their reprieve to beat Kynt/Vyxsin in the taxi race to the pit stop at Bandra Fort. In Ep.10 in Taiwan, Jennifer/Nathan elected the DETOUR Earth, to walk over 200 yards of rough stones barefoot and then do the reverse following tricky navigation by subway/bus or by taxi. Based on the recommendation of a local, they chose subway/bus and arrived behind the other 3 teams choosing taxi. It was bad advice and they were eliminated. Who most deserves AR12 saddest? For Azaria/Hendekea their own deficiencies brought them down. For Kynt/Vyxsin, stellar performance in recovering 30 minutes was wasted by a risky decision. Nathan/Jennifer get my AR12 "saddest" nomination.

AR13-- In Ep.8 in Almaty Kazakhstan two teams raced for the FAST FORWARD at Alasha Restaurant 15 to 30 minutes from the ROADBLOCK that other teams were doing. This FAST FORWARD was coveted by both Nick/Starr and Terence/Sarah. The task is to both eat a full bowl of korduk, a traditional Kazakh local delicacy including fat from the rear end of a sheep. When I attempted to verify this, I found only the Uzbek traditional quovurma shurva (mutton soup) likely served at the Alasha. Nick/Starr had no eating limits but Terence is vegetarian for 15 years and Sarah only eats kosher. Sarah/Terence had no chance to win this FAST FORWARD and should have abandoned it immediately once theynknew what it was. They stayed for quite a while hoping that Terence could eat it, but that did not happen. This time lost was critical later because they did eventually abandon it to return to DETOUR "Who's Feeling Peckish?" Finding a golden egg put them more than one hour behind the other teams (Ken/Tina, Toni/Dallas, and Andrew/Dan). Terence/Sarah constantly gained ground so that by the pit stop they were reportedly only 7 minutes behind. Imagine a different strategy on the FAST FORWARD (don't try at all or abandon quickly)! In leg 10 in Moscow Toni/Dallas reached the "Who's good at solving mysteries, Literally" ROADBLOCK and Dallas took it. He was performing average when, on a taxi ride to complete that ROADBLOCK, he left his Amazing Race pouch with passports and money in that cab after having to make microphone adjustments. They did get it back 1 day later, but in the interim they must beg for money for all transportation. A simple bus ride (and presumably a subway ride) is 20 or 25 rubles ($0.85 to $1.05 based on early May 2008 exchange rates) but a taxi ride is at least 400 rubles ($16.80). Moscow is a very expensive city, which Toni and Dallas found out the hard way. They travel each segment of a trip and then beg again for more money. They did not reach the choice of Ride the Lines (bus/tram/trolley) vs. Ride the Rails subway). They were eliminated by Phil in transit, as all other teams had checked in and they were not even halfway done. Because Terence/Sarah had their situation in their own control, I don't select them. Since Toni/Dallas did not deserve their fate, I nominate them for AR13 "saddest".

AR14-- Many viewers were saddened by the elimination of Brad/Victoria, stranded in Amsterdam missing a close connection of their Munich to Bucharest route overnight and eliminated in Bran at the end of that leg. I don't consider this "saddest" material because they did it to themselves with Brad's aggressive "let's separate from the pack" philosophy; their huge risks burned them. In Krasnoyarsk, Amanda/Kris were behind at the Construct DETOUR, allowing Margie/Luke to Blind U-Turn them. They were eliminated at the end of that episode, a result of redoing the Stack DETOUR (which they had failed at earlier). I feel they get some consideration for saddest. Christie/Jodi in Jaipur lost due to a rogue taxi driver who took them toward Pushkar when they requested Dhula Village. All the 30 minute deficit plus speed bump time was reclaimed by hard work except for 2 minutes at the pit stop. They were eliminated by that taxi driver's mistake. Christie/Jodi are AR14's "saddest."

Here are the "saddest" elimination nominations:
AR1-Nancy/Emily
AR2-Oswald/Danny
AR3-Derek/Drew
AR4-Jon/Al
AR5-Linda/Karen
AR6-Hayden/Aaron
AR7-no team
AR8-Gaghan family
AR9-Fran/Barry
AR10-Erwin/Godwin
AR11-Joe/Bill
AR12-Nathan/Jennifer

AR13-Toni/Dallas
AR14-Christie/Jodi

The three AR teams that get my designation for saddest eliminations are:
#1 Jon and Al
#2 the Gaghan family
#3 Christie and Jodi

AMAZING RACE ASIA

ARA1—In Ep.8 in Thailand, all teams were close at the end. Andy/Laura had been YIELDed but had overcome the resulting 30 minute deficit. At the dungcake ROADBLOCK Andy/Laura finished in 3rd place just ahead of Mardy/Marsio and Zabrina/JoeJer. Efforts to find a taxi succeeded for Mardy/Marsio and Zabrina/JoeJer snatched one away from Andy/Laura. My criteria when applied to their elimination make them a prime candidate for "saddest" despite Laura/Andy's role as the villains of ARA1. Mardy/Marsio were 1 of 4 teams in Ep.12 in Dubai. There was a full series of tasks, with Mardy/Marsio leaving from the Par 3 9-hole golf challenge in last place. Next is Eye of the Emirates ferris wheel where they reduce some of the time differential. Marsio takes the next task, ROADBLOCK "Who has the brains in the team?" The selected individual eats brains and bread for the clue. Now, what task do you think Mardy/Marsio would excel at? I would say an eating challenge, based on prior episodes and on their physiques. But Marsio lost rather than gained time because he doesn't eat organ meats, then had no real opportunity to make up time at Wild Wadi Water Park, Sheik al Maktoum's house or the short trip to the pit stop at Mina al Salaam Beach in Jumeirah. If they had left the eating challenge right after Sandy/Francesca, I doubt they could have prevented elimination. Although Mardy/Marsio have a minor excuse (100+ degree heat and choice of the wrong person to do the golf DETOUR), there's no excuse for them losing the eating challenge. My surpise nominee for "saddest" of ARA1 is Laura/Andy. I didn't expect to nominate them for anything positive, but criteria and no real competition make them the ARA1 nominee.

ARA2—In Ep.5, a double leg with TBC in between, Sawaka/Daichi went to their homeland Japan and completed many tasks around Tokyo, the last of which was a "figure out the name of this

Japanese city" puzzle which had them hours ahead of all other teams. However, the Bunching strategy of Michael McKay did them in, as all teams started even on and off the bullet train to Fukuoka, the solution to the puzzle. Daichi/Sawaka board a ferry traveling 320km to Busan Korea. Daichi, a black belt in karate, cannot break the boards at a Tae Kwan Do school (I find this weird). There was a YIELD at which they could have YIELDed Ann/Diane behind them but didn't know that and did not YIELD them. They reached DETOUR Slither or Deliver. Every other team chose Slither, which is squeamish but fast. They chose Deliver 3 trays of food, each one to a different location. Then they were lost for a while. The pit stop followed and Daichi/Sawaka arrived after Ann/Diane and are eliminated. Paula/Natasha in Ep.10 started in Budapest Hungary after non-elimination earned them a 30 minute Marked for Elimination penalty if they failed to place first. With the FAST FORWARD gone, there was little hope of that. Amidst the tasks was a YIELD which Marc/Rovilson used on Ann/Diane to help Paula/Natasha get into contention. Alas, Paula/Natasha could not recover as they were not able to make up enough ground on the earlier teams. After Ann/Diane's YIELD expired they were free to finish the last task and get to the pit stop. Paula/Natasha were eliminated without that penalty even being applied. In Ep.11 Ann/ Diane took a "safe but likely to put them behind some other teams" flight through London instead of gambling through Frankfurt like the other teams did and over one hour behind on arrival at the first task. Once arrived they had navigation issues in the fog (as did all the teams), but they definitely lost more time at the Killarney Motor Racing complex where they had to maneuver a 450 hp engine racecar around a track. The person who cannot drive manual shift well, Diane, had been chosen to do it and that prevented any catchup. Finally they reached the Aquila Game Reserve to shovel elephant dung. The pit stop was nearby; they were eliminated. If the delay was caused by weather or non-controllable factors I might be sympathetic, but that was not the case. Ann/Diane made the decisions which were responsible for their elimination. So, none of the 3 teams deserved the ARA2 "saddest" nomination.

ARA3– Mai/Oliver arrived in Taipei Taiwan in reasonable shape. The first task was at the New Sogo Department Store SONY Style Shop. All competing teams except Geoff/Tisha reached there soon after this task started. This was a mostly luck-based task to play

DVD Blu-Ray discs until one displayed CORRECT. This took over 6 hours for Mai/Oliver and they hadn't finished when the store closed but they were given their clue anyway. They were completely demotivated by then and elected to stay in their car rather than driving to the coal mine for the next of several tasks. In the early morning hours after all teams had checked in, Allan Wu eliminated them at their car. In Ep.8 teams had to fly Hong Kong to Cochin. There was a route through Delhi and another one through Singapore and Hong Kong. Bernie/Henry and Sam/Vince were on the last plane to arrive into the connecting point Delhi. Their connect time appeared OK to make the last flight that evening to Cochin, but for customs clearance reasons it didn't happen and they didn't arrive in Cochin until the next morning. Since the other teams had completed several tasks by that point, it was clear that the last 2 teams were fighting for 4th place. Both teams had the DETOUR choice of Fish or Fill. In Fish the team members carry 6 large swordfish to a nearby restaurant for their next clue. In Fill teams fill an intricate floor pattern using colored rice before receiving their next clue. Sam/Vince picked Fish and were quicker at finishing it. They were 4th and Bernie/Henry got eliminated. To the delight of many fans, Faeza/AD were still in ARA3 starting Ep.10. At Wadi Tanuf in Nizwah Oman, they reached ROADBLOCK "Who's ready for a cliffhanger?" and apparently it had to be done by Faeza for roadblock-count reasons. There could not have been other rationales for doing that, because the zipline was clearly visible. Sam was on a parallel zipline then, but he was able to declare a 4 hour penalty to start before unable-to-finish Faeza could do the same thing. As a result, Faeza/AD were eliminated. I nominate Mai/Oliver for "saddest" of ARA3.

Andy being on a sharp-edged team who would not hesitate to pursue their goal and hated by the other ARA1 teams and Mai/Oliver not being well thought of, the summary of my nominees is:
ARA1– Andy/Laura
ARA2—none
ARA3– Mai/Oliver

When I take other factors into consideration, I elect to not award any Amazing Race Asia team the coveted saddest elimination title.

Weakest Amazing Race/Amazing Race Asia Teams

My personal choices of the weakest teams (not the earliest out):
AR1:
Pat and Brenda—unable to find short-cut, last in the group exiting the train at Marseille to get taxis to Les Baux
Paul and Amie—4 episodes finishing in the bottom half but reaching Tunisia, their luck ran out; they were eliminated in the desert

AR2:
Hope and Norm—there are conflicting viewpoints on whether Blake/Paige finished last or Hope/Norm did at a jungle camp near Iguassu Falls, Brazil but even if the former, Blake/Paige petitioned for a time credit for vehicle breakdown (those rules were changed later); both teams were on the last bus from Rio de Janeiro to Iguassu Falls when Blake got a map that proved to be the decisive edge

AR3:
Sylvia and Gina---navigational error to pit stop near Mexico City
Trammel and Talicia—team TNT fizzled, second bus from Mexico City area to Cancun and then chose Trammel to do ROADBLOCK on a WaveRunner, at which he proved to be inept
Aaron and Arianne—they dissipated their energy with a ridiculous "Twin Hunt" concept; they would have been eliminated in Belem, Portugal if not for the penalty to Heather/Eve

AR4:
Debra and Steve—they really didn't have the physical fitness to do well in this race; most expected them first team out in Cortina area
Russell and Cyndi—inability to discern Gmundsen was not Gmund

AR5:
Dennis and Erika— I thank them for a last place finish in Punte del Este; their selfless giving up a cab to Colin/Christie kept the latter in
Donny and Allison—a mismatched team; Donny wanted to lose to get away from Allison; they took the slow bus and were passed by other teams on fast buses from Buenos Aires to the countryside

AR6:
Joe and Avi—they were hapless in the search to find the correct path to the pit stop next to the Blue Lagoon in Iceland

Meredith and Maria—why does another AR6 NY metro teams lag behind and can't overcome prior mistakes in the final drive to a rural farm in Norway? No experience driving a stick shift was a factor. Don and Mary Jean—#9 of 11, #7 of 10, #8 of 9, last forfeiting all their money, then eliminated; this record speaks for itself

AR7:
Ryan and Chuck–slow in finding the pit stop in Cuzco, Peru
Megan and Heidi—their competing against Brian/Greg led to their elimination when the latter were thinking ahead better and had the advantage on the final footrace to the pit stop in Santiago Chile

AR8:
The Black family—we hardly knew ye as Reggie Black chose a driving route to a farm pit stop near Lancaster PA that proved inferior and saved the Linz family from elimination in the process

AR9:
Joni and Lisa—publicly announced they'd wet themselves; they were eliminated the following episode as a result of inability to properly drive a stick-shift car in Brazil plus the ascender
Scott and John– this team exits on cue in the first leg in Sao Paulo; they appeared hapless to me; their genie power did not work
Wanda and Desiree—this team got behind searching for a gnome and then lost on the Autobahn on the way to a suburb of Munich

AR10: None

AR11:
John Vito and Jill—earned a reputation for poor navigation in AR3, failed to find the North entrance to Cotopaxi National Park; the road to Hacienda Yanahurco in Ecuador gave no opportunity to catch up
Kevin and Drew—near the back of the pack in the Valley of the Dead, then failed to use the 10 mph higher speed limit from there to the turnoff near San Pedro de Atacama and then made a right turn when the correct left turn to the pit stop would have saved them; with injuries Kevin had suffered, their elimination was a good thing
David and Mary—9th of 11, 9th of 10 and then 9th of 9; need I say more? Who decided to put them in AR11 "All-Stars" season?

AR12:

Ari and Staella– since Ari was an ass in his tricks against other teams, he deserved the "bad donkey" he got at Cleggan Farm
Kate and Pat– what were they were doing on this race?; although poor performance by 3 other teams put them in 8th place in leg 1, they quickly went to last place and stayed there; on the other hand, they are very nice and deserve great respect as Episcopal ministers

AR13:
Arthur and Anita- another nominee for "Why was this team here?" Award; they were slow/careful and who should be surprised at that?

AR14:
Steve and Linda– they were misplaced in this race as a team (Steve might win with another partner); Linda last leaving the top of the Rauschberg, missed a critical route marker for 4 hours behind Brad and Victoria– in the worst case of hubris I have seen in any Amazing Race, Brad wanted to "break away from the pack"; he succeeded in doing that at the expense of staying in the race when their connection in Amsterdam was disrupted by late arrival

AMAZING RACE ASIA
ARA1:
Aubrey and Jacqueline––quit the sand dig at Kuta Beach with a 4 hour penalty that put them in with 4 other teams that did the same, then fell behind going from Uluwatu Caves to the TanahLot Temple

ARA2:
Edwin and Monica– last in the non-elimination first leg, then had difficulties assembling a bicycle and finished last in the second leg
Brett and Kinar-she can't climb the rock wall; the waka DETOUR wasn't open while Sophie/Aurelia recovered from driving elsewhere
Sophie and Aurelia–earned 7 hour deficit then made up time in a no-Bunching leg to Rotorua. This team had most divisive relationship in ARA or in any AR except Allison and Dennis AR5

ARA3:
Neena and Amit—faltered reaching a DETOUR; they were last to the off-road buggies DETOUR, last to leave and last at the pit stop

FAVORITE AMAZING RACE TEAMS

I think a good approach is to make a case for multiple teams (if applicable) for each season and then look at the big picture to see what I conclude. This is an intensely personal approach, as many viewpoints have equal validity. I am giving you the benefit of my hindsight because in many cases the team I actually rooted for in each season may not be the one I select as my Favorite today. I offer you my subjective thinking on this topic:

AR1— I see 2 teams worth considering for this nomination, Kevin/ Drew and Nancy/Emily. Each of the final 3 has major deficiencies, so my AR1 favorites are the #4 and #5 teams. Kevin/Drew always had cute and witty remarks for each other. They also were willing to mix it up to see that right conquered efforts to derail it. Nancy/Emily were the sweethearts of the race. Many hearts dropped when they received a 24 hour penalty, which had the effect of eliminating them a little before that actually occurred. AR fans including me were incensed that wonderful Nancy/Emily were out and the villains Joe/Bill stayed alive despite the time they lost. I have to go with Kevin/Drew on this one. I made Nancy/Emily the saddest elimination of AR1, but I find Kevin/Drew to be my Favorite of AR1.

AR2—Oswald and Danny come to mind immediately. They are charming, good (but not top) racers. Their wit is a pleasure to listen to. I thought about Blake/Paige, but they just lacked something difficult to identify. It's Oswald/Danny for my AR2 Favorite.

AR3— one of my favorites is Zach, not Flo and Zach, but just Zach. He carried Flo on his back figuratively. I am sure he would have done so literally if required. John Vito/Jill were the team I was rooting for, but their elimination in Singapore was the last in a series of navigational mishaps that did them in. Ken/Gerard are worth a serious look. They share great humor and interact a bit like Kevin/Drew and are very competent racers. My AR3 Favorite is Ken/Gerard, who brightened up every episode of AR3.

AR4–another competitive situation; I rooted for Jon/Kelly in the Finale, but that's only because Jon/Al went out as the #4 team. Jon/ Kelly had a give-and-take relationship fun to watch unlike some dating couples on several Amazing Races. Jon/Al were always positive, always humorous, and willing to display their circus talents to make people laugh or applaud. It's Jon/Al for AR4 Favorite.

AR5—Karen/Linda deserve consideration because they are such nice, competent racers. My selection will not please many Amazing Race viewers. Most viewers disliked Colin and Christie because of Colin's tendency to fly way off the handle. They were pleased when in the Manila area they got YIELDed and later non-eliminated. I was horrified. However, what Colin did at the Lagan Wall to overcome Karen's 40 minute lead was astonishing. In my opinion this team is the greatest team in the history of the Amazing Race and they have the most episode wins of any Amazing Race team in one season. Even though they did not win AR5 due to multiple flukes, Colin's intensity and talent as an extreme athlete did appeal and still appeals to me. Colin and Christie are my AR5 Favorite team.

AR6— this one is easy. It's Kris and Jon; there is no other team I would consider for this honor. They had a positive attitude and treated each other so well, rare in Amazing Race dating couples. They lost about 10 minutes in arrival time at Chicago O'Hare Airport in the finale due to a rare mistake in not cross-checking flight information before deciding to take American Airlines rather than the actually-landing-earlier United Airlines. Then they almost eliminated that gap in the 4 Chicago tasks (two of which were taxi rides) in the race. They are the only choice I can make for AR6.

AR7— this has become competitive in retrospect, although at the time I was totally behind Uchenna and Joyce and anti-Boston Rob. Uchenna/Joyce are the likeable couple, willing to make any sacrifice including a head of hair and enduring major grief in Jamaica with no money and it being too early to easily beg for any. They persevered and convinced the pilot to pull back to the gate for the only flight that gave them a shot against Rob/Amber. Since that time, I have more appreciation for Rob/Amber, particularly Rob's ability to influence others and his planning and execution abilities. No, I do not think that Rob/Amber got shafted at the end of AR7 (some do). Nor do I think that Rob convinced any other individual doing the infamous Meat ROADLBOCK in Mendoza, Argentina to take the penalty. However, he brought a joie de vivre and irrepressibility in his racing approach not been duplicated by any other Amazing Racer. Amber brought the steady wisdom capable of

240

calming Rob down and keeping him in his place. I surprise myself but I am going to go with Boston Rob/Amber for my AR7 favorite.

AR8—there are a number of interesting families in this race, but only one is going to be my favorite. It is the Gaghans, Bill, Tammy, Billy, and Carissa. Although they were eliminated in Costa Rica as a result of the infamous "red bean" ROADBLOCK, they won the hearts of many AR8 viewers. I watched Bill Gaghan in Panama City hit a home run to keep the family in the race. I knew this family had something special. Actually many somethings: physical fitness, high intelligence, spirit, charm, wit. They are my pick for AR8 Favorite.

AR9—I rooted for BJ/Tyler during AR9. They have an insouciance and free-spiritedness I loved. They are my choice for AR9 Favorite.

AR10—don't even think about it! It's Dustin/Kandice, with great physical fitness, high intelligence, great beauty, Kandice's dancing skills and Dustin's musical skills. This team has everything except infallible navigation skills. They are my pick for AR10 Favorite.

AR11—when this race started I was rooting for John Vito and Jill; with them out in the first leg I switched to Uchenna/Joyce and stayed with them to their bitter ending in Kuala Lumpur. I found Joe/Bill to be reformed (it would be interesting if they see it that way) and much more likeable than in AR1. Oswald/Danny are back with the same charm. The team I picked to root for in the last 4 legs was Dustin/Kandice. I knew they could go all the way and I hoped they would win. They didn't due to a random choice of taxi drivers at Oakland International Airport, which gave Eric/Danielle a lead of 10 minutes on reaching the Old Mint and thus cemented the win. I will go with Dustin/Kandice as my AR11 Favorite.

AR12—I know many AR12 viewers doted on Kynt/Vyxsin. I did not, although I thought they were a decent team. Here I have to think about two other teams, both comprised of an older man and a younger relative. That gives it away, as the only teams that fit are Nicolas/Donald and Christina/Ronald. Both teams had ups and downs throughout AR12 but both made it to the Final 3. Nicolas is a funny guy and has decent physical skills, but he was not in the top half of braininess in this race. When the final ROADBLOCK was to sort out 14 objects and choose 10 to simultaneously meet multiple constraints, I knew it would not be his day. Ronald overcame his inherent crankiness and learned how to relate decently to his daughter most of the race. With her intelligence I expected she had an edge over Rachel in that final ROADBLOCK. It did not turn out that way, but I consider Ronald/Christina my AR12 Favorite.

AR13— Many people rooted for Terence/Sarah or Toni/Dallas or Kelly/Christy and maybe even a few for Ken/Tina. This is no contest for me; I rooted for Nick/Starr throughout. Though they were a bit shifty and sly from time to time, they had the most consistent racing performance leadership since AR9 and AR5. I liked them as individuals and the dynamic between Nick and Starr was very positive and suggested that the best Amazing Race team composition is two equals from a family who have known and worked with each other for a long time, such as brother/brother, sister/sister or brother/sister. They are my choice for AR13 Favorite.

AR14—I rooted for Tammy/Victor from the beginning. They are my Favorite AR14 team due to intelligence, geniality and using "Renaissance man" skills to handle a wide variety of tasks well.

When I consider all of the 14 nominations, I conclude that my favorite Favorite is the only team to be my Favorite for two separate races, Dustin/Kandice. I had the opportunity to meet them at TARCON XI and they ooze charm and beauty wherever they are and they look strong and powerful. You know from AR10 and AR11 that they are also highly intelligent. Dustin/Kandice are winners!

AMAZING RACE ASIA
ARA1—I was rooting for Sandy/Francesca the whole way. No other team had the combination of strength and smarts they did. A minor wrong turn in the parking lot at the Sarawak Cultural Center cost them the win, but that can happen to the best in such a tight race.

ARA2—This season was loaded with teams that I love. Marc/Rovilson, with their dominant performance up to the final task, were obnoxious and disliked among the viewer community outside of the Philippines so I dismiss them. Let's start with Paula/Natasha, quirky but beautiful and charming. Next is Pamela/Vanessa, the Chong sisters who were sleek and sometimes fast and strong (it was good enough for 2nd place overall). And finally there is the winning team, Adrian/Collin. They showed great courage and fortitude in their efforts to overcome Marc/Rovilson after finishing 2nd to them in most legs and were rewarded with Adrian's knowledge of flags being able to take them into first place at the final mat. I choose Pamela/Vanessa.

ARA3—I had several favorites in this race. I started with Bernie/ Henry and stayed with them through their untimely elimination in Cochin. I ask you to think about Pailin as an individual, who soldiered on when Natalie had quit on her and was as beautiful as her Miss Universe teammate. Next is AD/Faeza, that quirky and very funny team; you wondered how they would not fall way behind on some tasks. Finally it's Ida/Tania who during the telecasts of this season became my replacement for Bernie/Henry due to their charm and wit. My choice for Favorite is Pailin. She kept her team in it as long as possible, always with the right attitude.

When I look at Sandy and Francesca, Pamela and Vanessa, and Pailin, they are all wonderful. I chose Pamela and Vanessa as my favorite Favorite team of Amazing Race Asia.

AMAZING RACE MOST AMAZING MOMENTS

I review the best moments for each Amazing Race, then pick one from each season and one for the all seasons "most amazing."

AR1

Ep.9 has several exceptionally interesting moments. The first is Nancy/Emily want the lead and go for the FAST FORWARD at Temple of the Reclining Buddha against Joe and Bill in a coin counting task. Joe/Bill win, but erroneously think that the FAST FORWARD will protect them and delay departing to the south most of the day. Since they are tight on money as a result of overspending in Paris, they take a public bus rather than a quicker cab. They are saved by Nancy/Emily erring in not taking the public bus back in Bangkok; their 24 hour penalty eliminates them despite arriving hours before Joe/Bill. This arrival of teams at that pit stop in Krabi proved, although nobody knew at the time, to be decisive. The first 2 teams were Rob/Brennan and Frank/Margarita, 4 hours and 7.5 hours ahead of the other teams; task timing following Krabi allowed them to get a day ahead of Kevin/Drew and Joe/ Bill.

Ep.11 Kevin/Drew vs. Joe/Bill fight to avoid elimination at Temple of Heaven Park. They left a restaurant at the same time, but the taxi driver for the latter was quicker. Kevin/Drew took a risk and got off at West Gate; the pit stop was at South Gate. They are eliminated.

In Ep.13 the Finale, Frank learned the next clue would be found in Queens and expected his knowledge of the area would lead him and Margarita to victory after Vincent Daniels Square. Frank's northern route from Newark Airport contrasted a more direct route that Rob/Brennan's taxi driver used. The taxi driver was smarter than Frank; Rob/Brennan were 10 minutes and one subway ahead of Frank/Margarita.

I found Krabi's drama and tension most amazing, Nancy/Emily's penalty and Joe/Bill behind despite winning the FAST FORWARD.

AR2

Ep.8 had a unique exercise in language-Australian style. ROADBLOCK "For someone who speaks good Australian" has the selected individual (Alex, Wil, Blake, Oswald, Dave) navigate a

244

course from the Sydney Opera House past still models demonstrating specific behavior that has a well-known translation into Australian slang English. Each had to carefully follow the clue to earn the next clue from each of the models (males, females, child). Those words were surfie in the dairy laks, anklebiter, Sheila in the Aussie cozzie and bushie. Wil and Blake failed twice and returned to the beginning of the course to run it again.

Ep. 9 DETOUR in Coober Pedy Heat Up to play a round of golf in 100+degree summer temperatures or Cool Down mining for opals.

A fascinating Ep.10 is in Queenstown, South Island New Zealand area; first task is FAST FORWARD to search a stretch of Shotover River with a jet boat. A DETOUR next effectively forces choice of the Nevis Bungee Jump. At Inverary Sheep Station the simple task of separating 3 black sheep from 22 white ones proves formidable.

Ep.12 is the "follow that plane" ride to Trapper Creek Alaska. Wil and Tara lost their clue and couldn't remember instructions, so they follow the other teams to reach Trapper Creek and stay in AR2.

The Finale, Ep.13, remains the closest finish ever for any Amazing Race or Amazing Race Asia. Wil/Tara are desperate to have a big enough lead on Chris/Alex because they know in the final footrace they will lose if Chris/Alex can see them running. They need to reach East Fort Baker on the Marin County side of the Golden Gate Bridge. Those 2 teams get into taxis simultaneously, then Wil plays cat-and-mouse with the other team. He is successful in creating a lead, but Chris/Alex are close enough to compete in the footrace to the Finish Line. Wil has them beat but Tara is not a strong enough runner; Wil/Tara lose by about 10 seconds at the Finish Line to Chris/Alex.

The ARA2 Finish Line/maneuvering are the most amazing of AR2.

AR3
Ep.4, Heather/Eve took a taxi to the Tower de Belem in Lisbon instead of walking. A penalty of 37 minutes was eliminated them.

Ep.5 had the infamous Dieselgate, with 4 of the 8 teams filling their diesel tanks with unleaded fuel during a 250 mile drive from Cabo de Roca, Portugal to Algeciras, Spain. Three of those teams (Ian/Terri, Zach/Flo and Aaron/Ariane) made quick recoveries. Michael/Kathy decided to rest after a difficult day. They were eliminated. It should be noted that Aaron/Ariane finished 1 3/4 hours behind the other two teams, resulting in their elimination in the following Morocco episode.

Ep.11 was in Ho Chi Minh City with Ken/Gerard fighting Derek/Drew to find the cyclos needed to reach the pit stop. Flo inadvertently or maybe deliberately gave advice to Ken/Gerard but not to Derek/Drew until too late. Derek/Drew were eliminated as a direct result.

Ep.12 had Flo/Zach in An Hoi, Vietnam struggling with DETOUR Basket Boats vs. Basket Bikes. She couldn't handle either but Zach displayed unusual patience in talking her through it, hours behind but in the race.

Ep.13 the Finale had Zach and Ian battle in the "totem pole with various animals" ROADBLOCK to turn animal carvings to the order those animals appeared in the season. Zach was slightly faster at this which gave him the margin of victory, reported to be 2 minutes.

My choice for the best of AR3 is finding the HoChiMinh City cyclos.

AR4
Ep.2 the masked party at Palazzo da Mosto in Venice was rapid-fire. Teams had a tight time limit to find the matching mask and get the clue from the wearer. Many teams did it multiple times to finish.

Ep.5 Dave/Steve and Reichen/Chip competed in an open market near Amsterdam on the DETOUR "500kg", which was transport that exact weight of cheese with wooden shoes on their feet using a wooden stretcher. It was hilarious to the dozens of locals watching.

In Ep.7 Chip/Reichen and Tian/Jaree arrived at Alleppey India last. The DETOUR was Baskets vs. Trunks, deliver 2 fabric bales by Elephant Ride(at a slow speed dependent on how fast his handler wanted to take him) or use a basket on a bicycle wagon to deliver 10 chickens to a farm. Chip/Reichen made the choice of Baskets. Tian had trouble securing the load, delaying their departure and eliminating Tian/Jaree.

Ep.10 is South Korea 50km north of Seoul, near the DeMilitarized Zone. 4 teams at ROADBLOCK "Which of you has the colder personality?" swim under Hantan River ice in Sundam Valley, with medical supervision present but that was a frightening task.

Ep.11 had tragic consequences. Jon/Al chose Korean Airlines Seoul to connect in Singapore for Brisbane. There was intense ground fog and another airline the other 3 teams booked departed hours before Jon/Al were able to, with the credit card of Jon/Al apparently not accepted. There was a cover story of Korean Airlines having a later direct flight to Brisbane, but I don't believe it. I believe that Jon/Al arrived behind and late (even given the possibility that WRP production held the other teams a long time) and never caught up. Chip/Reichen were assessed a penalty in Mooloolaba for a taxi from Underwater World to Yacht Club pit stop, but Jon/Al were eliminated.

In Ep.13, the Finale, there was a catastrophic blunder by David/Jeff. All teams reached the Cairns airport to fly to Phoenix with little time to spare. Chip/Reichen and Jon/Kelly both chose to fly to Tokyo and then to Hawaii. David or Jeff decided that since some of the AR4 production team had gone to Sydney to get to Hawaii, it should be right for them to do that. Nice move, David and Jeff! Your decision to go south in order to get north will end up costing you the opportunity to get to the Finish Line. Cairns is 17 degree south of the Equator and Honolulu is 21 degrees north. Do you fly over 1500 miles due south to Sydney at 33 degrees south to get ultimately north? Maybe under some circumstances, but with that flight leaving momentarily for Tokyo (latitude 35 degree north), you should not hesitate to book it and get on it.

What is the most memorable event of AR4? I am going with the under-the-ice DETOUR swim on Hantan River in South Korea.

AR5
Ep.1's task in Uruguay requires a member of the team (it can change) to carry a 55 pound side of beef 0.5 miles to La Caniceria Rosada. Mirna starts but doesn't get far. Tiny Charla, who might weigh less than the beef, puts it on her shoulders and gets it done.

Ep.4 is in Pushkin, Russia at Old Tower Restaurant. The females are selected to eat 1 kg (2.2 pounds) of caviar. Caviar can be delicious but that much is overwhelming, the grossest eating challenge ever.

Ep.9 the Kolkata task is Heavy but Short DETOUR, push an engineless taxi 0.5 miles after getting to Land's Down by public transport. Kids observe and assist, helping to finish fast.

Ep.11 arrived in Manila area. Colin/Christie were slow off the plane and last to Malaguey Motors, YIELDed there and lost another 30 minutes. The other teams finished and headed for the pit stop when Colin does the DETOUR Plow on a marked field pulled by an ox. It goes poorly; Colin mutters the infamous line "My Ox is Broken". Colin/Christie finished last but are saved by non-elimination.

Colin/Christie start Ep.12 45 minutes behind with Linda/Karen as Brandon/Nicole and Chip/Kim are on the first plane to El Nido Island. Those two teams get to Lagen Wall where an ascender awaits. They finished in decent time. Linda/Karen get an edge of 40 minutes when Colin guessed wrong on which is Philippines flag, so Karen was halfway up the wall when Colin and Christie arrived. Colin takes the ROADBLOCK "Got vertigo? Don't go." and zooms past Karen. Linda/Karen were eliminated at the next cove. Colin made the Final 3 by the most impressive single performance ever.

In Ep.13 Finale, 3 teams arrive in Banff, Alberta to ride chairlifts and walk up to the Continental Divide and down to the buses taking them to Calgary Olympic Stadium and later to Calgary International Airport. Colin/Christie built a lead of 2.5 hours on Brandon/Nicole and 6 hours over Chip/Kim, then rest. Fog descended before Chip/Kim booked their flight to Dallas/Fort Worth, so the American plane did not arrive. They book United and arrive 18 minutes ahead of the other 2 teams not allowed on the United flight from Denver to DFW. They complete the Fort Worth and Dallas tasks to reach the finish line 10 minutes before Colin/Christie, delayed by a flat tire on the limo from driving on the shoulder to gain time. This is a ludicrous chain of events, but great TV.

Colin's feat on the ascender up Lagen Wall was the most dominant task performance in the history of the Amazing Race.

AR6

Jonathan started acting weird in Ep.2; this continued until elimination in Ep.9. His tirades against wife Victoria are part of Amazing Race lore, particularly the finish of Ep.5 in Berlin where he overly abused her.

Ep.3 had a sad, amazing moment. Lena/Kristy arrived at ROADBLOCK "Who's got hay fever?" to find clues within hay bales by unrolling them and finding one clue. Kristy unrolled them for 6 hours, but her eyesight was poor as there were apparently several clues later found in the 100+ hay bales she unrolled. They were eliminated "In the Field" by Phil.

In Ep.5 in Berlin Gus in the DETOUR Beer waited restaurant tables delivering beer to find tokens under the mugs to earn the clue. Gus indulged himself liberally sampling the beer before he delivered it. He was still trying to do so as Hera was dragging him out the door.

Ep.9 finished near Lion Rock in Sri Lanka. Teams bought a ticket to be allowed entry almost halfway up to the climb of 1000 steps to the top of Lion Rock, where good eyesight will figure out the direction of the pit stop below. This ROADBLOCK "Who has strong legs and a keen eye?" had Lori climbing; she was fast, but found Bolo hadn't given her the ticket. She descended and then had to go all the way up. Even though she was fast and motivated, there was no margin for error there and they're eliminated at that pit stop.

In Ep.11 on Mount Hua near Xian 4 females do a ROADBLOCK "Which of you is more methodical?" to use a single key to open the correct one of 3,000 locks. It takes hours for any progress. Kendra and Kris finished and left ahead of Hayden and Rebecca. It is almost 7pm, closing time for the last cablecar down; it appears they will both have 4 hour penalties for not completing the task, starting a fierce battle for 3rd place after the bus arrived back in Xian. Hayden/Aaron decided to take the penalty and leave. Rebecca, working for over 4 hours, all of a sudden was successful. She and Adam avoided any penalty and make the Final 3.

Ep.12 has a controversial ending. Kris/Jon battle Freddy/Kendra in Hawaii for a slight lead. Kris asks the American Airlines gate agent which flight is faster; she is American's flight but what she was not told is that American is scheduled to arrive Chicago 15 minutes behind the United flight. Freddy/Kendra book the United flight and reach Chicago about 10 minutes ahead. They go to the subway; their subway car starts moving before Kris/Jon get there. After multiple short tasks in Chicago, Freddy/Kendra reach Ping Tom Park one minute ahead of Kris/Jon before a passing train temporarily cuts off the latter's access.

I think the hay bale episode was the most amazing. A random task eliminated a fine female/female team.

AR7
Ep.3 is a return to gross eating challenge, probably the grossest ever except for the AR5 caviar. It is ROADBLOCK "Who's not a vegetarian?" with 9 teams competing; the men typically take the challenge except for Debbie/Bianca. It's in Mendoza Argentina, which rightly considers itself the world meat capital. It's 4 pounds of a traditional Argentinian parrillada (meat feast) containing cow rib, pork sausage, blood sausage, cow intestine, cow udder, cow kidney, and part of a cow's saliva gland. Several doing it size up their competition. Some believe they will finish and Alex and Uchenna actually do reasonably quickly (more than 1 hour but less than 2). Greg and Ron also finish. Rob, credited by many for twisting arms, really didn't do so in initiating a 4 hour non-completion penalty except by example. Meredith and Ray convinced themselves of the benefits of that position. Patrick initially took the penalty but reconsidered. He eats sparsely until Debbie and Bianca arrive; then he goes into high gear to eliminate them.

Ep.6 saw a brilliant example of catch-up by Greg and Brian. They arrived at the Xau Xarra cattle post to DETOUR Food or Water. All other teams were ahead of them doing Food, so they correctly reasoned that their only chance was on Water, filling 12 ostrich eggs(= 24 chicken eggs each) from an underground spring and burying them like a native. They finish just after Ray/Deanna but beat them in a pit stop footrace.

Ep.8 had 2 notable moments. Uchenna/Joyce go for a FAST FORWARD, requiring them to shave their heads. This is no problem for bald Uchenna but for Joyce it's a serious decision to lose her hair. She did it to win AR7 and I totally agree with Uchenna on how beautiful she is without hair. Gretchen/Meredith had the DETOUR choice Trunk or Dunk. Trunk has a 270 kg (600 pound) elephant directed through the downtown streets of Jodhpur. Gretchen gets to utter the world-famous line "We've got a bad elephant" when hers is not following directions and she had elected to ride on top of the elephant while Meredith has to push. Some locals save the day by helping to move the elephant.

In Ep.12 Finale, an extraordinary moment was at the San Juan Airport. Uchenna/Joyce had the initial lead going to that airport. Ron/Kelly missed the exit; the extra time doomed them to third place. Rob/Amber gained time driving by Rob breaking the speed limit or Uchenna conservative driving (I can't tell which). Rob/Amber arrived one minute before Uchenna/Joyce and Rob used that to get the gate agent on his side. He convinced her to allow them onto a boarding flight to Miami. Uchenna attempted to get on the same flight and is rejected. He appealed to the captain of the plane, who with the jetway already retracted extended it so Uchenna/Joyce can get on that plane. On arrival in Miami, both teams had an equal chance to win, but Uchenna/Joyce quickly found a Spanish language cigar store; Rob/Amber didn't.

The plane incident is the most amazing moment of AR7.

AR8
Ep.6 is at Doka Coffee Estate in Costa Rica; the challenge is find a single red bean among 800 pounds of green coffee beans. This was Roadblock "Search 800 pounds of coffee beans to find a red coffee bean" handled by mature females, except Tammy Gaghan couldn't find the red bean until 30 minute after the previous team, leading later to elimination of the Gaghans in AR8 due to this luck-based task.

Ep.11 The Finale has 2 tasks that created amazing moments. Finding the reamining 1 of 3 sets of charter plane tickets timed 5 minutes apart in 56,000 seat Olympic Stadium-Montreal, the Weaver females quit but Rolly kept on trucking and found the tickets. ROADBLOCK "Who paid attention in geography?" placed state shapes on a U.S. map so all 50 fit. Nick Linz beat Walter Bransen; the Linz family won AR8 as a result.

The most amazing task of AR8 was "find the red bean".

AR9
Ep.9 ended at Lake Bennett Wilderness Resort in Northern
Australia near Darwin. The simultaneous arrival of 3 teams in a
short footrace for the pit stop was the most exciting dash in
Amazing Race history. Ray/Yolanda checked in minutes earlier, so
this race was Eric/Jeremy vs. Joseph/Monica vs. BJ/Tyler. BJ took
a risk in an attempt to get ahead, but he slipped and was passed by
Monica. He ended up a fraction of a second in last place. This led to
non-elimination but involved the confiscation of all money and
clothing plus receiving none for the next leg. BJ was barefoot and in
shorts at that time, so he badly needed shoes and pants (which he
got at airport lost-and-found).

Ep.12, the Finale, ROADBLOCK "Who remembers most of the
places you've been?" before the finish line. BJ/Tyler fought to catch
Eric/Jeremy. BJ competed with Eric to place flags of countries used
in AR9 into correct order. They had to figure out which flag was
which (made easier by having only 3 extra flags to not select), but
placing them in correct order was difficult. BJ/Tyler won AR9.

The 3-way finish was the most exciting part of AR9.

AR10
Ep.11 has Dustin/Kandice leading, searching for a sign for a Horse
Farm Grind It DETOUR near Idelssan Morocco. They elected this
partially because it was in a direction they had come from. Despite
that, they drove by it and on for miles before returning. In that time
the other 3 teams, who had also selected Grind It, started their task
on the available 3 workstations. Dustin/Kandice arrived slightly after
the 3rd team, waiting until another team finished to start this task.
On completion all teams then had to drive more miles and at the pit
stop they were non–eliminated with a probable 30 minute penalty.

Ep.12 had a DETOUR of Lug It or Lob It. In Lug It, teams donned
giant costumes and walk more than a mile, navigating using
Spanish maps and signs to find a costumed female giant. In Lob It,
teams searched a giant pile of tomatoes to find one with a clue

inside. While they were searching, locals either lobbed or threw tomatoes at them as done in the Spanish festival called La Tomatina in Bunol Valencia. Dustin/Kandice chose Lug It against Tyler/James; Rob/Kimberly and Lyn/Karlyn chose Lob It. Dustin/Kandice gain no time and were eliminated. So endeth the AR10 stint of the best female/female team ever.

I have selected the La Tomatina task as most amazing.

AR11 All-Stars
Ep.4 started with Rob/Amber near the front of the pack. A task in Punta Arenas to simulate the route taken by Magellan in his 3 year round-the-world voyage starting in 1519 involved taking slabs of wood and having them point either EAST or WEST, but a sign had to be created of each slab naming a place on the voyage. Rob couldn't spell "Philippines" allowing most of the other teams to get ahead during the attempt. Approximately the same order was maintained until reaching staged boats to transport teams to Isla Redonda. Rob/Amber were put with Uchenna/Joyce ahead of Charla/Mirna. However, the Charla/Mirna boat arrived sooner than expected. The ROADBLOCK "Who's good at sorting things out?" was a random task to find mail addressed to a team in a large pile of letters at the southernmost post office in the non-Antarctic continents. Rob performed poorly and Mirna well, resulting in the elimination of Rob/Amber after they had won the first 3 legs.

Ep.5 had a classic moment at the pit stop in Maputo Mozambique. Oswald and Danny, full of coal dust and soot, wanted to share their riches with Phil. The video of Phil dodging them was hilarious.

Ep.6 started with flights Maputo, Mozambique to DarEsSalaam, but World Race Productions had not anticipated the demand for air travel in that direction due to Islamic pilgrims. Charla/Mirna were the only team to get standby on the nonstop flight that I believe WRP had intended to carry all teams. The other teams were frantic for alternatives among a small number of flight combinations, with the last teams Joe/Bill and Ian/Teri 2 days behind reaching DarEs Salaam. There was a legitimate weather issue for crossing to Zanzibar Island (but not warranting the delay edicted by WRP to allow teams to partially catch up). When finally released Charla/Mirna finished first. There is a rumor the original pit stop was at

Arusha Tanzania, so Phil was relocated to an improvised pit stop on Zanzibar Island; I can't say whether that is true is not.

During the following leg, adjustments were made to hold Dustin/ Kandice for 14 hours and the other teams for less in Warsaw to meet carefully scheduled charter bus departures.

I choose the elimination of Rob/Amber as most amazing.

AR12

Ep.1 has the classic animal encounter, with a jackass (no, I am not calling the competing individuals that). On Ireland's west coast at the Cleggan Farm in County Galway was the ultimate man vs. animal challenge. All teams select a donkey, direct it to an area to load up 15 pieces of peat and then direct it back to the starting point. This was as comic as television ever gets. The donkeys of several teams misbehaved and victimized their drivers. Ari/Staella were eliminated as a result of their inability getting their donkey to move at all for 7 hours.

In Finale, teams did Anchorage area tasks. Decisive ROADBLOCK "who wants to relive your experience on the race?" is a memory challenge to choose multiple AR12 objects which fit specific criteria. Teams had a list of types of objects and the episode they were from and had to select an object for each episode also meeting other criteria and place it on the scale. Only the exactly correct combination of objects would allow finishing. Rachel beat Christina; Rachel/TK win AR12.

I choose the donkey task as most amazing.

AR13

Ep.3 had one of the best ROADBLOCKs ever, "Who's ready to pick a fight?" at El Alto Municipal Arena features Los Titanes del Ring, fighting cholitas who are very talented female professional wrestlers. This task did not involve actual wrestling matches but required a member of each team to learn 6 professional wrestling moves and some choreography. To finish, each Amazing Race wrestler had to demonstrate competence in all six moves they were trained in. If they couldn't, they were sent back for retraining and another try. Mark/Bill arrived among the first but Mark's limited skills sent him back twice and they finished next-to-last before a 30 minute penalty for not following directions in the clue to walk (they took a taxi) eliminated them. The footage in the ring and in the practice ring is priceless. The locals in attendance and non-selected team members loved doing what is traditional at a professional wrestling match, cheering and heckling.

In Ep.4 there was an up to 3 hour trip to the Tauranga Bay of Plenty area of New Zealand and return to Auckland International Airport, a similar amount of time. This put the self-drivers in situations where non-compliance with the national speed limits brought out the local police. In the AR13 telecast Terence was ticketed for driving 117 km/hr with a fine by the police and a penalty from the Amazing Race producers. Not shown was a similar situation with Starr.

Ep.7 was ROADLBOCK "Who's ready for a colorful experience?" at the Deshbandu Apartments in Delhi where dozens of young Indians were celebrating an out-of-season (Feb./March is real and this was in early May) Holi Festival where individuals throw bright powdered colors. That includes the selected team member trying to maneuver to a ladder, climb up it, locate the correct Amazing Race envelope and get away with minimal damage. All seem to have many new skin tones, Tina had green hair and Kelly a many-color-array.

Ep.9 DETOUR Boots or Borscht at Kolosok Military Camp required all team members to don Russian military garb first. In Boots they join a marching squad for training/testing for good marching technique. Andrew had prior high school marching band experience, but Dan had a ridiculous gait that causing amusement among the troops and viewers.

Ep.11 the Finale has teams going to Bridge of the Gods where they ziplined to Thunder Island and its 150 clueboxes. Teams had to stay together and sequentially solve a puzzle with 10 slots (one for each prior episode) by inserting the correct photo requested by finding the right one from a given episode in any of the clueboxes. After they find it and test it and light up the game board, they do the next task. Jogging speed was critical to fast task completion. Nick/Starr arrived slightly behind Ken/Tina but finished slightly ahead and kept that through several tasks in downtown Portland Oregon to AR13 victory.

I rate the Holi Festival celebration as most amazing for AR13.

AR14
Ep.1—Teams visit Verzasca Dam in Switzerland near Locarno for a 622 foot bungee jump. That makes it one of the highest bungee jumps in the world. The visual impact on viewers was stunning.

Ep.3—Tammy/Victor get lost on a mountain near Bran Castle in Romania. Victor missed the red and yellow route markers going right and followed another red/white marker a long way up the mountain. Tammy questioned him several times. He needed to keep going and find the next clue. He was unable to second-guess himself until they were over an hour off the route. When Tammy finally convinced him to turn back, it took another hour to get back on course. If Brad/Victoria weren't delayed, Tammy/Victor would have been eliminated here.

Ep.5—TransSiberian Express is one of the most interesting railways in the world. How did World Race Productions take advantage of that? They schedule Krasnoyarsk to Novosibirsk mostly in the dark, with very little of this trip telecast. WRP seldom misses the biggest tourist attractions in an area, but missed on this.

Ep.6—Christie/Jodi selected a taxi driver on arrival at Jaipur Airport. He listened to them want to go to the Sacred Tree, but took them toward Pushkar. By the time this was discovered and turned around, Christie/Jodi arrived at the Amber Fort parking lot 30 minutes after the other teams. That is in addition to having to do a SpeedBump, typically taking another 30 minutes in task plus transportation. How did Christie/Jodi respond? They caught up with Mark/Michael by outstanding performances in the ROADBLOCK and DETOUR and left for the pit stop 2 minutes ahead of them. Mark/Michael's DETOUR was 1.5 miles closer to the pit stop, so they got there first by 2 minutes. Christie/Jodi were eliminated despite impressive performance.

Ep.7/8 Mark/Michael got two 30 minute penalties in Phuket and two 2 hour penalties in Bangkok. They survived the first but far behind from the second didn't reach Guilin until 10am next morning. That left insufficient tasks for recovery; they were eliminated.

Ep.10/11 Tammy/Victor had years of Chinese language instruction pay off. They were able to find task sites in China ahead of other teams. Their Chinese Waiter DETOUR was exemplary.

Ep.12 Victor arrived at ROADBLOCK "Who's Ready to Relive It" behind Luke as Luke had already correctly slotted 9 of 11 surfboards. The first two Victor found were the two Luke needed. Victor then went systematically but very rapidly through the pile of surfboards to find the other 9 that he needed. Jaime was catching up on him, but he finished first. Tammy/Victor went on to win.

Christie/Jodi's recovery effort is AR14's most amazing moment.

SUMMARY
What is the single most amazing moment in Amazing Race history?
AR1– Arrival in Krabi, Thailand of Nancy/Emily and Joe/Bill?
AR2– Wil/Tara lose footrace at East Fort Baker to Chris/Alex?
AR3– Ho Chi Minh City Derek/Drew vs. Ken/Gerard to find the cyclos?
AR4– under-the-ice swim in Hantan Rver, South Korea near DMZ?
AR5– Colin ascends the Lagen Wall near El Nido Island, Philippines?
AR6– Kristy unrolls more than 100 hay bales in Sweden?
AR7– San Juan International Airport "bring back the plane" incident?
AR8– Find the red bean at the Doka Coffee Estate?
AR9– 3 way finish at Lake Bennett Wilderness Resort?
AR10– La Tomatina reenactment in the Barcelona area?
AR11– Rob/Amber lose on Isla Redonda after poor mail identification?
AR12– Ari/Staella can't get their donkey to cooperate on Cleggan Farm?
AR13– Holi Festival celebration, Delhi?
AR14—Christie/Jodi almost recover 1 hour in Jaipur?

My judgment on which is the "best of the best" is between AR2 and AR5. I thought the close finish of AR2 was thrilling in the multiple times I have seen it. However, nothing beats Colin on the ascender at the Lagen Wall. That is the most amazing Amazing Race moment I have ever seen.

Amazing Race Asia Most Amazing Moments

ARA1

Australians have a justifiable pride in their music. In Ep.4 teams use a Sony HD Camera to record a video of an individual they select singing a local bushman ballad "Click Goes the Shears". It's popular in Australia but not everyone knows it. Once done filming, they go back to SONY Central and play the video on a screen. If the person filmed had sung the lyrics of "Click Goes the Shears" right, regardless of their singing skills, that team is done; if not they try again with another individual.

Ep.5 in New Zealand has a deceptively simple task. After crossing from Auckland to Devonport by ferry, teams search for a small girl on a swing. Devonport is not a big place (population 11,000), but walking around this town left most teams clueless. 2 teams discovered that the swing was located only a few hundred meters from the Ferry Terminal. The rest meander around town. Sahil/Prashant illegally accepted 3 rides in private cars, resulting in a penalty causing their elimination.

Ep.6 teams fly to Dunedin and drive to Queenstown, the central point of New Zealand's South Island. The tasks in the Queenstown area are the extreme adventure type. At Bob's Peak the DETOUR is Ledge or Luge. Ledge is much scarier, a giant swing which sends you multiple times out to 400 meters above Queenstown. Luge requires rapid movement to get back to the top of that run. ROADBLOCK "Who can drop 134m in 8.5 seconds?" is the famous Nevis Valley Bungee Jump of 134 meters.

Ep.7 has the most amazing knucklehead moment ever. Michael McKay and his ActiveTV/AXN group take teams to Singapore for the sole purpose of washing a car at a Caltex service station. They may never live that down. Product placement can be OK but this just wasn't right.

Ep.10 Dubai ROADBLOCK "Who's ready to play a round?" is playing 9 holes golf at Emirates Golf Club Par3 course in summer heat averaging 104 an ordeal, like AR2 golf in Cooper Pedy.

Ep.11 also in Dubai uses the Eye of the Emirates (a gondola ferris wheel similar to the London Eye) for a random task. Teams picked a numbered gondola car to enter. The Eye rotates after each selection (including theirs) of a gondola car number. If the number selected isn't correct, they stay on the Eye. Sandy/Francesca battle Zabrina/JoeJer and had systems to sequentially nominated new numbers. Zabrina/JoeJer win this battle when Sandy/Francesca abandoned their system; the number they logically would have picked won for Zabrina/JoeJer.

In Ep.13, finale, an important task was ROADBLOCK "Who can swing like Tarzan?", Francesca vs. Zabrina on a rope obstacle challenge course. Zabrina started with a slight lead. That was enough since it was the last task where any differential timing could happen. Teams go by boat to Bako National Park mangrove swamp area near the Finish Line. Zabrina and JoeJer won by 2 minutes over Sandy/Francesca.

I choose the Devonport New Zealand "girl on a swing" task as the most amazing moment of ARA1.

ARA2
In Japan Ep.5 the ROADLBOCK "Who is cold and calculating" is spell the name of a Japanese city at Tokyo Ice Bar. The selected team member arranges the order of the 6-sided blocks that can only be correctly combined to spell one Japanese city. That is Fukuoka, which is the next destination for ARA2. High-speed train schedules caused extreme Bunching.

Ep.12, the Finale has a memory challenge. They are given a box of flags to choose from and must choose the 12 countries that ARA2 actually visited, placing them in correct order and discarding the 3 that don't apply. It was Rovilson, then Pamela, then Adrian reaching this ROADBLOCK "Who can flag their worldly knowledge?" in that order. However, Adrian blitzed through it correctly and won first place for he and Adrian. Pamela finished 2nd and Rovilson, was left with 3rd place. Adrian had played with and memorized national flags as a child.

ARA2 had few amazing moments. The best of them is the Finale ROADBLOCK where Adrian provides the margin of ARA2 victory.

ARA3

Ep.5 in Taipei teams went to New Sogo Department Store SONY Style Store to use a dedicated BLU-RAY player. Any of 1,000 discs are chosen to find one of 10 with the message "Correct!" when played on the Blu-Ray unit showing they were done and could claim the clue. Others display "Sorry. Try again." Early teams finished quickly. Mathematically the last 3 teams will take hours longer as fewer correct discs are left.

Ep.8 in Pune, India has ROADBLOCK "Who has the better pheta?" with 50 local men walking a garden. Clues are inside only a few of those pheta (think turban). The selected individual asks the wearer if he has the clue, then repeats this process with the next one. I believe this was normalized (clues not taken away) so each individual competing has an equal chance, unlike with the SONY Blu-ray discs where those found are taken away.

Ep.10 at Wadi Tanuf, Nizwa, Oman performance depends on the strength and weight of the competitor to handle the distance over a gorge by level zipline. In ROADBLOCK "Who's ready for a cliff-hanger?" each competitor takes a crack at it. Ida completes it and takes first place. Sam is stuck midway. Geoff passes in the second lane and finishes with ease to capture second place. Fuzzy goes and can't get back from the far side. Sam wisely protects his position by taking the 4 hour non-completion penalty. Fuzzy is forced by her strength/weight ratio to take the same penalty but doing so eliminates her team.

Ep.11, Finale Ida/Tania get unusually poor travel agency help in Muscat airport; with insufficient time to deal with it, their flight combo arriving into Phuket 45 minutes behind the other 2 teams.

The best of the above is Oman zipline gorge ROADBLOCK.

The most amazing moments of Amazing Race Asia are:
ARA1—"girl on a swing" task in Devonport
ARA2—pick and order those national flags ROADBLOCK
ARA3—Oman zipline gorge ROADBLOCK

All 3 are ROADBLOCKs, which create important outcomes late in these races. The "girl on a swing" wins my award as best of ARA.

SUMMARY OF SUCCESSFUL FAST FORWARDS IN ALL AMAZING RACES

The idea for this chapter came from a question while writing another chapter: "How many Amazing Races have had the team finishing the FAST FORWARD not finish that leg in first place?" The answer:

AR1 in Thailand—Joe/Bill dally in Bangkok with money for a taxi, but wait for a cheaper bus to Krabi and finish last except Nancy/Emily get a 24 hour penalty; Joe/Bill are checked in next-to-last

AR3—in a desperate attempt to get back into the race, Andrew/Dennis need instant transportation to Scotland; timely completion of the obstacle course tank piloting is not enough to save them from elimination, but they do go in style with a limo and champagne

AR4 in the Dolomites near Cortina D'Ampezzo—Monica/Sheree win the FAST FORWARD with a snowshoe trek up a hill, but finish 4th

AR10 in Antananarivo Madagascar where the Intersected team of Tyler/James/Rob/Kimberly eats cows lips at a market stand. Their problems slow them enough for Dustin/Kandice to take first place

It should be interesting to take a look at where FAST FORWARDS were, which team won each one, and which other teams contested unsuccessfully (as best I can determine that; there may be some omissions here). You could take it one step farther and calculate the time by which teams finished ahead of the #2 team, but I have not done so. I can say that it is generally a 1 to 3 hour advantage. Two major exceptions to that are Colin/Christie Moscow to Cairo with a finish in leg 5-5 of over 7 hours ahead and Frank/Margarita ending with an 11 hour lead in leg 1-7 Italy to the Taj Mahal

The biggest issue with FAST FORWARDs is that there have not been many since AR4. The first 4 seasons of Amazing Races had FAST FORWARDs on many legs, but after that there haven't been more than 2 taken in any season. There may have been an additional FAST FORWARD opportunity, but the declining advantage from doing them and the challenges that FAST FORWARDs involve have been generally escalating. Let's look at the history of successful FAST FORWARDs :

AR1

Ep.1—at Boiling Pot Victoria Falls there was a steep walk down to the edge of the Zambezi River. Rob/Brennan beat Dave/Margaretta. Taking the FAST FORWARD here was a big advantage for Rob/Brennan later in the race. They had used it and were ineligible, so they could focus on regular tasks without losing time considering FAST FORWARD strategy.

Ep.2—White Water Rafting on Zambezi River near Songwe Village, Pat/Brenda

Ep.3— Paris Mariage Freres Tea shop, Kevin/Drew

Ep.7— search Ferrara Estense Castle moat, Frank/Margarita

Ep.9— Bangkok Reclining Buddha monastery, the famous confrontation of Joe/Bill versus Nancy/Emily; Joe/Bill won

AR2

Ep.2—Copacabana Beach Rio de Janeiro score 10 points against a Brazilian volleyball team, Shola/Doyin beat Gary/Dave; Peggy/Claire withdrew

Ep.4— Windhoek Swapkopmund hotel swimming pool capture the flag, Oswald/Danny

Ep.7—Wong Tai Sin Temple Hong Kong face-reading session with fortune teller, Gary/Dave beat Mary/Peach

Ep.9—Sydney Harry's Cafe de Wheels eat a meat pie, Chris/Alex beat Blake/Paige

Ep.10—Queenstown Shotover River Jet Boat ride to find flag, Blake/Paige beat Wil/Tara

Ep.11— Mt. Tarawera, New Zealand scree run, Wil/Tara

AR3

Ep.1—Mexico City Plaza Santo Domingo search for street typist, Ken/Gerard beat Derek/Drew

Ep.2—Mexico National Museum of Anthropology fly with voladores, Derek/Drew

Ep.3—Cambridge, England Duxford Imperial War Museum, pilot a tank through an obstacle course in 90 or less seconds, Andrew/Dennis

Ep.6—Marrakesh, search through a pile of Oriental rugs for an Amazing Race logo, Ian/Teri beat John Vito/Jill and Flo/Zach dropped out

Ep.7—Innsbruck get the attention of a stationary surfer in the Inn River, Flo/Zach

Ep.9—Kanderstag, Switzerland eat cheese cubes to uncover clue, John Vito/Jill

AR4
Ep.1—Dolomites near Cortina d'Ampezzo snowshoe up a hill, Monica/Sheree

Ep.2—Venice street theatre with Commedia dell Arte, Steve/Dave

Ep.3—Vienna Schonbrunn Palace amidst waltzing couples each safely bring a tray of champagne flutes across the floor, Steve/Josh

Ep.4—Marseilles assemble a mural at the Musee des Tapisseries of the pit stop Chateau des Alpilles, Tian/Jaree

Ep.5—Holland Molen van Sloten Windmill take a ride each attached to a vane, Millie/Chuck

Ep.9—hand-feed 4 pieces of fruit to orangutans at Sepilok Orangutan Rehabilitation Center, Reichen/Chip beat Jon/Kelly

Ep.11—Sunshine Coast of Australia safe water rescue, Dave/Jeff

AR5
Ep.5—Cairo Pharaonic Temple move a sarcophagus, Colin/Christie

Note– Ep.9- famous refusal to do head-shaving by Brandon/Nicole

AR6
Ep.7(TBC of 6)—Budapest Budavari Larinitus drink a goblet of pig's blood, Lori/Bolo

Ep.8—Ajaccio Corsica walk on ocean floor with ancient diving suit, Adam/Rebecca

AR7
Ep.5-Soweto, South Africa Orlando Cooling Tower rope bridge walk, Ray/Deanna beat Rob/Amber
Ep.9 (TBC of 8)—Jodhpur Hindu Temple head shaving, Uchenna/Joyce

AR8
Ep.5—Panama City Power Station Tandem Bungee Jump, Paolo family beat Gaghan family

AR9
Ep.6—Stamatopolous Tavern Athens break plates, Eric/Jeremy beat Monica/Joseph

Ep.10—Lopburi Thailand eat a bowl of crickets and Grasshoppers, BJ/Tyler beat Ray/Yolanda

AR10
Ep.6—Kuwait City put out an oilwell fire, David/Mary are unopposed due to some help by feinting a try from Erwin/Godwin

Ep.8—Antananarivo Madagascar eat Cows' Lips, intersected Rob/Kimberly and Tyler/James

AR11
Ep.8—Krakow Poland count steps for Town Hall and St. Mary's Basilica, intersected Oswald/Danny and Uchenna/Joyce

Ep.10—Hong Kong participate in high speed stunt sequence, Oswald/Danny

AR12

Ep.7—each get a tattoo at Fabio's Studio Empoli Italy,
Nicolas/Donald

AR13
Ep.4—climb mast of Auckland Sky Tower to retrieve gnome,
Ken/Tina

Ep.8—Almaty Kazakhstan eat a traditional local delicacy containing
sheep's butt, Nick/Starr beat Terence/Sarah

AR14
Note—there was an unaired and unused one at the Phuket Zoo
involving spending scarce cash to buy presents for local charities

ARA1
Ep.2 Sahil/Prashant—beat earlier-starting Ernie/Jeena to a school
for "Find SONY Walkman" challenge systemically questioning the
50 students there until they found the clue in a message.

Ep.8 Mardy/Marsio go to Pranang Bay Thailand in a 2-man kayak to
find the clue hidden among numerous caves along the coastline

ARA2
Ep.10 Adrian/Collin count posts against Marc/Rovilson on the Elizabeth Bridge in Budapest to see who gets the correct count of 2377
first. There is big-time gamesmanship by Marc/Rovilson but they
missed two attempts and Adrian/Collin got their second correct.

ARA3
First at SONY Blu-Ray disc challenge gave Vince/Sam the chance
at the FAST FORWARD site before any other team could compete.
They went to Kevin's tattoo parlor for a small "FF" on their arms.

AMAZING RACE PERFORMANCE for CATEGORIES of TEAMS

Some Amazing Race superfans express a strong desire for a Female/Female team Amazing Race U.S. win. It is interesting to analyze how each Female/ Female teams got eliminated or finished in the Finale of their race. I later decided to look at Male/Male teams, then also for Male/Female Couples, and Other Family Relationships. Team totals by category were 33 F/F, 34 M/M, 64 Couples and 26 Other Family.

The Female/Female category, why teams were eliminated or didn't win:

AR1, Ep.2 Kim/Leslie—couldn't locate cluebox at Arc de Triomphe fast
AR1, Ep.3 Pat/Brenda—found the wrong Foucault's Pendulum in Paris
AR1, Ep.9 Nancy/Emily—incurred 24 hour penalty for taking taxi when only bus or car (they couldn't find) to Kanchanburi allowed

AR2, Ep.1 Deidre/Hilary - slow on rappel down from Sugarloaf Mountain
AR2, Ep.3 Peggy/Claire - went to CapeTown from Sao Paulo via NYC
AR2, Ep.7 Mary/Peach - exhaustion at tea-drinking ROADBLOCK

AR3, Ep.1 Gina/Sylvia—could not find pit stop near Mexico City
AR3, Ep.4 Heather/Eve—incurred 37 minute penalty for taking a taxi to Torre de Belem instead of required walking

AR4, Ep.6 Monica/Sheree—generally lagging behind in Mumbai
AR4, Ep.7 Tian/Jaree—lost to Chip/Reichen on elephant vs. on bicycle

AR5, Ep.7 Charla/Mirna—delayed flight then lost finish to Kami/Karli
AR5, Ep.10 Kami/Karli—lost finish of leg at zorb to Chip/Kim
AR5, Ep.12 Linda/Karen—Karen lost the Lagen Wall ascender task

AR6, Ep.2 Meredith/Maria—poor stick shift driving in Norway
AR6, Ep.3 Lena/Kristy—couldn't find clues in hay bales near Stockholm

AR7, Ep.2 Megan/Heidi—lost finish to Greg/Brian in Santiago park
AR7, Ep.3 Debbie/Bianca—went 100+ miles each way out of the way driving north in Chile when they needed to take exit going east

AR9, Ep.2 Joni/Lisa—problems driving a VW stick shift in Brazil
AR9, Ep.3 Wanda/Desiree—poor driving skills navigating Autobahn
AR9, Ep.4 Dani/Danielle—YIELDed by Lake/Michelle

AR10, Ep.2 Kellie/Jamie—poor navigating Nat. Park to Mongolia House
AR10, Ep.12 Dustin/Kandice—drove by North African Horse Ranch and Olive Farm sign in Idelssan Morocco for last place
AR10, Finale Lyn/Karlyn—to Orly Airport for NYC flight, then arrived CharlesdeGaulle Airport late so no chance at seats on full flight; inferior flights Paris to Dublin to Newark, landing 1 hour behind top 2

AR11, Finale Charla/Mirna—inferior taxi performance from Oakland International Airport to Grateful Dead House
AR11, Finale Dustin/Kandice—inferior taxi performance from Oakland International Airport to Grateful Dead House

AR12, Ep.2 Kate/Pat–missed last #30 bus to Ransdorp, last to vaulting
AR12, Ep.3 Marianna/Julia-problems milking camel, doing DETOUR fast
AR12, Ep.5 Shana/Jennifer-lost battle vs. Nicolas/Donald in Vilnius

AR13, Ep.4 Marissa/Brooke—bad driving skills in New Zealand
AR13, Ep.7 Kelly/Christy—lost electric system tag task to Dan/Andrew

AR14, Ep.6 Christie/Jodi—poor taxi driver in Jaipur area overwhelmed otherwise excellent recovery effort
AR14, Ep.11 Lakisha/Jennifer—inability to locate Birds Nest Stadium
AR14, Finale Jaime/Cara—bad taxi performance put them behind

There are 33 female/female teams shown above. This invites comparison to why the male/male teams were eliminated or finished where they did in the Finale if not first. Here is the same analysis for

Male/Male teams. Brother/brother teams are shown here but father/son or grandfather/grandson are Other Family Relationships:

AR1, Ep. 11 Kevin/Drew-lost taxi race South Gate Tiantan Park Joe/Bill

AR1, Ep. 13 Finale Joe/Bill—24 hours behind in Alaska as race finishes in NYC due to not seizing the Fast Forward opportunity in Thailand; 3rd

AR1, Ep. 13 Finale Brennan/Rob—won

AR2, Ep. 4 Shola/Doyin—lost driving in the sands of Namibia

AR2, Ep. 9 Gary/Dave—to Cooper Pedy last; not on 1st charter flight

AR2, Ep. 11 Oswald/Danny—slower in Lost World Caves than Alex/Chris

AR2, Ep. 13 Finale Alex/Chris—won

AR3, Ep. 7 Andre/Damon—screwed up in flight connection in Paris, so behind arriving in Germany and never caught up

AR3, Ep. 11 Derek/Drew—inability to locate cyclos in Ho Chi Minh City

AR3, Ep. 13 Finale Ken/Gerard—finished 3rd animal head ordering task

AR4, Ep. 4 Steve/Josh—driving to Gorges du Blavet, went to wrong place

AR4, Ep. 5 Steve/Dave—lost to David/Jeff after both missed half-hour connection Charles de Gaulle to Orly airports 21 miles apart

AR4, Ep. 11 Jon/Al—flight delay problems Seoul to Brisbane

AR4, Ep. 13 Finale David/Jeff—went to Sydney from Cairns to reach Hawaii when they should have connected in Tokyo

AR4, Ep. 13 Finale Reichen/Chip—won

AR5, Ep. 6 Marshall/Lance—slow on DETOUR

AR6, Ep. 1 Avi/Joe—slower navigation in Iceland vs. Gus/Hera

AR7, Ep. 1 Ryan/Chuck—lost taxi race in Cuzco Peru to Ron/Kelly

AR7, Ep. 7 Brian/Greg— make wrong turn navigating in Botswana

AR7, Ep. 8 Lynn/Alex—lose race to finish line with Gretchen/Meredith after going to the wrong Indian castle in a taxi

AR9, Ep. 1 Scott/John— behind before arriving at Rotors DETOUR
AR9, Finale Eric/Jeremy—Eric loses to BJ on flag challenge; 2nd
AR9, Finale BJ/Tyler—won

AR10, Ep. 1 Billel/Saeed—had taxi problems in reaching Meridian
Gate, Beijing where Phil Keoghan unexpectedly eliminated them
AR10, Ep. 4 Tom/Terry—rowing problems in Vietnam
AR10, Ep. 10 Erwin/Godwin—had huge navigational problems in
Ukraine
AR10, Ep. 13 Finale Tyler/James—won

AR11, Ep. 2 Kevin/Drew—drove under speed limit in Atacama
Desert, turned right when unmarked left would have saved them
AR11, Ep. 8 Joe/Bill—design of legs leaves them behind after flight
problems that started in Mozambique and continued in Tanzania
AR11, Ep.12 Danny/Oswald—Guam ground navigation faulty; 4th

AR13, Ep. 3 Mark/Bill—30 minute penalty taking a taxi, not walking
AR13, Finale Andrew/Dan—finished 3rd; taxi problem in Oregon

AR14, Ep. 7 Mel/Michael—poor taxi driver in Phuket
AR14, Ep. 9 Mark/Michael—unable to catch up after penalties in
Bangkok plus flight schedules make10 hours behind arriving Guilin

There are 34 Male/Male teams; 5 of them won their Amazing Race.
Here is the list of teams composed of Male-Female couples:

AR1, Ep. 1 Matt/Ana—navigation issues finding Songwe village
AR1, Ep. 4 David/Margaretta—David loses El Jem Coliseum
Tunisia ROADBLOCK battle to Emily
AR1, Ep. 5 Paul/Amie—lost in Sahara Desert searching for an oasis
AR1, Ep. 7 Lenny/Karen—bad taxi ride Agra airport to Taj Khema
Hotel
AR1, Ep. 13 Finale Frank/Margarita—Frank overvalues his ability to
navigate to Queens so they are 10 minutes behind Rob/Brennan

AR2, Ep. 2 Hope/Norm—lose to Blake/Paige Iguassu Falls to jungle
camp
AR2, Ep. 5 Cyndi/Russell—can't navigate to Bangkok's bird
marketplace

AR2, Ep. 13 Wil/Tara—inability to get ahead of Chris/Alex on taxi ride to East Fort Baker, Marin County

AR3, Ep. 5 Michael/Kathy—on drive through Spain, Michael puts diesel fuel into unleaded tank; engine won't perform; 3 other teams who find a way to stay in the race, but Michael/Kathy do not
AR3, Ep. 6 Aaron/Ariane—other team to pay price for DIESELGATE; they survived Ep. 5, but behind other teams, unable to catch up in Morocco
AR3, Ep. 8 John Vito/Jill—navigation problems self-driving in Singapore
AR3, Finale Ian/Teri—2nd; animal head twirling ROADBLOCK slow
AR3, Finale Flo/Zach—win

AR4, Ep. 1 Deborah/Steve—last bus tickets from Milan, then lack of physical fitness for both of them is decisive in tasks in the Dolomites
AR4, Ep. 2 Amanda/Chris—Masked Ball in Venice is mad scramble for matching real masks with photos; they miss multiple times
AR4, Ep. 3 Rusell/Cindy—ticket agent mistake Gmundsen for Gmund
AR4, Ep. 9 Millie/Chuck—bad navigating in Sarawak lost to Jon/Kelly
AR4, Finale Jon/Kelly—miss close connection Tokyo-Narita airport; behind until flight Honolulu to Phoenix boarding; Chip/Reichen used lead to earn navigation edge after arriving in Phoenix; finished 2nd

AR5, Ep. 1 Dennis/Erika—are involved in taxi shortage at key point in Uruguay; Dennis offers their taxi to Colin, so later they're out
AR5, Ep. 2 Allison/Donny—Buenos Aires to countryside; they take local bus; later other teams on express buses pass
AR5, Ep. 4 Bob/Joyce—later flights from Buenos Aires to St. Petersburg doom this team to being last at every task in Russia
AR5, Finale Brandon/Nicole—checking bag at Calgary forced them to take a later Denver to Dallas flight on American Airlines
AR5, Finale Colin/Christie—checking a bag at Calgary forced them to take later Denver to Dallas flight on American airlines, then their limo driver got a flat driving on the shoulder making up lost time
AR5, Finale Chip/Kim—won

AR6, Ep. 4 Don/MaryJean-lost to Lori/Bolo soapbox derby, walking
AR6, Ep. 7 Jonathan/Victoria—failure to take 2 donkeys from pen

AR6, Ep. 9 Lori/Bolo—failure to follow clue sends Lori up Lion Rock in Sri Lanka without a needed ticket; Freddy did same but turned around quicker to identify the location of the pit stop from the top
AR6, Ep. 11 Hayden/Aaron—Rebecca vs. Hayden for last Final 3 spot; Rebecca finds lock for her key at last moment after Hayden/Aaron had taken 4 hour ROADBLOCK non-completion penalty
AR6, Ep.12, Finale Rebecca/Adam-don't perform Hawaii tasks fast; 3rd
AR6, Ep.12, Finale Jon/Kris—bad decision at Honolulu Airport for American Airlines arriving 10 minutes after United Airlines flight in Chicago; can't catch Freddy/Kendra at Finish Line; 2nd
AR6, Ep.12, Finale Freddy/Kendra—won

AR7, Ep. 6—Ray/Deana lost out in footrace from car to pit stop less than 100 yards away to Brian/Greg at Makgadikani Pans
AR7, Ep. 10 Gretchen/Meredith—lost time carrying 5 160 pound boats in London's Battersea Park
AR7, Finale Ron/Kelly—missed turn to San Juan Airport so missed plane to Miami that other two teams made; 3rd
AR7, Finale Rob/Amber—could not find Cuban cigar store that only speaks Spanish language in Miami's Little Havana; 2nd
AR7, Finale Uchenna/Joyce—won

AR9, Ep. 5 Dave/Lori—lagged behind on this entire leg
AR9, Ep. 6 Lake/Michelle—driving in a rainstorm at night in a contest against BJ/Tyler, Lake gets behind and arrives last
AR9, Ep. 8 Fran/Barry—bad taxi karma; reserved taxi never came
AR9, Ep. 10 Joseph/Monica—lose FAST FORWARD to BJ/Tyler
AR9, Ep. 12 Ray/Yolanda—slow getting Denver Airport to Red Rocks area for tasks, finished 3rd

AR10, Ep. 1 Vipul/Arti—trailing most of the episode in China
AR10, Ep. 6 Peter/Sarah—inability to navigate around Kuwait City
AR10, Ep. 8 David/Mary—one task after Intersection didn't allow recovery from 30 minute MARKED FOR ELIMINATION penalty
AR10, Finale Rob/Kimberly—taxi driver crossing Queens didn't have EZPass and didn't know the way to News Building in Manhattan; 2nd

AR11, Ep. 1 John Vito/Jill—inability to navigate
AR11, Ep. 3 David/Mary—distracted while driving to LaMaquina,

went 3 hours out of the way and were last by about 10 minutes
AR11, Ep. 4 Rob/Amber—did poorly in Punta Arenas to fall behind, then Rob lost ROADBLOCK to Mirna at Isla Redonda post office
AR11, Ep. 6 Ian/Teri—Joe/Bill beat on Zanzibar Island by 2 minutes
AR11, Ep. 9 Uchenna/Joyce—risky connection in Frankfurt from Krakow to Kuala Lumpur; ticket problems caused them to miss flight
AR11, Ep. 13 Finale Eric/Danielle—won

AR12, Ep. 1 Ari/Staella—balky donkey Cleggan Farms outwits them
AR12, Ep. 4 Lorena/Jason—poor Ep. 3, 1.5hours behind; couldn't recover
AR12, Ep. 8 Kynt/Vyxsin—tried to U-Turn Nicolas/Donald unsuccessfully; with better information they U-Turn Nathan/Jennifer, survive
AR12, Ep. 10 Nathan/Jennifer—used subway/bus advice by Taipei local; 3 other teams took taxis to Earth DETOUR arriving earlier
AR12, Ep. 11 Finale TK/Rachel—won

AE13, Ep. 1, Arthur/Anita—lagged behind throughout this episode
AR13, Ep. 2 Anthony/Stephanie--last to figure out solution to ROADBLOCK to discover name of pit stop location on painted wall
AR13, Ep. 8 Terence/Sarah eating challenge FAST FORWARD but unable to eat quickly enough to compete with Nick/Starr

AR14, Ep. 1 Preston/Jennifer—on Milan flight; late for connection to rail; almost recovered but later lost pit stop footrace to Christie/Jodi
AR14, Ep. 2 Linda/Steve—she made a wrong turn jogging down Rauschberg Mountain in Germany; they lost 4 hours and were out
AR14, Ep. 3 Brad/Victoria—made risky decision to connect in Amsterdam to reach Bucharest 15 minutes ahead of several teams; flight Munich to Amsterdam was delayed; they were stuck overnight
AR14, Ep. 4 Amanda/Kris—average on tasks but YIELDed to fall 30 minutes behind; they finished 10 minutes behind Mark/Michael

There were 64 male/female couples in Amazing Races (without those in families). 6 male/female couples won Amazing Races. Finally, we have the family relationships, which include 8 families with children, 2 families without children, 4 father/daughter teams, 3 mother/son teams, 6 brother/sister teams and 1 father/son team and 1 grandfather/grandson team (6 brother/brother teams were categorized under male/male). 2 brother/sister teams and 1 family team won. The Family Relationships list is:

AR2, Finale Blake/Paige—slower navigation around San Francisco; 3rd

AR3, Ep. 2 Tramel/Talicia—Tramel can't handle a WAVERUNNER
AR3, Ep. 3 Dennis/Andrew—couldn't get timely flight Mexico to London

AR5, Ep. 3 Jim/Marsha—inability to get earlier flights dooms them to one hour after the next earlier flight Buenos Aires to Bariloche

AR6, Ep. 7 Gus/Hera—in a race with Freddy/Kendra, Gus/Hera lose out by getting behind in Budapest and unable to catch up

AR7, Ep. 4 Susan/Patrick—water trip around Tigre Argentina their boat engine died, requiring replacement; unable to regain time lost

AR8, Ep. 1 Black Family-Linzes won route to Lancaster Rohrer Farm
AR8, Ep. 2 Rogers Family—lost race battlefield task to Paolos
AR8, Ep. 3 Aiello family--lost race at U.S.RocketCenter to Gaghans
AR8, Ep. 4 Schroeder Family—slow to finish gambling, unable to use New Orleans home-town advantage
AR8, Ep. 6 Gaghan Family—Tammy last "Find Red Bean" ROADBLOCK
AR8, Ep. 8 Paolo Family— had trouble navigating to Glen Canyon dam, arrived last there, then last after task and last at pit stop
AR8, Ep. 10 Godlewski Family—had trouble navigating around Montana to Red Lodge Mountain Golf Course and pit stop Green Meadow Ranch
AR8, Finale, Finale Weaver Family—slow getting to Joseph Davis State Park, then could not compete on the 50 state map puzzle; 3rd
AR8, Finale Branson Family—Wally did that puzzle quickly, but not quickly enough to beat Nick Linz; 2nd
AR8, Finale Linz Family—won

AR10, Ep. 3 Duke/Lauren—lost navigating around Vac, Vietnam

AR12 Ep. 6 Azaria/Hendekea—screwed by travel agent ticketing, then Azaria didn't notice anchor preventing him from rowing
AR12, Ep. 11 Finale Nicolas/Donald—finished 3rd due to inferior memory challenge ROADBLOCK performance

AR12, Ep. 11 Finale Christina/Ronald—lost lead to Rachel at memory challenge ROADBLOCK; finished 2nd

AR13, Ep. 5 Aja/Ty—were behind for Ep.4 finish, not able to reach Singapore to make a critical flight connection to Siem Reap
AR13, Ep. 10 Toni/Dallas—loses pack/money/passports during ROADBLOCK; begging money for transportation delays them
AR13, Ep. 11 Finale Nick/Starr—won

AR14, Ep. 7 Mel/Michael—poor taxi driver in Phuket
AR14, Finale Margie/Luke—Luke lost ROADBLOCK find and place 11 surfboards with icons for AR14 episodes in correct order; 3rd
AR14, Finale Tammy/Victor—won

You can see that World Race Productions attempts a good cross-section of the different categories of teams. 26 teams are in the above Family Relationships category.

For AR14, CBS announced footage of racers making flight reservations and flying would be cut drastically versus prior seasons. I believe that's a mistake. The Amazing Race is a circumnavigation of the globe. Are there any land routes around the globe not part of the Arctic or Antarctic that can do that? You know the answer. With 11 or 12 episodes and the shortest route about 20,000 miles, the average distance of each episode will be above 2,000 miles. Travel time by land varies, but is a minimum of 2 days on the road or rails. Air travel is necessary for any prompt circumnavigation of the globe. Interesting things happen at travel agencies, airline offices and airports that change the outcome of races.

The scenes we typically see are teams visiting travel agents or airport airline booking agents. Air travel can be fiendishly complex. On a leg Phuket to Bangkok it is a single nonstop flight. Other times like Novosibirsk to Jaipur it takes over 24 hours from when teams are released from the pit stop, find out where they have to go and get there via Moscow and Delhi. From Kuwait City to CapeTown, South Africa was the ultimate indignity. Flying 9,400 miles via London to get there compares to the more logical direct route of 5,500 miles through Dubai that only flies other days of the week.

The ultimate nightmare for an AR producer is teams strung out across 2 days getting to their destination, found in AR11 on the route Maputo, Mozambique to DarEs Salaam, Tanzania. There is a nonstop flight on the date teams wanted to go but it was full. Teams had to backtrack to Johannesburg and from there to DarEsSalaam (DES), an unusual mess because of Hajj for Moslem religious pilgrims. One team reached DES the afternoon of pit stop release, several teams followed the next morning and 2 teams didn't get out until the third morning (through Blantyre Malawi). WRP apparently had a rare planning error and were surprised by problems.

The extreme range of pit stop times in Zanzibar directly translated to problems on the next leg when teams flew to Warsaw. Dustin/ Kandice booked Addis Ababa and Frankfurt as connect points while Uchenna/Joyce booked Johannesburg and Frankfurt. Johannesburg/Frankfurt flight was delayed and they missed the earliest flight to Warsaw but caught one less than 2 hours later. Charla/Mirna and Oswald/Danny were booked connecting through Nairobi and Amsterdam and landed a half hour after Dustin/Kandice. Eric/Danielle and Joe/Bill were much later than the rest. They booked through Arusha and Frankfurt but a KLM pilot screwed them in Arusha by not letting them on with 50 minutes connect time. They took a flight the next morning and arrived in Warsaw long after others had finished. This caused Joe/Bill to be last on that leg and eliminated next leg by a Marked for Elimination 30 minute penalty.

One of the better examples of an exciting difference in route strategies occurred leaving Krakow, Poland for Kuala Lumpur, Malaysia, 5,500 miles as the crow flies. The crow wasn't flying on the routes chosen by the teams. First place on arrival more than 2 hours ahead of other teams were Charla/Mirna, who either due to their own research (which was top-notch) or by the assistance of an excellent travel agent, got a connection in Vienna that involved minimal backtracking and arrived at 445am. The next team departing from Krakow was Uchenna/Joyce with minimum connect time in Frankfurt. When their flight arrived slightly late and there were ticket complications they missed the one nonstop flight to Kuala Lumpur. 3 other teams routed themselves through Paris with more connect time and arrived in Kuala Lumpur 2 3/4 hours behind Charla/Mirna. Uchenna/Joyce's next best alternative was a flight through Hong Kong arriving at dusk, causing them to be given the "mercy finish" of elimination. There are many who believe that this leg was designed to be a non-elimination leg originally but was altered because the time spread for Uchenna/Joyce versus the other teams was too great for Bunching to get them back into the race. I find most interesting attempting to duplicate Charla/Mirna's flight reservation from Vienna to Kuala Lumpur a week after the actual race happened there (not later when telecast on CBS) was not possible for an individual with serious international flight booking experience. The conclusion was they took flight OS1 Vienna to Kuala Lumpur, not supposed to operate that day. Go figure!

Another example is the AR14 saga of Brad and Victoria from Munich, Germany to Bucharest. The other teams flew nonstop. Brad and Victoria wanted to "break away from the pack" and they chose a tight connection in Amsterdam (serious backtracking again) for minimal gain. When their flight from Munich to Amsterdam was delayed they didn't have enough connect time to make the last flight from Amsterdam to Bucharest. They were stranded until the next morning, which effectively eliminated them soon after arrival at the beginning of the 5+ hour Romanian portion of this episode.

ARA3 Ep. 8 required travel Hong Kong to Cochin India. 5 teams left Hong Kong. Geoff/Tisha were first to arrive and booked via Singapore, connecting there to Cochin. Vince/Sam flew later through Singapore to Mumbai and Bernie/Henry duplicated that. Ida/Tania found a nonstop Hong Kong to Mumbai flight, with time to connect there to Cochin and AD/Fuzzie duplicated that. The flights of Ida/Tania and AD/Fuzzie got them to Mumbai in time for an easy connection. Vince/Sam and Bernie/Henry are in trouble. Their flight Singapore to Mumbai is late and they miss their connection Mumbai to Cochin and cannot get to Cochin until about 7am the next morning. The first 3 teams have already finished the Cochin portion of the leg by then so 1 of these 2 teams will finish last. Vince/Sam pick a different DETOUR; Bernie/Henry are eliminated.

AR14 flying Bucharest to Krasnojarsk is similar. 8 teams used 4 different routes (via Istanbul, Sofia, Munich, Frankfurt). All teams went through Moscow's Sheremetyevo airport, although through some connection points to there they could alternatively have chosen Moscow's Domodedovo airport. The first 3 teams arrive with sufficient connect time for security/customs. They made the 8:55pm flight. All teams connecting through Germany (backtracking) were later and although they theoretically had enough connect time in actuality they didn't reach the gate at Sheremetyevo in time. The next flight left and arrived 3.5 hours behind the first one.

The AR12 flights from Ouagadougou Burkina Faso to Vilnius Lithuania illustrate the impact of different connecting points. The 7 teams all flew the same nonstop Ouagadougou to Paris-Charles de Gaulle. There they connect through Amsterdam, Paris, Frankfurt and Prague. This is not one of those horror stories, as all team had on-time connections and arrived in Vilnius within a 45 minute range.

AR12 from Vilnius to Dubrovnik connections mattered a great deal. We had 6 teams who wanted to fly that route. The possibilities are: 3 teams chose an early flight to Warsaw, connecting in Vienna and arriving Dubrovnik 1120am

2 teams chose an early flight to Prague that left late, so the connection to Vienna and then Zagreb is missed; this caused one team to elect to continue on that route and arrive 240pm and the other team to connect in Zagreb and arrive late at 345pm
1 team is mistakenly put into business class by the airline agent (24 hour penalty if they actually fly there) as those are the only seats available; they discover this in time, but then their options are limited to connecting in Amsterdam and Frankfurt and arriving 415pm. As a result plus weak rowing, Azaria/Hendekea lost.

AR12 flying 4,000 miles Mumbai India to Osaka Japan illustrates that teams tend to book identical flights. The team breaking away from the pack is sometimes brilliant (AR5's Colin/Christie or AR11's Charla/Mirna Krakow to Kuala Lumpur) and sometimes foolish like Brad/Victoria in AR14. 3 teams got the same flight connecting in Hong Kong, arriving together. TK/Rachel booked a different routing through Delhi and Beijing, arriving 3 hours later. If that leg had been elimination, they were toast. They were fortunate it was non-elimination and they could recover despite a SpeedBump next leg.

One of the neatest things on AR13 was the trans-South Pacific flight that teams took from Santiago Chile (reached by plane from LaPaz Bolivia via Buenos Aires) nonstop for 13 hours to Auckland New Zealand about 6,000 miles west. The CBS Amazing Race map implied that this trip was done eastward from LaPaz to the east coast of South America, then to South Africa and then to Australia, but it happened east to west on a single flight Santiago to Auckland.

Ability to complete bookings rapidly can be decisive. In ARA3 Finale, Ida/Tania reached Muscat airport ahead of Vince/Sam but due to problems with an airport ticketing agent did not get the same flight as Geoff/Tisha and Vince/Sam who connected through Dubai and Bangkok to get to Phuket. Ida/Tania got a later flight to Dubai and was forced to fly to Singapore to connect to Phuket, but a 45 minute deficit stayed with them. Ida/Tania finished third in ARA3.

The wrong decision in flight routing can be fatal. The best example is ARA2. Ann/Diane played it safe with a Budapest to London to CapeTown routing while the others took risks with a Budapest to Frankurt to CapeTown routing. The more direct routing arrived about 3 hours earlier, causing the elimination of Ann/Diane.

Amazing Race Self-Driving Highlights

Amazing scenes from Amazing Races occur when teams must drive themselves. Driving in the U.S. does not pose serious challenges most of the time, but in foreign countries where little English is spoken the results of self-driving can be chaotic. Teams must interact with locals to find destinations or be very talented at map reading and navigating. Following are the most interesting incidences of self-driving in AR10-14 and ARA1, ARA2 and ARA3.

My favorite case study for this happens when AR12 teams receive a marked car in Ancona Italy at 940pm, navigating to Empoli about 200 miles away but not a simple "take this autostrada from point A to point B" experience. Here are the different routes used:
Nathan/Jennifer-A13 north to Forli, SS27 east to Firenze, SW on SP127, A1 W, Strada Grande Comunicazione Firenze-Pisa-Livorno W to Empoli
Nicolas/Donald, Christina/Ronald, Kynt/Vyxsin—A14 north to Bologna, A1 SW to Firenze, A11 west and local roads SW to Empoli
TK/Rachel-A14 south to Giulianova, A24 SW to Borgorose, E80 south toward Rome, A1 north to Firenze, A11 west + local roads SW to Empoli
The terrain was difficult crossing the spine of Italy, the Apennine Mountains. Nathan/Jennifer arrived first in darkness. TK/Rachel arrived at dawn. Teams on A14 north reach a temporary road blockage before the Firenze/Milan cutoff. 2 teams try local roads. Nicolas/Donald waited out the road delay until 6am; it reopened; they made it around 7am. Christina/Ronald arrived soon after 7am. Kynt/Vyxsin were lost and arrived 1.5 hours after the opening hours of operation for the airfield.

In Mongolia AR10 teams left Ulaanbaatar for Gorkhi Terelj National Park about 45 miles away in old Russian military jeeps. They encountered breakdowns. Tyler/James had a mechanical break-down. Jamie/Kellie had one and difficulty getting the engine restarted. Lyn/Karlyn had a similar problem. Jamie/Kellie were clueless about navigating, leaving the National Park to get 47 miles to Mongolia Hotel. Poor navigating was the cause of elimination.

For me the saddest incidence of poor self-driving occurred in AR10

279

in Morocco where Dustin/Kandice in first place chose a DETOUR returning to Idelssan area from Café Pirgola. They overestimated their navigational skills and missed the sign for the North Africa Horse Ranch and Olive Farm. It's 4 miles away from Café Pirgola. They took too long to realize their mistake. They reached it last and later were non-eliminated. A 30 minute Marked for Elimination penalty minimized their chances in the next leg (Barcelona).

ARA3 Finale teams released from a desert pit stop had to find Said's Camel Farm and do a ROADBLOCK with major risk of getting stuck in the sand. It happened to 2 of the 3 teams, with Vince/Sam able to regain valuable time and catch up at Muscat airport.

Teams in ARA2 had to navigate the difficult navigational challenge of South Korea from Busan through Seoil Farm at Anseong to Woncheon Resort at Suwon and Korean Folk Village in Youngin to Seoul airport. Vanessa as driver made a wrong turn, went out of the way and had to make a U-turn at a toll booth to retrieve the route.

Reaching Chennai, AR10 teams found a ROADBLOCK classes at Karthik Driving School needed to obtain an India driving permit to allow driving a School vehicle 10 miles in Chennai to the pit stop.

In AR11, teams drove from Quito to Cotopaxi National Park and then on to Hacienda Yanahurco. John Vito/Jill had a history of poor navigation from getting to Mt. Faber in Singapore in AR3. They have the same problems here. They miss the northern entrance to Cotopaxi National Park and use the longer southern entrance route. Charla/Mirna made the same mistake but they were well in front of John Vito/Jill. Kevin/Drew were also ahead of them and got to the pit stop next to last after suffering a tire blowout and driving the last several miles on the rim. John Vito/Jill were eliminated.

In AR11 in Chile, teams drive from Metri, southern suburb of Puerto Montt, to La Maquina on the Petrohue River near Petrohue. Joe/Bill took off with only half the clue to get 50 km away from the next clue. By a miracle they run across Charla/Mirna in the same area who had the full clue and shared it. Both teams shared resources to avoid elimination. David/Mary were reportedly distracted in conversation with the WRP soundman and missed the turnoff for 3 hours extra. They were barely last and eliminated.

Any self-driving in India (examples already provided) is perilous. Congestion, animals in the streets, honking of horns, and the poor driving skills of the natives always make this a treat for the eyes.

AR13 teams released from the pit stop near Tauranga New Zealand had to get 2.5+ hours to Auckland airport by taking a northwest route on some major highways. This was difficult but compounded by the strict enforcement of speed limits in New Zealand. The telecast showed a ticket to Terence/Sarah for going 117 km/hr in a 100 km/hr zone. It did not show the similar ticket that Starr received.

In AR11 in southwest Poland teams self-drive 20 miles from Krakow to Pieskowa Skala. Charla/Mirna elected to hire a taxi to follow; the driver attempted to rip them off along the way. Mirna argued her way out of it; they arrived at the castle soon enough to not be last.

In Ep.1 of ARA1, Mardy/Marsio and Jacqueline/Aubrey hired taxis to follow, still a common practice in Amazing Race Asias.

The finale of ARA1 finished in the Sarawak region of Malaysia. Marked cars are driven around Kuching and then 35 miles to Sarawak Cultural Village, then 32 km to Permai Rain Forest Resort. 2 teams hired taxis to follow and battled for the Finish Line. Andrew/Syeon relied on a Lonely Planet guide, fell behind and finished 3rd.

You didn't think you would see the end of this chapter without my views on self-drivers hiring taxis to follow, did you? I despise this practice. It happens because it is not prohibited by Amazing Race rules (it should be) and because teams do begging not shown in telecasts to raise enough money to fund an only slightly limited number of insurance policies via hiring the taxi to follow. I don't like those insurance policies and I want to see them disappear from future Amazing Races. No purpose is served, because instead of seeing a self-driving experience with all its uncertainties, we are effectively seeing that team in a taxi ride. Bertram van Munster and Michael McKay, are you listening? Please change the rules to prohibit self-drivers following hired taxis.

AMAZING RACE and TAXIS

The random selection of a taxi driver can be the difference between who wins and who finishes lower in an Amazing Race. Since the finale of a race is Bunched at an important point in the last leg, small things will lead to the differentiation of team performance. In non-final legs, getting a poor taxi driver can spell doom for a team.

A fine example of the taxi driver or taxi equipment happened in the finale of AR10 when Tyler/James were racing in cabs against Rob/Kimberly for first place from Kennedy Airport to the News Building in Manhattan. At a Queens toll plaza, the taxi Tyler/James were in had EZ-Pass and went through quickly while Rob/Kimberly's lost time in the cash lane. Those minutes were the final difference in that race.

Let's review some favorite taxi driver situations in anecdotes from Amazing Races 10 to 14 and Amazing Races Asia 1 to 3. One example of taxis making a difference was the finale of AR11. Eric/Danielle raced by taxi from Oakland International Airport to the Grateful Dead House in San Francisco's Haight/Ashbury, did a brief unaired task there, then the taxi took them to the Old Mint. By arrival there they had built an edge of 5 to 10 minutes over Dustin/Kandice which remained at the finish line at Strybing Arboretum.

In Moscow in AR13, Ken/Tina had an excellent taxi driver with a GPS system who spoke English. When Ken fell behind Nick on the ROADBLOCK, Nick was able to take over that taxi and made it part of his campaign to develop a strong lead by the end of that episode.

Another taxi borrowing scheme was by ARA1's Andy/Laura in Kolkata after the teams finish a task at Kaniska's Sari boutique. Andy/Laura were done that task ahead of Sandy/Francesca and offered the taxi driver more money to work for them. Immediately after that the To Be Continued (TBC) directive and the Bunching at Sealdah Station meant that this had no impact on the outcome of the race. However, it did have an impact on the reputation of Andy/Laura as sharp dealers who would do anything to win.

AR10 near Chennai, India Dustin/Kandice were in first place on the way to the DETOUR Wild Things at the Madras Crocodile Bank when their taxi's tire went flat. That gave Peter/Sarah the chance to take first place by a small margin; they never relinquished it.

In Dubrovnik in AR12, the teams could elect to row around the city to get to the other side and most did. Nathan/Jennifer were leading as they reached the taxi pickup, but their wet bathing suits caused many taxi drivers to not allow them into their cabs. That caused Nathan/Jennifer to fall from first place to third place.

In Taipei, failure to use a taxi cost Nathan/Jennifer the race. They used a combination of subway and bus based on the advice of locals to avoid rush hour congestion. They arrived for the Earth DETOUR after all of the 3 other teams which used taxis to Youth Park. Later that episode, they were eliminated as a result.

Another example of "do or die" involving taxis was AR13 in Moscow for the penultimate episode where Dallas was sent by his mother Toni to do a complicated ROADBLOCK. One of the parts of it involved transportation between the Fallen Monument Park and a bookstore and Mikhail Bulgakov's house. Somewhere in there Dallas took off his money/passport belt during some type of filming preparation and he forgot to retrieve it. The taxi driver at some point discovered it and dropped it off at the U.S. Embassy in Moscow, but Dallas/Toni could not function effectively without money. Even with begging they were not able to raise enough funds to not fall behind and out of the race. After the other 3 teams had been checked in at the pit stop, Dallas/Toni were eliminated on the street.

In AR14, 2 or 3 teams had to get from their arrival point by flying from Novosibirsk at Moscow's Domodedovo airport to Sheremetyevo airport where their flight to New Delhi would originate from. It's possible to do this by taxi or a non-trivial subway trip. Tammy/Victor and maybe the other team/teams with them took the subway to eliminate the uncertainty. They reached Sheremetyevo and made the flight to Delhi.

In AR14 in Jaipur Christie/Jodi were at the mercy of a taxi driver who did not believe their destination and wanted to take them to the Pushkar Camel Fair, which was happening at the same time and drawing many foreign visitors. They reached Amber Fort parking lot with the loss of about 30 minutes. Despite excellent performance overcoming that plus the deficit of about 30 minutes from a Speed

283

Bump, Christie/Jodi arrived at the pit stop 2 minutes after the prior team and they were eliminated. Thank you, Mr. Taxi Driver.

In AR14 at Phuket teams landed and took taxis to try to find a statue of a gorilla. 5 teams discovered after floundering in downtown Phuket that it was at Phuket Zoo. Mel/ Michael got some bad advice from locals and went to Patong Beach instead. His taxi driver did not know the correct location. The 30 minutes or so that they lost was decisive in their elimination.

Hiring taxis to follow to the intended destination goes back to early Amazing Races. I find it an abhorrent practice to be outlawed along with begging. In AR14 in Phuket, Mark/Michael had minimal harm when they received a 30 minute penalty for tampering and another 30 minute penalty for following a taxi prohibited by clue pulling a rickshaw 1.4 miles to the pit stop, missing first place by 4 minutes.

In ARA3's finale the taxis taken from Thai Trade Food Ice Factory to the Kong Sam Temple provided the decisive edge for Vince/Sam over Geoff/Tisha. Vince/Sam had a much better taxi driver and got ahead 30 minutes when the others had trouble finding that temple.

In ARA1, episode 2 Ernie/Jeena were first after the first task and went for FAST FORWARD at the SMA60 School by taxi, but their taxi driver could not find the school. After searching, Ernie and Jeena attempted to find the school on foot. By the time they had done so, it was too late as Sahil/Prashant had gotten there ahead of them and had completed the FAST FORWARD task. Ernie/Jeena were forced to regular tasks, finished last and were eliminated.

In ARA1, the elimination of Andy/Laura occurred after the ride from the Tibetan Monastery market to the pit stop at Jain Mandir Dada Bari. Andy/Laura had finished third at the monastery market just ahead of Zabrina/Joe Jer and Mardy/Marsio. It is a tough call as to whether Zabrina/Joe Jer actually stole their taxi but they definitely left Andy/Laura behind and finished ahead of them at the pit stop.

AR10 Ep.1 teams go by taxi from Beijing airport to Gold House restaurant. Teams with poor taxis were Dustin/Kandice and Erwin/ Godwin. At ROADBLOCK completion, they easily got a second taxi to the Meridian Gate. The bad driver curse then fell on Billel/Saeed.

TRAINS in AMAZING RACES AND AMAZING RACE ASIAs

Trains are used occasionally by Amazing Races and Amazing Race Asias. Some of them are 24 hours long, making them draining for the racers. That episode is typically designed so that all teams get on these trains. Here are the AR10 to 14 and ARA1 to 3 train trips:

In AR10, the teams leave China by taking a train from the border with Mongolia to the Mongolian capital of Ulaanbaatar.

Later in AR10, teams get from Haiphong back to Hanoi on a train which goes the over 100 km distance.

In AR10 in Finland, teams using the rail system to get from Helsinki to Tampere, 125 miles, and later from Tampere to Turku, 104 miles.

In the final episode of AR10, teams had to take trains from Paris–Gare St. Lazare to Caen in Normandy and later back from Bayeux through Caen back to Gare St. Lazare.

In AR12, teams in Ougadougou take a train about 25 miles north into the bush to find a whistle or request stop at the small village of Bingo.

Later in AR12, teams in Taiwan must take the Taiwan High Speed Rail trains from Taipei to Taichung, just under 100 miles, in 36 minutes. After doing tasks in central Taiwan they take a high-speed train in the reverse direction back to Taipei.

In AR14 the first episode has teams arriving from Los Angeles into either Zurich or Milan-Malpensa airports and then transferring to trains there. Train service exists from Zurich airport that connects to Locarno Switzerland, their joint destination, but teams have to take bus or taxi to a rail station along the Milan to Locarno train line. The combination of flights and train schedules puts the Zurich connectors ahead of the Milan connectors into Locarno. After tasks in the Locarno area, all teams must go from Locarno to Interlaken. Brad/Victoria and Christie/Jodi are both doing this but Christie/Jodi take a train via Lucerne at 939am while Brad/Victoria wait for the direct route train at 1050am, which gets into Interlaken earlier.

AR14 teams took trains from Salzburg to Munich International Airport to get flights to Romania. Once there after tasks in Bucharest, they took a 2.9 hour train from Bucharest to Brasov. It is unclear whether they went from Bran back to Bucharest by train but they may have.

Once checked out of the pit stop at Krasnojarsk, AR14 teams find out that they must take the TransSiberian Railroad as far as Novosibirsk about 400 miles away, a slightly more than 12 hour trip.

In ARA1 as teams receive To Be Continued instructions, they must get to Kolkata's Sealdah station for a 19 hour train ride from Kolkata to New Delhi.

In ARA2 all teams are sent on a Shinkansen high speed train in Japan from Tokyo to Fukuoka which is all the way down Honshu to its southwestern tip and across to near the northwest corner of Kyushu.

ARA2 teams did a task in Frankfurt, but then got on the overnight 1138pm train for Prague (except for Henry/Terri who had to wait until the following morning). Teams next take a local train from Prague to Beroun, then another train back after a pit stop. From Prague they take another train to Budapest. Adrian/Collin find a 5am train through Vienna which takes an hour longer but arrives 1.5 hours before the 730am nonstop. They parlay that into their first victory of an ARA2 leg.

BOATS in AMAZING RACES AND AMAZING RACE ASIAs

The use of water transportation in Amazing Races is necessitated by the facts that about 70% of the earth's surface is water and that many of the world's great cities started on coasts or rivers. I have attempted to find out major instances in AR10 to 14 and ARA1, ARA2 and ARA3 where boats play a role. Much of the time that role is a bunching opportunity and sometimes it differentiates the teams.

Let's start with some simple situations. In AR10 episode 4, the first boat used was the one teams selected themselves from Hydrofoil Harbor to Hon Yen Ngua Island for a ROADBLOCK. After a task they need to go by boat to Sung Sot Cave for a DETOUR. Over has teams row to a supply ship, load cargo into their rowboat, deliver it to 2 addresses, row back to a junk and take the junk to Soi Sim Island. All this is in beautiful and famous Ha Long Bay.

In a later episode off the southwest tip of Mauritius teams elect Sea DETOUR, take a captained sailboat with tiny engine to an island 2.5 miles offshore. A treasure map helps find a mast and sail belonging to the boat which they rig up to sail the boat back to the mainland.

In AR11 as the teams are trying to reach the southernmost post office in the Western Hemisphere at Isla Redonda, teams take a supply boat from the National Park to Isla Redonda. These were supposed to leave every 20 minutes. However, after Rob/Amber and Uchenna/Joyce arrived they saw Charla/Mirna only 5 minutes behind. That caused Rob and Mirna to compete with almost an even start in the task of sorting mail in that post office. Rob/Amber were eliminated as a result of Rob's difficulties finding one of two letters addressed to him and to Amber.

AR11 teams needed to get from the mainland at DarEsSalaam to Zanzibar Island by dhow. World Race Productions used a minor storm as an opportunity for partial compression of time differences between teams by essentially stopping Charla/Mirna overnight. Once on the water, the transit time by dhow was 4 to 9 hours.

Something you will never see unless there is a "what we cut" edition of the Amazing Race is the Laziensky Park Palace on the Water where teams did something with boats in an unaired segment and the AR10 Mauritius "canoe" paddle in or near Grand Baie.

One of the favorites of ARs and ARAs is the harbor in Hong Kong. This has been the site of important water transportation; the preferred method of travel is the Star Ferry between Kowloon and Hong Kong Island. In AR11, teams had to get the Star Ferry from Kowloon to Hong Kong Island. Due to miscommunication with their taxi driver, Charla/Mirna went to Hong Kong Island by mistake and rode the Star Ferry both ways to follow their clue.

In AR12 at Dubrovnik Croatia the mishandling of a rowboat caused elimination of a top team. Azaria/Hendekea, arriving at Dubrovnik airport 35 minutes behind Nicolas/Donald, after 2 tasks had a DETOUR and elected to do Long & Short, mostly rowing around the tip of Dubrovnik to reach the other side harbor. Nicolas/Donald had a sizeable lead as Azaria took the oars, but it looked possible for Azaria to catch them. For about a half hour Azaria rowed hard but made almost no headway until he discovered that their rowboat was attached to a line which was attached to an anchor preventing them from moving forward. Once that was released, they moved fast but by then it was too late. Azaria had rowed his team into oblivion.

In AR12, teams took buses from Dubrovnik to Split and then a high-speed ferry from Split to Ancona, Italy. This Bunched all the teams.

In AR13, teams had to take boats on Tonle Sap Lake in Cambodia near Ankgor Wat. The leading team Terence/Sarah lost time when their boat's engine conked out. It took a while for its captain to get restarted after rowing it a short distance to their destination.

In ARA3 the Star Ferry became a vital link again. Teams had to take it Tsim Shat Tsui to Central and later take TurboJet high speed ferry to Macau. That trip was crucial in determining the outcome of the episode Hong Kong to Macau. Since it is a very busy route and there are departures at least every 15 minutes throughout the day, Geoff/Tisha created a lead with a very smart move to trade tickets with other passengers to get the 5 minute earlier departure. That slim lead expanded when they got to Macau and gained the #1 position for the Macau Tower, where there was both a YIELD (used on Bernie/Henry) and ROADBLOCK. Next in that same episode teams paddled a dragon boat around a buoy in Sai Van Lake.

In ARA3 Finale, long-tailed fishing boats were used to transport teams from Lan Hin Pier Phuket out to the sea between islands to find a fisherman in a marked boat and get a clue for the DETOUR.

In ARA1 Ep. 4 there were both regular and high-speed ferries with schedules. If you could decipher the schedule or you had great luck and arrived at the right time, you could get on a high-speed ferry. Otherwise, it was the regular ferry from downtown Sydney to Manly Wharf for its Ocean World attraction and later back.

The most exciting, simplest task of ARA1 started with a ferry ride from Auckland to Devonport, a north shore suburb. On exiting, teams had to find a girl on a swing (who was 300 yards along the harbor from the ferry terminal), then take the ferry back to downtown Auckland.

Once teams got to Krabi, Thailand there were several on-water or near-water tasks. A FAST FORWARD claimed by Mardy/Marsio uses a 2-person kayak to Pranang Bay to find the clue in a cave. That sent them direct by boat (not kayak) to the pit stop at Ko Phak Bia Island. The other teams had to take long-tailed boats from Hat Phi Phi National Marine Park to Ko Poda Island. Later when finished with the Port Riley East 123 Wall, teams had to take boats to Koh Hong Lagoon.

ARA1 teams on arrival in Dubai were directed to the Burj Dubai water taxi station; they took an abra water taxi to the Dubai Creek Golf & Yacht Club.

The Auckland DETOUR in ARA2 included the choice of Waka, a Maori boat. Team rowed them to gather 3 flags. On the next leg, all teams went to Lake Tikitapu and piloted a 450hp AgroJet boat around a course.

After a Shinkansen ride from Tokyo to the southwest end of the line, ARA2 teams took the 24 hour ferry crossing to Busan, formerly Pusan, South Korea.

Later in Prague, ARA2 teams rowed a rowboat on a course navigated on the Vltava River by compass to Strelecky Island.

BUSES in AMAZING RACES 10 - 14, ARA1, ARA2, ARA 3

Here are favorite anecdotes about buses in these Amazing Races:

In AR10 in Vietnam a bus goes Hanoi to Vac. The following episode teams go from Hanoi to Ha Long Bay Hydrofoil Harbor by bus.

AR11 second Poland episode teams take a bus 4 hours Warsaw to Auschwitz, then continue by bus another hour to Krakow.

In AR12 from Amsterdam teams rode the #30 bus to Ransdorp. Kate/Pat missed it and had to wait for the after-hours #44 bus.

In AR12, teams took a 4 hour bus Dubrovnik to Split. It crossed the Neum corridor, a 9 km strip of Bosnia/Herzegovina that is north of the southern part of Croatia and south of the northern part of Croatia. This area is reportedly about 90% inhabited by Croatians.

ARA3 Bangkok a bus took teams 3 hours north to Wat Phai Rong Wua to search a cemetery; teams got 8 hour buses to Chiang Mai.

Later in Vietnam teams rode buses from Ho Chi Minh City to Cai Be and after tasks there returned to Ho Chi Minh City by bus.

Vietnam is a haven for bus travel. An episode later teams traveled 25 hours by bus Ho Chi Minh City about 1000 km north to Hue.

In ARA1, the ultimate bus challenge was the result of poor judgment by 3 teams. Teams traversed the southern half of Thailand by bus from Bangkok to Krabi for 880km. 3 teams intelligently took express buses and arrived at 630pm. Another 3 teams attempted to make it in coordinated segments southward, but the first segment Bangkok to Prachuap was only 1/3 of the total when they expected it to be 1/2. Next connection is Champon, then Menang Mai and finally to Krabi when a driver arranged for a special bus to meet them. They arrived Krabi at 730pm.

In India for AR10, teams went Chennai to Mamallapararm and returned to Chennai. Bus was the quickest and most convenient way to do that.

INDEX of AMAZING RACES, RACERS and PIT STOPS

11-1 Hacienda Yanahurco, Ecuador 48
11-2 San Pedro de Atacama, Chile 50
11-3 Playa Petrohue, Chile 52
11-4 Isla Redonda, Chile near Ushuaia, Argentina 54
11-5 Fortaleza of Maputo, Mozamique 55
11-6 Old Fort, StoneTown, Zanzibar Island 57, 58
11-7 NONE (although pseudo-pit-stop for leaders in Warsaw)
11-8 Pieskowa Skala, Poland 61
11-9 Caricosa Sera Negara, Kuala Lumpur 63
11-10 Happy Valley Race Course, Hong Kong Island 65
11-11 Trilho da Taipa Pequena 2000, Macau 66
11-12 Fort Soledad, Guam 68
11-13 FINISH LINE Strybing Arboretum, San Francisco 70

AR12: 71 - 92
TK/Rachel 71-92, 242, 254, 272, 273, 278, 279
Christina/Ronald 71-92, 241, 242, 254, 274, 279
Nicolas/Donald 71-92, 230, 241, 265, 274, 278, 288
Nathan/Jennifer 71-90, 227, 231, 232, 272, 279, 283
Kynt/Vyxsin 71-86, 230, 231, 241, 272, 279
Azaria/Hendekea 71-82, 230, 231, 273, 278, 288
Shana/Jennifer 71-81, 267
Jason/Lorena 71-77, 221, 272
Marianna/Julia 71-76, 221, 267
Kate/Pat 71-74, 238, 267
Ari/Staella 71-72, 221, 238, 254, 257, 272
12-1 Connemara Heritage and History Center, Ireland 72
12-2 Durgerdam Yacht Club near Amsterdam 74
12-3 Bingo, Burkina Faso 76
12-4 Ouagadougou Hotel de Ville 77
12-5 Aukstaitija Windmill, Lithuanian Outdoor Museum, Vilnius 80-1
12-6 Stone Cross Overlook near Dubrovnik, Croatia 82
12-7 Boboli Gardens, Florence 84-5
12-8 Bandra Fort, Mumbai 86
12-9 Tempozan Park, Osaka 88
12-10 Chiang Kai-shek Memorial Hall Plaza, Taipei 90
12-11 FINISH LINE - Girdwood Airport near Anchorage, Alaska 92

AR13: 93 -120
Nick/Starr 93-120, 231, 242, 255, 265, 272, 274, 282
Ken/Tina 93-120, 231, 242, 255, 265, 282

14-9 Banyan Lake, Guilin China 143
14-10 NONE (pseudo-pit-stop at Drum Tower, Beijing) 145
14-11 Niao Chao Bird's Nest Stadium, Beijing 148
14-12 FINISH LINE - King Kamehameha Colf Club, Maui 151

ARA1: 152-173
Zabrina/Joe Jer 152-173, 233, 259, 284
Sandy/Francesca 152-173, 233, 242, 259, 282
Andrew/Syeon 152-173, 281
Mardy/Marsio 152-172, 233, 235, 265, 271, 284, 289
Andy/Laura 152-169, 223, 235, 265, 281, 284
Howard/Sahran 152-166, 222
Melody/Sharon 152-162
Sahil/Prahsant 152-159, 258, 265, 284
Aubrey/Jacqueline 152-157, 238, 281
Ernie/Jeena 152-155, 265, 284
A1-1 Kuala Lumpur Tower 153
A1-2 Monas National Historic Monument, Jakarta 155
A1-3 TanahLot Temple, Denpasar Bail 157
A1-4 Tall Ship Bounty in Sydney Harbor 159
A1-5 Auckland Museum 160
A1-6 Chard Farm Winery near Queesntown 162
A1-7 Wat Pho, Bangkok 164
A1-8 Ko Phak Bia Island near Krabi Thailand 165-166
A1-9 NONE (pseudo-pit-stop at Schiava Train Station, Kolkata) 167
A1-10 Jain Mandir Dada Bari temple, Delhi 169
A1-11 Margham Desert Camp near Dubai 170
A1-12 Miran A' Salam Beach, Dubai 172
A1-13 FINISH LINE - Bako National Park, Sarawak, Malaysia 174

ARA2: 175-199
Collin/Adrian 175-199, 235, 260, 265, 277, 278, 280, 284
Pamela/Vanessa 175-199, 242, 243, 257, 271
Marc/Rovilson 175-199, 234, 242, 243, 259, 265
Ann/Diane 175-197, 234, 278
Paula/Natasha 167-194, 232, 242
Henry/Terri 167-191, 285
Sawaka/Daichi 167-184, 234-235
Sophie/Aurelia 167-180, 238
Brett/Kinar 167-179, 238
Edwin/Monica 167-178, 238

Kevin/Drew 223, 239, 240, 241, 256, 257, 266
Nancy/Emily 9, 223, 224, 232, 239, 244, 256, 260, 261, 266
Karyn/Lenny 269
Paul/Amie 236, 269
Dave/Margaretta 262, 269
Pat/Brenda 236, 262, 265
Kim/Leslie 266
Matt/Ana 269

AR2:
Chris/Alex 224, 234, 244, 245, 257, 261, 262, 268
Tara/Wil 224, 244, 245, 261, 262, 273
Blake/Paige 233, 234, 244, 245, 246, 262, 266
Oswald/Danny 224, 232, 239, 244, 262, 266
Gary/Dave 224, 244, 262, 268
Mary/Peach 262, 266
Russell/Cyndi 268
Shola/Doyin 262, 268
Peggy/Claire 262, 266
Hope/Norm 236, 269
Deidre/Hillary 266

AR3:
Flo/Zach 234, 245, 246, 262, 263, 270; just Zach 239, 246
Ian/Teri 245, 246, 262, 263
Ken/Gerard 224, 239, 239, 245, 261, 268
Derek/Drew 224, 225, 232, 246, 257, 261, 264, 268
John Vito/Jill 224, 232, 239, 262, 270
Andre/Damon 268
Aaron/Ariane 236, 246, 270
Michael/Kathy 270
Heather/Eve 9, 245, 266, 273
Dennis/Andrew 261, 262, 273
Tramel/Talicia 236, 273
Gina/Sylvia 236, 266

AR4:
Chip/Reichen 225, 246, 263, 268
Jon/Kelly 225, 239, 263, 270
David/Jeff 8, 215, 247, 263, 268
Jon/Al 225, 232, 239, 240, 247, 268

Millie/Chuck 262, 270
Tian/Jaree 225, 246, 263, 266
Monica/Sheree 261, 263, 266
Steve/Dave 246, 262, 266
Steve/Josh 263, 268
Russell/Cindy 236, 270
Amanda/Chris 270
Debra/Steve 237, 270

AR5:
Chip/Kim 248, 270
Colin/Christie 225, 226, 240, 248, 257, 261, 263, 270, 278
Brandon/Nicole 248, 264, 270
Linda/Karen 225, 232, 240, 248, 266
Karli/Kami 266
Charla/Mirna 247, 266
Marshall/Lance 7, 268
Bob/Joyce 270
Jim/Marsha 273
DonnyAllison 236, 270
Dennis/Erika 236, 270

AR6:
Freddie/Kendra 249, 250, 271, 273
Kris/Jon 240, 248, 250, 271
Adam/Rebecca 226, 249, 264, 271
Hayden/Aaron 226, 232, 249, 271
Lori/Bolo 221, 248, 264, 271
Jonathan/Victoria 238, 271
Gus/Hera 273
Don/MaryJean 237, 270
Lena/Kristy 7, 225, 226, 249, 257, 266
Meredith/Maria 237, 266
Avi/Joe 236, 268

AR7:
Uchenna/Joyce 226, 240, 250, 251, 264, 271
Rob/Amber 240, 241, 251, 264, 271
Ron/Kelly 250, 251, 271
Gretchen/Meredith 226, 268, 271
Lynn/Alex 227, 250, 263

AMAZING RACE PLACES INDEX (for multiple citations;air connection cities not included; note city/country list Countries Visited)

Made in the USA
San Bernardino, CA
07 December 2013